India Studies in Business and Economics

India is one of the fastest growing economies of the world, with the country being an important G20 member. It is a significant player in the global market with a notable demographic advantage, and an important geo-political and geo-trade position. Additionally, due to its position of being not only the most populous country in the world, but also the world's largest youth population, India has a pivotal role to play in meeting global SDG goals. This makes research from the country to be of immense interest to the global community.

With this backdrop, this series aims to bring forth the latest studies and research specific to India from all areas of economics, finance, business, trade, and management science, often with strong social science and political economy linkages. The titles featured in this series present rigorous research, both empirical and non-empirical in nature, usually accompanied by policy recommendations. They evoke and evaluate various aspects of the economical and/or the business and management landscape in India, with a special focus on India's relationship with the world. The series also tracks research on India's position on social issues, on health, on politics, on agriculture, on rights, and many such topics which directly or indirectly affect sustainable growth of the country.

The series welcomes contributions from scholars or practitioners belonging to the academic community, corporates, think tanks and/or non-governmental organizations, and also policymakers to publish their work in the form of authored monographs, edited volumes or collection of case studies. Each proposal undergoes at least two double blind peer review where a detailed concept note along with extended chapter abstracts and/or a sample chapter is peer reviewed by experienced academics. The reviews may be more detailed if recommended by reviewers. The series follows the Ethics Statement as per Springer Nature's standard guidelines.

Shveta Singh · Samridhi Suman

Corporate Governance Monitoring Mechanisms and Corporate Performance and Valuation

Lessons from India

Springer

Shveta Singh
Department of Management Studies
Indian Institute of Technology Delhi
New Delhi, Delhi, India

Samridhi Suman
University of Southampton Delhi
Gurgaon, Delhi, India

ISSN 2198-0012 ISSN 2198-0020 (electronic)
India Studies in Business and Economics
ISBN 978-981-96-9735-9 ISBN 978-981-96-9736-6 (eBook)
https://doi.org/10.1007/978-981-96-9736-6

This Springer imprint is published by the registered company Springer Nature Singapore Pte Ltd.
The registered company address is: 152 Beach Road, #21-01/04 Gateway East, Singapore 189721, Singapore

To
The Almighty
and
Our Family Members

Acknowledgments

At the outset, we would like to thank the Almighty for his blessings for inspiring us to accomplish this academic endeavor. This work has been possible because of the help, encouragement, cooperation and guidance of many people and we convey our heartfelt thanks to all of them. We are grateful to Prof. Rangan Bannerjee, Director, IIT Delhi for his encouragement and support.

To thank the Head of the Department may seem to be a ritual. But it is not so in the case of Prof. S. P. Singh, Head (DMS). He has been supportive throughout. We thank all our colleagues in the Department of Management Studies (DMS) for their good wishes for this endeavor.

Prof. Shveta Singh takes this opportunity to express her deepest gratitude to her gurus, Prof. P. K. Jain and Prof. Surendra S. Yadav, for their valuable guidance and inspiration in the completion of this project. She also thanks her husband Anil and her son Shashvat for their unwavering support and encouragement.

Dr. Samridhi Suman would like to profess profound gratitude to Prof. Shveta Singh for recognizing and helping her realize her potential as a researcher by constantly pushing her to do better to reach new heights. She also extends a heartfelt thank you to the strong pillars of her life, her parents, Mr. Ravi Sawlani and Mrs. Sangeeta Sawlani and her brother, Saksham Sawlani.

Last but not the least, we are thankful to all those, not mentioned above, who helped in carrying out the study, our family members and loved ones for their continuous encouragement and support.

Shveta Singh
Samridhi Suman

Contents

About the Authors

Shveta Singh is PFS Chair Professor and Area Chair of Finance at the Department of Management Studies (DMS), Indian Institute of Technology (IIT) Delhi, India. She is also the coordinator of the National Centre on Corporate Governance. She has contributed to various research and consulting assignments for organizations like the CIO Foundation, CISO Foundation, Lok Sabha, National Foundation for Corporate Governance (NFCG), Directorate General of Supplies and Disposals (DGS&D), National Buildings Construction Corporation (NBCC), Indian Council of Social Science Research (ICSSR), UK-India Education and Research Initiative (UKIERI), ReNew Power, the Ministry of Agriculture and Farmers' Welfare, the Ministry of Food and Consumer Affairs, the Indian Navy, and the Indian Air Force. She is also a member of the International Organization for Standardization (ISO) and Bureau of Indian Standards (BIS) sectional committees on Sustainable Finance. She is the Associate Editor of *Journal of Advances in Management Research* (JAMR). In addition to publishing more than 180 research papers, she has co-authored a textbook and four research monographs, all published by Springer. She has been honored twice with the "Literati" award for outstanding research and is a recipient of the Lok Sabha Fellowship and the Fetzer Fellowship from the Academy of Management, USA as well as the National Stock Exchange—Indira Gandhi Institute of Development Research (NSE-IGIDR) Corporate Governance Research Initiative Grant. She has also been honored by the "Leadership" award in research from the Institute of Business and Finance Research in USA.

Dr. Samridhi Suman has completed her Ph.D. in finance from the Department of Management Studies, IIT Delhi, India. Presently, she is working as a Lecturer at University of Southampton Delhi, Gurgaon, India. Prior to this she was a Lecturer at Jindal School of Banking & Finance, O.P. Jindal Global University, Sonipat, India. Her research interests are in the field of corporate governance and corporate finance. She has published her manuscript in high-ranked journals including *American Business Review* and *International Journal of Productivity and Performance Management*. She has also presented her research work at several conferences organized by eminent institutes and associations.

Abbreviations

ASEAN	Association of South East Asian Nations
CEO	Chief Executive Officer
FRQ	Financial Reporting Quality
HHI	Herfindahl-Hirschman Index
IPO	Initial Public Offering
LODR	Listing Obligations and Disclosure Requirements
MLS	Multiple Large Shareholders
NPV	Net Present Value
NWC	Net Working Capital
R&D	Research and Development
SEBI	Securities and Exchange Board of India
SGA	Selling, General, and Administrative
U.K.	United Kingdom
U.S.	United States
VIF	Variance Inflation Factor

List of Figures

List of Tables

Chapter 1
Introduction

The unveiling of major corporate failures and malfeasance over the past decade, including the exposé of the LIBOR[1] scandal in the U.K., Wirecard fraud in Germany, and the PNB-Nirav Modi scam in India, has renewed focus on corporate governance (Ashton & Christophers, 2015; Hanumantu et al., 2019; Teichmann et al., 2024). In the wake of these corporate frauds, regulators across the globe have been prompted to strengthen and strictly enforce corporate governance provisions to ensure better protection of stakeholders' interests and a company's long-term survival (Jones, 2022; Titus & Mittal, 2018).

Considering the primacy of robust governance mechanisms in a company, this chapter first elaborates on the background of the conception of corporate governance in Sect. 1.1. Section 1.2 provides a brief overview of the corporate governance framework in India. Section 1.3 underlines the motivation for the study and presents the emerging research questions. The research objectives and significance of the study are emphasized in Sect. 1.4. Section 1.5 discusses the analytical framework adopted for the current study. The layout of the book is outlined in Sect. 1.6. Section 1.7 concludes the chapter.

1.1 Background

Corporate governance refers to "the system by which companies are directed and controlled" (Cadbury, 1992). This system describes the rights and responsibilities of all the parties with a share in the firm (Aoki, 2014). It assures the suppliers of capital to the corporates that they will get a return on their invested capital (Shleifer & Vishny, 1997).

---

[1] LIBOR is an acronym for the London Interbank Offer Rate.

S. Singh and S. Suman, *Corporate Governance Monitoring Mechanisms and Corporate Performance and Valuation*, India Studies in Business and Economics,
https://doi.org/10.1007/978-981-96-9736-6_1

The genesis of corporate governance can be traced to the Berle and Means (1932) description of modern corporations[2] that gave rise to the concept of separation of ownership and control. According to the underlined concept, the ownership of such corporations is dispersed across small investors, but the control is concentrated in the hands of managers. These managers are appointed as agents to shareholders to perform day-to-day business operations on behalf of the latter (Mittal & Singh, 2025). As a result, modern corporations have an inherent agency issue between managers and shareholders (Jensen, 1986).

The agency problem occurs when managers take actions that are not in the interests of shareholders (Prakash et al., 2022). They may divert funds to companies they set up, waste away corporate surplus funds on consuming expensive perquisites, or overinvest them into sub-optimal projects to enhance their power (Jensen, 1986; Shleifer & Vishny, 1997). Managers are able to carry out these self-serving activities because they possess more information about the firm than the shareholders (Jacobson & Aaker, 1993). This disparity in knowledge between corporate insiders and outside investors concerning a company's functioning constitutes the issue of information asymmetry.

The classical agency problem between managers and shareholders, which is also termed the Type I agency problem, occurs in consonance with the free-rider problem that characterizes widely diffused ownership structures (John & Senbet, 1998). The free-rider problem arises because shareholders of most modern corporations have dispersed significantly smaller stake that do not provide sufficient incentive to scrutinize the management closely (Jensen & Meckling, 1976). Therefore, corporate governance mechanisms are required to limit managerial discretion in modern corporations and protect the interests of their shareholders. Figure 1.1 provides a visual representation of the standard agency issue.

Contravening the Berle and Means (1932) construct of modern corporations, La Porta et al. (1999) observe that concentrated ownership structures are a common organizational form across the world, including India (Rajagopalan & Zhang, 2008). The authors affirm that a present-day corporation is characterized by the presence of a dominant shareholder who usually exercises significant control owing to substantial stakeholding (Khosa, 2017; Sarkar & Sarkar, 2008). Correspondingly, controlling owners have the incentive and the ability to use corporate assets for personal benefit at the expense of minority shareholders. Hence, the primary agency problem in such closely-held companies is between the controlling and minority owners. The controlling-minority shareholder conflict, also known as the Type II agency problem, is briefly summarized in Fig. 1.2.

[2] There is no doubt that the idea of corporate governance is as old as the existence of the corporate form of business entity. Its significance can be observed from the frequent occurrences of manager-shareholder conflicts at former historical corporations, such as the Dutch East India Company (Cheffins, 2013; Wells, 2009). However, the present-day conception of corporate governance issues came into being with the growth of modern companies during the twentieth century (Cheffins, 2013). These modern corporations were giant industrial enterprises where ownership was dispersed across a multitude of small investors (Berle & Means, 1932).

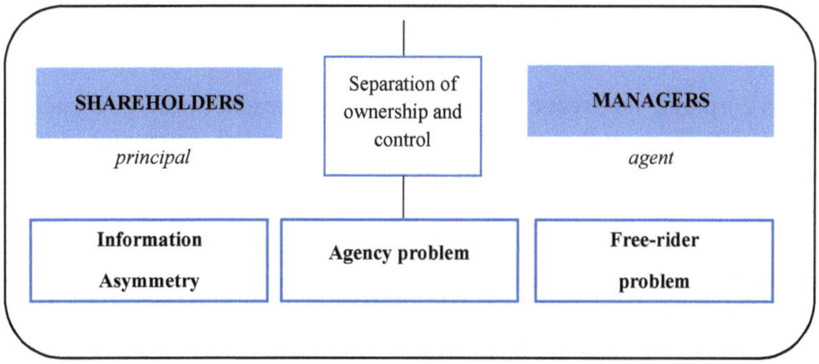

Fig. 1.1 Illustration of manager-shareholder agency conflict. *Notes* This figure presents an overview of the manager-shareholder agency conflict

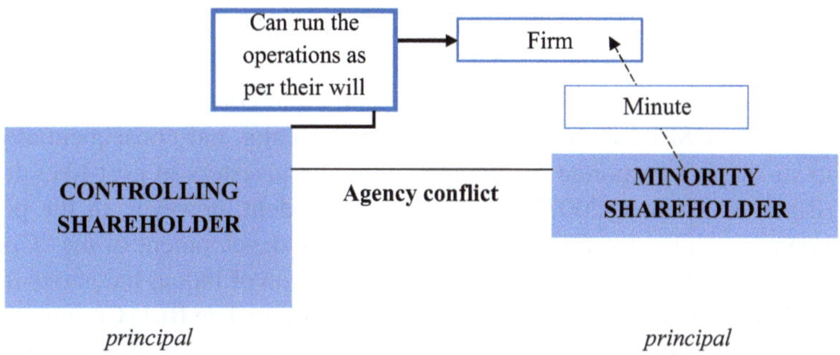

Fig. 1.2 Illustration of controlling shareholder-minority shareholders agency conflict. *Notes* This figure presents an overview of the controlling shareholder-minority shareholders agency conflict

The occurrence of manager-shareholder conflict and controlling-minority shareholder conflict necessitates the need for corporate governance mechanisms to minimize agency costs. However, the issue of corporate governance gained prominence among regulators after a series of infamous corporate frauds and scandals like those of WorldCom and Enron in the U.S. (Brown & Caylor, 2006). In India, active discourse on corporate governance also began after a spate of stock market scams in the early 1990s and rampant incidents of fly-by-night companies fleeing away with investors' money (Chakrabarti et al., 2008). A brief review of the evolution of the corporate governance milieu in India follows in the next section.

1.2 Corporate Governance in India

The Indian corporate landscape is dominated by the presence of large owners. Sarkar and Sarkar (2012) report that about 93% of publicly traded companies in India have a minimum of one blockholder who holds at least 5% of a corporation's shares. A substantial portion of block shareholding is usually retained by the strategic and inside shareholders, who are known as promoters[3] in the local parlance (Balasubramaniam & Anand, 2013; Sarkar & Sarkar, 2012). These large owners wield significant control over the firm's business (Banerjee & Homroy, 2018; Sarkar & Sarkar, 2008). Consequently, the agency conflicts between controlling and minority shareholders are more salient in Indian entities (Suman & Singh, 2022).

In order to regulate agency issues and limit expropriation by the controlling owners, policymakers in India have undertaken a multitude of corporate governance reforms. Prior to the liberalization reforms in India in 1991, the Companies Act of 1956 stipulated rules to ensure the basic functioning of Indian companies. However, after a series of stock market scandals, the Securities and Exchange Board of India (SEBI) was authorized in 1992 to regulate corporate conduct (Joshi, 2020). The empowerment of SEBI is one of the most fundamental and consequential developments in shaping corporate regulations to protect investors in post-liberalization India (Black & Khanna, 2007). The earliest antecedent, however, of the present-day corporate governance framework in India is the development of the "Code for Desirable Corporate Governance" by the Confederation of Indian Industries in 1998 (Selarka, 2018). SEBI, too, constituted the "Kumar Mangalam Birla Committee" and the "Narayana Murthy Committee" in 1999 and 2003, respectively, to address the corporate governance issues in India (Singla & Singh, 2018). These two committees are responsible for shaping the corporate governance landscape in India by formulating SEBI's Clause 49 of the Listing Agreement in 2005, which augmented the provisions relating to board composition (Narayanaswamy et al., 2012; Singh et al., 2013).

The Department of Corporate Affairs of the Government of India has also played an instrumental role in strengthening corporate governance rules. In consideration of the corporate scandals in the U.S. in 2002, it set up the "Naresh Chandra Committee," which made recommendations about auditors and audit committees (Selarka, 2018). This regulatory effort was followed by the constitution of the "J.J. Irani Committee" in 2004 for reviewing the Companies Act of 1956 (Srivastava et al., 2018) and the issuance of the "Corporate Governance Voluntary Guidelines" in 2009 as a response to the Satyam scam (Narayanaswamy et al., 2012). The introduction of the Companies Act of 2013 and SEBI (Listing Obligations and Disclosure Requirements) Regulation of 2015 brought about significant reforms in corporate governance regulations in India (Hasan et al., 2024). One of the most sweeping changes it ushered in is the mandated quota for women directors to enhance board gender diversity (Sarkar &

---

[3] Section 2(69) of the Companies Act, 2013 defines a promoter as "a person who has control over the affairs of the company, directly or indirectly whether as a shareholder, director or otherwise" (PwC India, 2013).

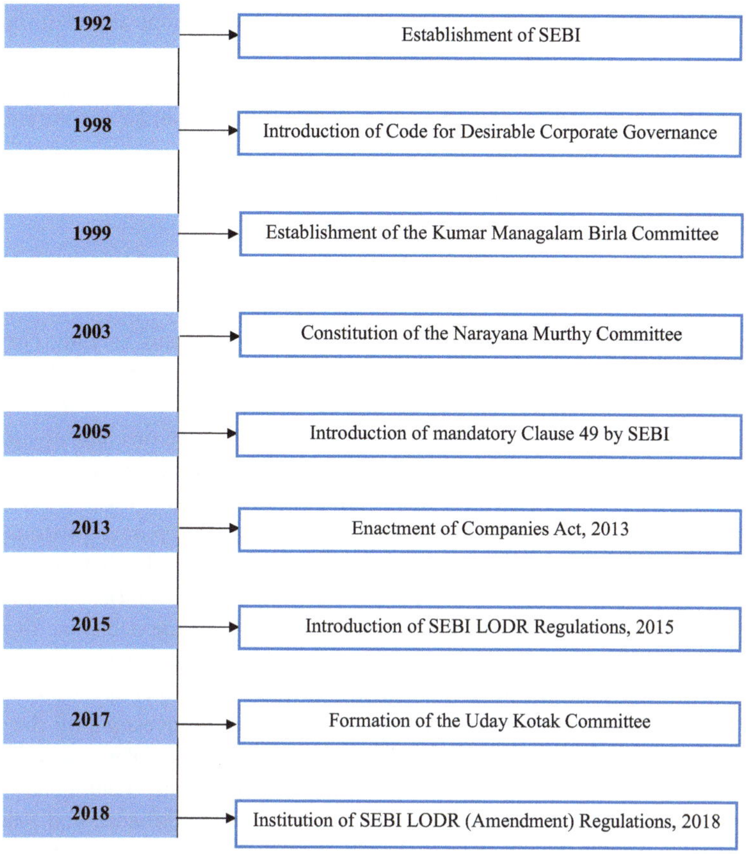

Fig. 1.3 Evolution of corporate governance framework in India. *Notes* This figure depicts important developments in the corporate governance regulatory framework in India

Selarka, 2021). It also imposed stricter independence requirements for hiring independent directors on the board and raised the maximum limit of sitting directors, among many other changes (Grant Thornton, 2013).

In 2017, SEBI constituted the "Uday Kotak Committee" to further improve the quality of corporate governance in India and adopted most of its recommendations in March 2018.[4] Some of the amendments included ensuring a minimum board size of 6 directors, appointment of independent women directors, a reduction in the maximum number of directorships, and stringent related party transaction approval (Securities & Exchange Board of India, 2018). Although SEBI had also mandated the separation of the CEO and Chairman posts, this provision was later made voluntary in 2022 (Biju, 2022). Figure 1.3 summarizes some of the important corporate governance developments in India.

[4] The enforcement of these provisions commenced from April 1, 2019 onwards.

In 2023, SEBI also instituted additional regulatory provisions aimed at reducing entrenchment by prescribing declaration of any shareholders' agreements and requiring shareholders' assent on the continuation of directors on the board beyond the tenure of five years (Jayachandran & Aakulu, 2023; Krishnan & Subramanian, 2023).

1.3 Motivation for the Study

As can be inferred from the corporate collapses of Enron and Satyam, corporate governance is fundamental to a firm's survival and success (Mülbert, 2009; Saini & Singhania, 2018). Regulators and policymakers worldwide are also making sustained efforts to improve the effectiveness of corporate governance mechanisms to limit corporate frauds and enhance investors' confidence in the business (Jones, 2022; Titus & Mittal, 2018). Despite these observed realities, the extant literature furnishes indeterminate empirical evidence regarding the impact of corporate governance on a company's valuation and performance (Aguilera et al., 2008; Pandey et al., 2023). The study attempts to address the underlined dichotomy by empirically examining the effect of corporate governance on those corporate finance decisions that have been noted to affect a corporation's value. Investment, capital structure, and dividend decisions are reported to influence a firm's value (Dahiya et al., 2023; Fama & French, 1998). Therefore, the current research focuses on investigating the implications of corporate governance devices on specific aspects of the stated financial management decisions. The proposed analyses will help in understanding how effective governance mechanisms can generate higher firm performance and valuation (Bøhren et al., 2007). It will also provide a renewed business case for practicing good corporate governance by evaluating its influence on value-driving financial metrics (Fama & French, 1998).

Corporate governance can affect corporate financial decisions by regulating the agency issues that may afflict the outcome of these decisions. Corporate insiders[5] can accumulate excess cash to over-invest in negative net present value (NPV) projects to pursue their empire-building aspirations (Jensen, 1986). On the other hand, they may avoid investing in risky but value-enhancing innovations for fear of losing their jobs and undiversified wealth in the case of project failure (Caixe et al., 2019; Lu & Wang, 2015). Similarly, they can also steer away from borrowings to minimize the risk of bankruptcy (Chakraborty, 2018; Fama, 1980). Furthermore, they can restrict dividend payments to retain funds for tunneling (La Porta et al., 2000). These self-serving actions can upset a corporation's cost of financing and its value (Hashim & Amrah, 2016; Lugo, 2019). Since robust corporate governance mechanisms are set up to limit the entrenchment of executives and dominant owners, it can be deduced that these devices will also curtail the adverse effects of their discretion on investment, financing, and payout decisions. Hence, the ramifications of corporate governance on

[5] Corporate insiders include managers and the controlling owner.

financial management decisions are checked to comprehend their influence beyond the direct metric of profitability or valuation.

The dichotomy posed by the inconclusive corporate governance-firm value association is also tackled by examining the contingent effects of governance attributes. The standard corporate governance theories and frameworks posit a universal linkage between governance mechanisms and corporate decisions without giving consideration to an organization's context (Filatotchev & Allcock, 2010; Pandey et al., 2023). As per Aguilera et al. (2008), such an isolated investigation of the influence of corporate governance engenders ambiguous findings. The efficacy of the governance devices is likely to vary according to a firm's environmental situation (Dedman & Filatotchev, 2008; Zona et al., 2013). Therefore, it becomes imperative to analyze the conditional effects of corporate governance mechanisms to determine their boundary conditions.

The study is also inspired to examine the effectiveness of corporate governance mechanisms in relation to financial management decisions in the context of the developing economy of India. As discussed earlier, Indian corporations are characterized by the presence of a controlling owner or promoter (Banerjee & Homroy, 2018; Sarkar & Sarkar, 2008). In spite of the high percentage of stakeholding by the inside owners, Indian entities follow a corporate governance framework based on the Anglo-American model (Banerjee & Homroy, 2018; Reed, 2002). The Anglo-American model emerged in the U.S. and U.K. to protect the interest of dispersed shareholders of widely-held entities from managerial expropriation (Jeffers, 2005; Piesse et al., 2012). Therefore, it will be intriguing to investigate the performance of corporate governance practices adopted from the U.S. or U.K. in the Indian corporate milieu, where principal-principal agency conflicts are more salient. Furthermore, by setting up the study in India, the impact of the Companies Act of 2013 on the functioning of corporate governance devices can also be addressed.

Lastly, the research is also impelled to examine the implications of such corporate governance mechanisms that tend to affect the monitoring of corporate insiders. Continuous and strict supervision can restrict the extraction of private benefits by managers and dominant shareholders (Khanchel, 2007). In this connection, the empirical analyses consider the impact of the board of directors, which is regarded as the cornerstone of internal corporate governance (Guest, 2009). Its importance is also emphasized by the recent regulatory interventions to improve its effectiveness by raising the minimum number of sitting directors, enhancing gender diversity, and bolstering the independence requirements (Securities & Exchange Board of India, 2018). In addition, the effect of controlling owners is also taken into account because they play a predominant role in the Indian corporate sector (Sarkar & Sarkar, 2008). The risk of abuse of their commanding position by the dominant shareholders creates an urgency to monitor and question their actions to inhibit them from swaying corporate decisions in their favor (Claessens et al., 2002; La Porta et al., 1999). Besides the main controlling shareholder, the influence of non-controlling large owners on corporate finance decisions is also analyzed. They can utilize their significant voting rights to enhance governance by scrutinizing and challenging any self-serving decisions by the dominant shareholder (Jiang et al., 2019; Maury & Pajuste, 2005). Finally, the monitoring function of auditors is also addressed by concentrating on their ability to conduct independent audits. Policymakers are making continuous efforts to ensure auditors' objectivity by either expanding the ambit of prohibited non-audit services or curtailing the proportion of non-audit fees (Deloitte, 2015; Prasad, 2020).

In line with the underscored motives, the following research questions are investigated by the study:

i. What is the impact of corporate governance monitoring mechanisms on the investment efficiency and cash holdings level for firms listed in the developing economy of India?
ii. What is the impact of corporate governance monitoring mechanisms on the leverage ratio and cost of capital for firms listed in the developing economy of India?
iii. What is the impact of corporate governance monitoring mechanisms on dividend payout intensity and dividend stability for firms listed in the developing economy of India?
iv. How is the observed impact of corporate governance monitoring mechanisms affected by the introduction of the Companies Act of 2013?
v. How does the observed impact of corporate governance monitoring mechanisms vary according to different organizational contexts?

In consonance with the identified research questions, the research objectives of the study are stated as follows:

i. To examine the impact of corporate governance monitoring mechanisms on select investment decisions of a firm.
ii. To analyze the impact of corporate governance monitoring mechanisms on select capital structure decisions of a firm.
iii. To investigate the impact of corporate governance monitoring mechanisms on select dividend decisions of a firm.

1.4 Analytical Framework

Scope of the study

The ambit of the study is stated as follows:

i. The corporations that comprise the NIFTY 500 index in India form the target sample of the study. As NIFTY 500 firms represent about 96.10% of the free-float market capitalization of all the firms listed on the National Stock Exchange in India as of March 29, 2019,[6] they are regarded to constitute a suitable sample.
ii. The period for conducting empirical investigations spans over a decade, extending from FY 2010 to FY 2019.

---

[6] Source: https://www1.nseindia.com/global/content/investor_rel/nseil_shp_home.htm.

iii. In line with the previous literature, observations pertaining to financial entities are eliminated from the initial sample due to differing regulatory requirements that govern these entities (Chen et al., 2016; Pandey et al., 2023).
iv. Observations with missing data are excluded from the analyses.

Research methodology

Corporate governance monitoring mechanisms serve as the primary explanatory variables of the study. The analysis considers the board of directors' attributes to proxy for its effectiveness, the influence of large owners, and the independence of auditors. A succinct review of each monitoring mechanism, along with their definition, is presented in Table 1.1. The measurement of the examined financial management decisions is expounded in the respective chapters.

The impact of corporate governance monitoring mechanisms on financial management decisions is investigated using dynamic panel data modeling. A dynamic panel data model is based on the premise that the contemporary value of the dependent variable is affected by its previous year's level (Roodman, 2009). For example, Lintner (1956) notes linkages between consecutive dividend payments as firms adjust their dividends gradually toward a target level to avoid drastic cuts in these payments. Therefore, this approach addresses the persistent nature and partial adjustment behavior of financial management decisions (Ban & Chen, 2019; Dang et al., 2015).

The consideration of dynamic linkages posits the problem of autocorrelation and endogeneity. Endogeneity concerns can also arise due to corporate governance variables. These concerns are minimized by employing the two-step system GMM estimator. System GMM provides more efficient estimates by helping tackle the endogeneity issue arising from omitted variable bias, simultaneity bias, and measurement error (Arellano & Bond, 1991; Blundell & Bond, 2000).

Statistical software used

The study was mainly carried out using Microsoft Excel® and Stata®.

1.5 Organization of the Book

The book is structured as follows. This chapter introduces the book by providing a background of the conducted study. The subsequent chapters expound on the results from the empirical examination of stated research objectives. The analyses of the effects of corporate governance on investment decisions are undertaken by focusing on long-term investment efficiency in Chap. 2 and short-term investments in cash holding in Chap. 3. Further, the implications of corporate governance on financing decisions are checked by concentrating on the capital structure composition and

Table 1.1 Summary of corporate governance variables used in the study

Variables	Benefits	Costs	Measurement
Board size *(BSIZE)*	Larger boards augment board effectiveness: • Provide an enhanced supply of resources in terms of knowledge, experience, expertise, and skills (Anderson et al., 2004) • Strengthen the ability of the firms to procure critical resources such as external financing (Dalton et al., 1999; Pfeffer, 1972) • Can lead to better governance as they present scope for establishing several monitoring committees for overseeing managerial activities (Monks & Minow, 1995; Klein, 2002) • The likelihood that at least one director will question the executive's actions is higher in the case of oversized boards (Upadhyay & Sriram, 2011)	Larger boards can be easily controlled by CEOs (Jensen, 1993): • Provide directors with an opportunity to free-ride (Lipton & Lorsch, 1992) • The directors may also be less participative as they may be disincentivized by the little impact that their contributions have on business decisions (Zona et al., 2013) • Board members of such boards usually do not hold honest and frank discussions and can devolve into conflicting factional groups (Goodstein et al., 1994) • These boards suffer from problems of communication, coordination, and delayed decision-making that are intrinsic to larger groups (Guest, 2009)	Total number of directors on the board (Suman & Singh, 2021; Zona et al., 2013) *Source*: Bloomberg®

(continued)

Table 1.1 (continued)

Variables	Benefits	Costs	Measurement
Board independence *(BIND)*	• Independent directors are able to bring unbiased and objective judgment on various corporate matters to the board as no pecuniary interests in the corporation (Chen et al., 2016; Solomon, 2007) • They contribute valuable knowledge, experience, expertise, and diverse perspectives that aid in better decision-making (Adams & Mehran, 2012; Rashid, 2015)	• Independent directors have little information about the day-to-day workings of the business, which can impede their ability to monitor properly	Number of independent directors as a percentage of board size (Lu & Wang, 2015; Rashid, 2015) *Source*: Bloomberg®
CEO duality *(CEODUAL)*	• CEO duality confers substantial decision-making power in the hands of a CEO and also creates a conflict of interest as the person responsible for steering executive decision-making is also required to appraise the effectiveness of managerial actions (Finkelstein & D'aveni, 1994)	• CEO duality establishes a clear-cut authority and maintains the unity of command (Chancharat et al., 2012) • A combined CEO-Chairman position provides stronger leadership and superior firm-specific knowledge that is requisite for undertaking swift decision-making in response to the dynamic environment (Finkelstein & D'aveni, 1994)	A binary variable that assumes a value equal to one when the CEO-Chairman position is combined, zero otherwise (Chen et al., 2016; Guizani 2018) *Source*: Bloomberg®

(continued)

Table 1.1 (continued)

Variables	Benefits	Costs	Measurement
Board gender diversity *(BGD)*	Female directors contribute bring unique human capital to the board (Terjesen et al., 2009), which results in: • Facilitating the board to examine an issue from a fresh and different viewpoint (Campbell, 1996). Consequently, the board of directors is enabled to consider a comprehensive set of responses for making an informed decision (Carter et al., 2003) • Reducing the groupthink problem and strengthening board independence (Carter et al., 2010)	• Extant literature on gender and psychology also indicates that women are risk-averse and adopt a conservative approach to decision-making (Jianakoplos & Bernasek, 1998; Nadeem et al., 2019). Correspondingly, female directors may make low-risk and economically cautious business choices that may not necessarily be optimal (García-Meca et al., 2022)	Number of women directors as a percentage of board size (Low et al., 2015; Yarram & Adapa, 2021) *Source*: Bloomberg®
Controlling shareholder *(PROMOTER)*	• Owing to substantial ownership and accompanying voting rights, controlling owners may be tempted to undertake decisions activities detrimental to the small shareholders' interests (Claessens et al., 2002; La Porta et al., 1999)	• As the ownership stake of controlling shareholders increases, they are more likely to bear the adverse effects of their private consumption, considering that their economic and human capital depends upon the corporation's performance (Chau & Gray, 2010). Hence, the controlling owners may minimize their self-serving behavior in light of the possible erosion of their wealth (Boubaker et al., 2014)	Equity percentage shareholding of the promoter, who is regarded as the controlling owner in the Indian context (Banerjee & Homroy, 2018; Bhaumik & Selarka, 2012) *Source:* Prowessdx®

(continued)

Table 1.1 (continued)

Variables	Benefits	Costs	Measurement
Non-controlling large shareholders *(NPD)*	• Other blockholders can discipline the controlling shareholder to minimize its rent extraction behavior (Maury & Pajuste, 2005). They can do so by exerting pressure through control contestability (Pagano & Röell, 1998), participation in decision-making (Edmans, 2014), or divestment of their holdings (Hope et al., 2017)	• Additional blockholders may collude with the controlling owner to engage in value-destroying activities for furthering personal wealth at the expense of minority shareholders (Jiang et al., 2019; Zwiebel, 1995)	A dummy variable coded as one if a non-promoter owner holds a minimum of 10% share in the equity capital, zero otherwise (Jiang et al., 2019; Maury & Pajuste, 2005) *Source:* Prowessdx®
Auditor independence *(NAF)*	• The provision of non-audit services also enables an auditor to give client-specific expertise that can improve a company's performance and productivity (Carcello et al., 2002; Shi et al., 2023). They possess significant private information about the client's business gathered over the course of the audit process and frequent interactions with the management (Cai et al., 2016; Dhaliwal et al., 2016). Further, auditors have a vast knowledge base that has been developed over the years from auditing numerous corporations across multiple industrial sectors (Bae et al., 2017). Consequently, auditors are knowledge repositories that can provide valuable advice on various corporate affairs	• Auditor independence is affected by the provision of non-audit services to client firms. Payment of non-audit fees strengthens the financial association between a firm and its auditors (Naiker et al., 2013; Prasad, 2020). In such a case, the auditor is at the risk of bearing a greater loss of income due to which they may be unwilling to report any breaches by the client firm (Mitra, 2007)	Ratio of non-audit fees to audit fees (Naiker et al., 2013; Shi et al., 2023) *Source:* Prowessdx®

Notes This table provides a brief overview of all the corporate governance variables used in the study

cost of capital in Chaps. 4 and 5, respectively. In addition, the ramifications of corporate governance monitoring mechanisms on dividend decisions are detailed in Chap. 6. Finally, the relevant recommendations and concluding remarks are presented in Chap. 7.

1.6 Summary and Concluding Observations

This chapter presents an overview of the study. It introduces the concept of corporate governance and briefly traces its evolution in the Indian context. It also delineates the motivation for undertaking research, which extends an opportunity to formulate appropriate research questions and objectives of the study. The significance and analytical framework of the study are also succinctly covered in the chapter. Lastly, it also covers the outline of the book. The succeeding chapters present the empirical investigations for the stated research objectives.

References

Adams, R. B., & Mehran, H. (2012). Bank board structure and performance: Evidence for large bank holding companies. *Journal of Financial Intermediation, 21*(2), 243–267.

Aguilera, R. V., Filatotchev, I., Gospel, H., & Jackson, G. (2008). An organizational approach to comparative corporate governance: Costs, contingencies, and complementarities. *Organization Science, 19*(3), 475–492.

Anderson, R. C., Mansi, S. A., & Reeb, D. M. (2004). Board characteristics, accounting report integrity, and the cost of debt. *Journal of Accounting and Economics, 37*(3), 315–342.

Aoki, Y. (2014). How does the largest shareholder affect dividends? *International Review of Finance, 14*(4), 613–645.

Arellano, M., & Bond, S. (1991). Some tests of specification for panel data: Monte Carlo evidence and an application to employment equations. *The Review of Economic Studies, 58*(2), 277–297.

Ashton, P., & Christophers, B. (2015). On arbitration, arbitrage and arbitrariness in financial markets and their governance: Unpacking LIBOR and the LIBOR scandal. *Economy and Society, 44*(2), 188–217.

Balasubramanian, B. N., & Anand, R. (2013). *Ownership trends in corporate India 2001–2011: Evidence and implications*. Retrieved January 4, 2025 from https://www.iimb.ac.in/sites/default/files/2018-07/WP_No._419_0.pdf

Bae, G. S., Choi, S. U., Dhaliwal, D. S., & Lamoreaux, P. T. (2017). Auditors and client investment efficiency. *The Accounting Review, 92*(2), 19–40.

Ban, M., & Chen, C. C. (2019). Ambiguity and capital structure adjustments. *International Review of Economics & Finance, 64*, 242–270.

Banerjee, S., & Homroy, S. (2018). Managerial incentives and strategic choices of firms with different ownership structures. *Journal of Corporate Finance, 48*, 314–330.

Berle, A., & Means, G. (1932). *Private property and the modern corporation*. Mac Millan.

Bhaumik, S. K., & Selarka, E. (2012). Does ownership concentration improve M&A outcomes in emerging markets? Evidence from India. *Journal of Corporate Finance, 18*(4), 717–726.

Biju. R.M. (2022). *SEBI Makes Splitting CEO and Chairperson roles voluntary.* Retrieved January 4, 2025 from https://www.bqprime.com/business/listed-companies-have-option-to-split-ceo-md-and-chairman-posts.

Black, B. S., & Khanna, V. S. (2007). Can corporate governance reforms increase firm market values? Event study evidence from India. *Journal of Empirical Legal Studies, 4*(4), 749–796.

Blundell, R., & Bond, S. (2000). GMM estimation with persistent panel data: An application to production functions. *Econometric Reviews, 19*(3), 321–340.

Bøhren, Ø., Cooper, I., & Priestley, R. (2007). *Corporate governance and real investment decisions.* Retrieved January 4, 2025 from https://ssrn.com/abstract=891060

Boubaker, S., Cellier, A., & Rouatbi, W. (2014). The sources of shareholder wealth gains from going private transactions: The role of controlling shareholders. *Journal of Banking & Finance, 43*, 226–246.

Brown, L. D., & Caylor, M. L. (2006). Corporate governance and firm valuation. *Journal of Accounting and Public Policy, 25*(4), 409–434.

Cadbury, A. (1992). *Report of the committee on the financial aspects of corporate governance.* Gee & Co., Ltd.

Cai, Y., Kim, Y., Park, J. C., & White, H. D. (2016). Common auditors in M&A transactions. *Journal of Accounting and Economics, 61*(1), 77–99.

Caixe, D. F., Kalatzis, A. E. G., & de Castro, L. R. K. (2019). Controlling shareholders and investment-risk sensitivity in an emerging economy. *Emerging Markets Review, 39*, 133–153.

Campbell, R. H. (1996). Letters to the editor: CEO vs. Nun: It's a draw. *Wall Street Journal*, August 12, Section A.

Carcello, J. V., Hermanson, D. R., Neal, T. L., & Riley, R. A., Jr. (2002). Board characteristics and audit fees. *Contemporary Accounting Research, 19*(3), 365–384.

Carter, D. A., D'Souza, F., Simkins, B. J., & Simpson, W. G. (2010). The gender and ethnic diversity of US boards and board committees and firm financial performance. *Corporate Governance: An International Review, 18*(5), 396–414.

Carter, D. A., Simkins, B. J., & Simpson, W. G. (2003). Corporate governance, board diversity, and firm value. *Financial Review, 38*(1), 33–53.

Chakrabarti, R., Megginson, W., & Yadav, P. K. (2008). Corporate governance in India. *Journal of Applied Corporate Finance, 20*(1), 59–72.

Chakraborty, I. (2018). Effects of ownership structure on capital structure of Indian listed firms: Role of business groups vis-à-vis stand-alone firms. *Emerging Markets Finance and Trade, 54*(10), 2315–2332.

Chancharat, N., Krishnamurti, C., & Tian, G. (2012). Board structure and survival of new economy IPO firms. *Corporate Governance: An International Review, 20*(2), 144–163.

Chau, G., & Gray, S. J. (2010). Family ownership, board independence and voluntary disclosure: Evidence from Hong Kong. *Journal of International Accounting, Auditing and Taxation, 19*(2), 93–109.

Cheffins, B. R. (2001). History and the global corporate governance revolution: The UK perspective. *Business History, 43*(4), 87–118.

Cheffins, B. R. (2013). *The history of corporate governance.* Retrieved January 4, 2025 from https://ssrn.com/abstract=1975404

Chen, X., Sun, Y., & Xu, X. (2016). Free cash flow, over-investment and corporate governance in China. *Pacific-Basin Finance Journal, 37*, 81–103.

Claessens, S., Djankov, S., Fan, J. P., & Lang, L. H. (2002). Disentangling the incentive and entrenchment effects of large shareholdings. *The Journal of Finance, 57*(6), 2741–2771.

Dahiya, M., Singh, S., & Chaudhry, N. (2023). Corporate social responsibility and dividend policy in India. *Management Decision, 61*(10), 3144–3168.

Dalton, D. R., Daily, C. M., Johnson, J. L., & Ellstrand, A. E. (1999). Number of directors and financial performance: A meta-analysis. *Academy of Management Journal, 42*(6), 674–686.

Dang, V. A., Kim, M., & Shin, Y. (2015). In search of robust methods for dynamic panel data models in empirical corporate finance. *Journal of Banking & Finance, 53*, 84–98.

Dedman, E., & Filatotchev, I. (2008). Corporate governance research: A contingency framework. *International Journal of Managerial Finance, 4*(4), 248–258.

Deloitte. (2015). *Nonaudit services: Restrictions and fee cap.* Retrieved January 4, 2025 from https://www2.deloitte.com/content/dam/Deloitte/global/Documents/Audit/gx-deloitte-non-audit-services.pdf

Dhaliwal, D. S., Lamoreaux, P. T., Litov, L. P., & Neyland, J. B. (2016). Shared auditors in mergers and acquisitions. *Journal of Accounting and Economics, 61*(1), 49–76.

Edmans, A. (2014). Blockholders and corporate governance. *Annual Review of Financial Economics, 6*(1), 23–50.

Fama, E. F. (1980). Agency problems and the theory of the firm. *Journal of Political Economy, 88*, 288–307.

Fama, E. F., & French, K. R. (1998). Taxes, financing decisions, and firm value. *The Journal of Finance, 53*(3), 819–843.

Filatotchev, I., & Allcock, D. (2010). Corporate governance and executive remuneration: A contingency framework. *Academy of Management Perspectives, 24*(1), 20–33.

Finkelstein, S., & D'aveni, R. A. (1994). CEO duality as a double-edged sword: How boards of directors balance entrenchment avoidance and unity of command. *Academy of Management Journal, 37*(5), 1079–1108.

García-Meca, E., López-Iturriaga, F. J., & Santana-Martín, D. J. (2022). Board gender diversity and dividend payout: The critical mass and the family ties effect. *International Review of Financial Analysis, 79*, Article 101973.

Goodstein, J., Gautam, K., & Boeker, W. (1994). The effects of board size and diversity on strategic change. *Strategic Management Journal, 15*(3), 241–250.

Grant Thornton. (2013). *Implications of Companies Act, 2013.* Retrieved January 4, 2025 from http://gtw3.grantthornton.in/assets/Companies_Act-Governance.pdf

Guest, P. M. (2009). The impact of board size on firm performance: Evidence from the UK. *The European Journal of Finance, 15*(4), 385–404.

Guizani, M. (2018). The mediating effect of dividend payout on the relationship between internal governance and free cash flow. *Corporate Governance: THe International Journal of Business in Society, 18*(4), 748–770.

Hanumantu, K. D., Worlikar, V., & Narayanaswami, S. (2019). The Punjab National Bank scam: Ethics versus robust processes. *Journal of Public Affairs, 19*(4), Article e1952.

Hasan, I., Singh, S., & Kashiramka, S. (2024). Does socially responsible investing outperform conventional investing? A cross-country perspective. *Asia-Pacific Financial Markets.* Advance online publication. https://doi.org/10.1007/s10690-024-09489-0

Hashim, H. A., & Amrah, M. (2016). Corporate governance mechanisms and cost of debt: Evidence of family and non-family firms in Oman. *Managerial Auditing Journal, 31*(3), 314–336.

Hope, O. K., Wu, H., & Zhao, W. (2017). Blockholder exit threats in the presence of private benefits of control. *Review of Accounting Studies, 22*(2), 873–902.

Jacobson, R., & Aaker, D. (1993). Myopic management behavior with efficient, but imperfect, financial markets: A comparison of information asymmetries in the US and Japan. *Journal of Accounting and Economics, 16*(4), 383–405.

Jayachandran, A., & Aakulu, S. (2023). *SEBI amendments to the LODR—An overview of key changes.* Retrieved January 4, 2025 from https://corporate.cyrilamarchandblogs.com/2023/07/sebi-amendments-to-the-lodr-an-overview-of-key-changes/

Jeffers, E. (2005). Corporate governance: Toward converging models? *Global Finance Journal, 16*(2), 221–232.

Jensen, M. C. (1986). Agency costs of free cash flow, corporate finance, and takeovers. *The American Economic Review, 76*(2), 323–329.

Jensen, M. C. (1993). The modern industrial revolution, exit, and the failure of internal control systems. *The Journal of Finance, 48*(3), 831–880.

Jensen, M. C., & Meckling, W. H. (1976). Theory of the firm: Managerial behavior, agency costs and ownership structure. *Journal of Financial Economics, 3*(4), 305–360.

Jiang, F., Cai, X., Jiang, Z., & Nofsinger, J. R. (2019). Multiple large shareholders and dividends: Evidence from China. *Pacific-Basin Finance Journal, 57*, Article 101201.

Jianakoplos, N. A., & Bernasek, A. (1998). Are women more risk averse? *Economic Inquiry, 36*(4), 620–630.

John, K., & Senbet, L. W. (1998). Corporate governance and board effectiveness. *Journal of Banking & Finance, 22*(4), 371–403.

Jones, H. (2022). *UK audit shake-up targets big firms after spate of corporate failures*. Retrieved January 4, 2025 from https://www.reuters.com/markets/financials/uk-audit-shake-up-targets-big-firms-after-spate-corporate-failures-2022-05-30/.

Joshi, M. (2020). *Harshad Mehta scam in 1992 ushered regulatory regime in Indian capital market*. Retrieved January 4, 2025 from https://www.moneycontrol.com/news/business/markets/harshad-mehta-scam-in-1992-ushered-regulatory-regime-in-indian-capital-market-5944281.html.

Khanchel, I. (2007). Corporate governance: Measurement and determinant analysis. *Managerial Auditing Journal, 22*(8), 740–760.

Khosa, A. (2017). Independent directors and firm value of group-affiliated firms. *International Journal of Accounting & Information Management, 25*(2), 217–236.

Klein, A. (2002). Economic determinants of audit committee independence. *The Accounting Review, 77*(2), 435–452.

Krishnan, R., & Subramanian, U. G. (2023). *How SEBI's norms for enhanced disclosures promote better governance*. Retrieved January 4, 2025 from https://www.livemint.com/money/personal-finance/sebi-introduces-new-amendments-431to-listing-regulations-for-better-corporate-governance-and-transparency-in-india-11688497626326.html

La Porta, R., Lopez-de-Silanes, F., & Shleifer, A. (1999). Corporate ownership around the world. *The Journal of Finance, 54*(2), 471–517.

La Porta, R., Lopez-de-Silanes, F., Shleifer, A., & Vishny, R. W. (2000). Agency problems and dividend policies around the world. *The Journal of Finance, 55*(1), 1–33.

Lintner, J. (1956). Distribution of incomes of corporations among dividends, retained earnings, and taxes. *The American Economic Review, 46*(2), 97–113.

Lipton, M., & Lorsch, J. W. (1992). A modest proposal for improved corporate governance. *The Business Lawyer, 48*(1), 59–77.

Low, D. C., Roberts, H., & Whiting, R. H. (2015). Board gender diversity and firm performance: Empirical evidence from Hong Kong, South Korea, Malaysia and Singapore. *Pacific-Basin Finance Journal, 35*, 381–401.

Lu, J., & Wang, W. (2015). Board independence and corporate investments. *Review of Financial Economics, 24*, 52–64.

Lugo, S. (2019). Insider ownership and the cost of debt capital: Evidence from bank loans. *International Review of Financial Analysis, 63*, 357–368.

Maury, B., & Pajuste, A. (2005). Multiple large shareholders and firm value. *Journal of Banking & Finance, 29*(7), 1813–1834.

Mitra, S. (2007). Nonaudit service fees and auditor independence: Empirical evidence from the oil and gas industry. *Journal of Accounting, Auditing & Finance, 22*(1), 85–107.

Mittal, A., & Singh, S. (2025). Does CEO gender impact dividends in emerging economies? *International Journal of Disclosure and Governance, 25*, 165–176.

Monks, R. A., & Minow, N. (1995). *Corporate governance*. Blackwell.

Mülbert, P. O. (2009). *Corporate governance of banks after the financial crisis-theory, evidence, reforms*. Retrieved January 4, 2025 from https://ssrn.com/abstract=1448118.

Nadeem, M., Suleman, T., & Ahmed, A. (2019). Women on boards, firm risk and the profitability nexus: Does gender diversity moderate the risk and return relationship? *International Review of Economics & Finance, 64*, 427–442.

Naiker, V., Sharma, D. S., & Sharma, V. D. (2013). Do former audit firm partners on audit committees procure greater nonaudit services from the auditor? *The Accounting Review, 88*(1), 297–326.

Narayanaswamy, R., Raghunandan, K., & Rama, D. V. (2012). Corporate governance in the Indian context. *Accounting Horizons, 26*(3), 583–599.

Pagano, M., & Röell, A. (1998). The choice of stock ownership structure: Agency costs, monitoring, and the decision to go public. *The Quarterly Journal of Economics, 113*(1), 187–225.

Pandey, N., Kumar, S., Post, C., Goodell, J. W., & García-Ramos, R. (2023). Board gender diversity and firm performance: A complexity theory perspective. *Asia Pacific Journal of Management, 40*(3), 1289–1320.

Pfeffer, J. (1972). Size and composition of corporate boards of directors: The organization and its environment. *Administrative Science Quarterly*, 218–228.

Piesse, J., Strange, R., & Toonsi, F. (2012). Is there a distinctive MENA model of corporate governance? *Journal of Management & Governance, 16*, 645–681.

Prakash, N., Singh, S., & Sharma, S. (2022). A non-parametric framework for evaluating governance–efficiency–productivity associations in commercial banking. *Journal of Economic Studies, 49*(7), 1159–1180.

Prasad, G. C. (2020). *Govt. mulls banning non-audit services by statutory auditors, breaking oligopoly of Big Four*. Retrieved January 4, 2025 from https://www.livemint.com/news/india/govt-mulls-banning-non-audit-services-by-statutory-auditors-breaking-oligopoly-of-big-four-11581093069988.html

Rajagopalan, N., & Zhang, Y. (2008). Corporate governance reforms in China and India: Challenges and opportunities. *Business Horizons, 51*(1), 55–64.

Rashid, A. (2015). Revisiting agency theory: Evidence of board independence and agency cost from Bangladesh. *Journal of Business Ethics, 130*(1), 181–198.

Reed, A. M. (2002). Corporate governance reforms in India. *Journal of Business Ethics, 37*(3), 249–268.

Roodman, D. (2009). How to do xtabond2: An introduction to difference and system GMM in Stata. *The Stata Journal, 9*(1), 86–136.

Saini, N., & Singhania, M. (2018). Corporate governance, globalization and firm performance in emerging economies: Evidence from India. *International Journal of Productivity and Performance Management, 67*(8), 1310–1333.

Sarkar, J., & Sarkar, S. (2008). Debt and corporate governance in emerging economies Evidence from India. *Economics of Transition, 16*(2), 293–334.

Sarkar, J., & Sarkar, S. (2012). *Corporate governance in India*. SAGE Publications.

Sarkar, J., & Selarka, E. (2021). Women on board and performance of family firms: Evidence from India. *Emerging Markets Review, 46*, Article 100770.

Securities and Exchange Board of India. (2018). *Securities and Exchange Board of India (Listing Obligations and Disclosure Requirements) (Amendment) Regulations, 2018*. Retrieved January 4, 2025 from https://www.sebi.gov.in/legal/regulations/may-2018/sebi-listing-obligations-and-disclosure-requirement-amendment-regulations-2018_38898.html

Selarka, E. (2018). *Corporate governance practices in India*. Retrieved January 4, 2025 from http://www.mse.ac.in/wp-content/uploads/2018/08/Working-Paper-173.pdf

Shi, L., Hong Teoh, S., & Zhou, J. (2023). Non-audit services in audit committee interlocked firms, financial reporting quality, and future performance. *Journal of Accounting, Auditing & Finance, 38*(4), 804–832.

Shleifer, A., & Vishny, R. W. (1997). A survey of corporate governance. *The Journal of Finance, 52*(2), 737–783.

Singh, S., Yadav, S. S., & Jain, P. K. (2013). Corporate governance practices: Empirical evidence from Indian corporates. *International Journal of Global Business and Competitiveness, 8*(1), 11–22.

Singla, M., & Singh, S. (2018). Impact of institutional set-up on the responsiveness to change in a firm's governance structure: A comparative study of public and private sector enterprises in India. *Global Journal of Flexible Systems Management, 19*, 159–172.

Solomon, J. (2007). *Corporate governance and accountability*. John Wiley & Sons.

Srivastava, V., Das, N., & Pattanayak, J. K. (2018). Corporate governance: Mapping the change. *International Journal of Law and Management, 60*(1), 19–33.

Suman, S., & Singh, S. (2021). Corporate governance mechanisms and corporate investments: Evidence from India. *International Journal of Productivity and Performance Management, 70*(3), 635–656.

Suman, S., & Singh, S. (2022). The role of multiple large shareholders in dividend payouts: Evidence from India. *American Business Review, 25*(1), 120–151.

Teichmann, F. M. J., Boticiu, S. R., & Sergi, B. S. (2024). Wirecard scandal. A commentary on the biggest accounting fraud in Germany's post-war history. *Journal of Financial Crime, 31*(5), 1166–1173.

Terjesen, S., Sealy, R., & Singh, V. (2009). Women directors on corporate boards: A review and research agenda. *Corporate Governance: An International Review, 17*(3), 320–337.

Titus, D., & Mittal, R. S. (2018). *Kotak Committee recommendations on corporate governance get SEBI sanction.* Retrieved January 4, 2025 from https://www.moneycontrol.com/news/business/economy/kotak-committee-recommendations-on-corporate-governance-get-sebi-sanction-2540971.html

Tran, D. H. (2014). Multiple corporate governance attributes and the cost of capital—Evidence from Germany. *The British Accounting Review, 46*(2), 179–197.

Upadhyay, A., & Sriram, R. (2011). Board size, corporate information environment and cost of capital. *Journal of Business Finance & Accounting, 38*(9–10), 1238–1261.

Wells, H. (2009). The birth of corporate governance. *Seattle University Law Review, 33*(4), 1247–1292.

Yarram, S. R., & Adapa, S. (2021). Board gender diversity and corporate social responsibility: Is there a case for critical mass? *Journal of Cleaner Production, 278*, Article 123319.

Zona, F., Zattoni, A., & Minichilli, A. (2013). A contingency model of boards of directors and firm innovation: The moderating role of firm size. *British Journal of Management, 24*(3), 299–315.

Zwiebel, J. (1995). Block investment and partial benefits of corporate control. *The Review of Economic Studies, 62*(2), 161–185.

Chapter 2
Corporate Governance and Investment Efficiency

This chapter presents and discusses the empirical examination of the impact of monitoring mechanisms of corporate governance on long-term investments by focusing on the efficiency of these decisions. Investment decisions are critical to a corporation's goal of maximizing shareholders' wealth (Mangesti Rahayu, 2019; Singh et al., 2012). Further, these decisions are imperative for economic growth and productivity (O'Toole et al., 2016; Pindado et al., 2011). However, efficient capital allocation can be disrupted by the issues of agency conflicts and information asymmetry, which results in the implementation of sub-optimal projects (Jensen, 1986; Myers & Majluf, 1984). A company's governance structure attempts to ameliorate managerial opportunism and information disparity between corporate insiders[1] and outside investors (Nguyen et al., 2015; Shleifer & Vishny, 1997). Therefore, the current research study seeks to disentangle the role of governance attributes pertaining to the board of directors, large ownership, and auditor independence in a firm's investment decisions. The underlined objective is conducted by analyzing the efficient investment expenditure of non-financial firms traded on NIFTY 500 from FY 2010 to FY 2019. The main analyses are supplemented with an additional investigation to ascertain how the effectiveness of corporate governance attributes has changed in response to reforms introduced by the Companies Act, 2013. Further, consistent with the growing emphasis on the need to identify contingent effects and boundary conditions of corporate governance (Aguilera et al., 2008; Oehmichen, 2018), sub-sample analyses are conducted by considering a CEO's tenure, a company's size, its age, growth prospects, financial condition, and the level of industry concentration.

The overall chapter has been structured as follows. Section 2.1 introduces the chapter. Section 2.2 presents and elaborates on the main empirical findings of this study. The results from the additional analyses have been summarized and described in Sect. 2.3. Lastly, Sect. 2.4 concludes the chapter by recapitulating observations from the empirical investigation undertaken.

[1] Corporate insiders include the controlling owner and managers.

S. Singh and S. Suman, *Corporate Governance Monitoring Mechanisms and Corporate Performance and Valuation*, India Studies in Business and Economics,
https://doi.org/10.1007/978-981-96-9736-6_2

2.1 Introduction

The association between corporate governance and long-term investment outlay can be expounded by understanding the problem of agency conflicts and information asymmetry that distort capital allocation decisions (Jensen, 1986; Myers & Majluf, 1984). In a frictionless world, optimal investment levels are determined solely by growth opportunities (Biddle et al., 2009; Richardson, 2006). However, it has been widely documented that the actual investment expenditure diverges from the target[2] level, resulting in inefficient capital allocation (Chen et al., 2011; Dahiya et al., 2024). This observed reality implies that companies undertake investment spending that is not in line with their growth options, which is reflected in the form of under-investment and over-investment (García-Sánchez & García-Meca, 2018).

Under-investment can be driven by the information disparity between corporate insiders and external investors (Biddle et al., 2009). The management of an organization has better knowledge and awareness about the worth and profitability of investment opportunities compared to external capital providers (Myers & Majluf, 1984). As a result, outside investors are willing to supply funds at a higher risk premium only (Cheng et al., 2013). The costly external financing thus forces the management to let go of positive net present value (NPV) investment projects, thereby leading to under-investment (Benlemlih & Bitar, 2018; Naeem & Li, 2019). Inadequate investment outlay can also be a consequence of the prioritization of personal interests by corporate insiders over minority shareholders' interests. They may prefer to pursue a quiet life as identifying and deliberating on the prospective investment opportunity set is a time-consuming and laborious process (Bertrand & Mullainathan, 2003; Ward et al., 2020). Since investments into new projects would expand a manager's work, they may be tempted to avoid complex decisions and turn down optimal projects in the absence of robust monitoring (Bertrand & Mullainathan, 2003).

Under-investment may also occur because of the distinctive risk preferences of corporate insiders and external shareholders. Career concerns and the limited diversification of wealth may make the executives and controlling owners risk-averse and persuade them to adopt a conservative approach (Amihud & Lev, 1981). Many long-term investment decisions, as in the case of research and development (R&D) projects, tend to be risky and have high failure rates (Lee & O'Neill, 2003; Lu & Wang, 2015). Since the prospect of loss can threaten their job security and reputation in the labor market, managers may cut spending on risky but valuable projects (Block, 2012). Similarly, dominant shareholders may avoid risky investments as their wealth is mostly tied to the firm (Caixe et al., 2019; Chen & Hsu, 2009). The under-investment in risky projects can also be a by-product of short-termism, whereby management focuses on immediate or near earnings rather than a business' long-term valuation (Stein, 1989). As expenditure on R&D can depress the current profits, it may shun related projects with long gestation periods.

[2] Target and optimal level of investment are used interchangeably.

Over-investment is a manifestation of the agency problem of free cash flows, which entails corporate insiders engaging in empire-building by investing excess cash flows into negative NPV projects (Jensen, 1986; Richardson, 2006). They overspend on sub-optimal investments to expand the firm size and enjoy the accompanying benefits of enhanced power and prestige (Stulz, 1990). A larger firm also enables management to have more resources under its control that can be used to extract private benefits at the expense of minority owners (Shleifer & Vishny, 1989). Hence, in the presence of surplus cash flows and poor monitoring, corporate insiders are likely to fulfil their aspiration of building empires.

Corporate governance structures have been established to regulate agency conflicts and informational asymmetry between corporate insiders and outside minority investors (Shleifer & Vishny, 1997). Therefore, it is expected that various governance devices would affect the severity of distortions to optimal investment outlay. Table 2.1 succinctly summarizes the theoretical relationship between corporate governance variables and investment efficiency.

2.2 Main Empirical Analysis and Discussion

Sample description

The target sample of the research study is NIFTY 500 firms that are analyzed from FY 2010 to FY 2019. After the exclusion of financial corporations from the initial sample on account of divergent regulatory requirements and investment activities (Benlemlih & Bitar, 2018; Biddle et al., 2009), some firm-year observations are also dropped due to missing financial and corporate governance data. The final sample consists of 3121 firm-year observations representing about 363 companies.

Regression model and variables

The dependent variable of the empirical study is investment efficiency (*INVEFF*). Its computation is based on the deviation of the actual investment spending from the optimal level. The target level is estimated using the expected investment expenditure model of Richardson (2006). Richardson (2006) regresses the actual investment expenditures on the previous year's investment outlay and the lagged values of other firm-level variables discussed in Table 2.2. The predicted values obtained from the model are taken as the optimal investment amount. The difference between actual and optimal investment amounts can be positive or negative, representing over-investment and under-investment, respectively (Chen et al., 2011). In order to standardize differences and capture efficiency, the multiplication of the absolute value of deviations with minus one is undertaken (Rajkovic, 2020). Thus, the higher value of deviation will imply greater investment efficiency.

The baseline regression model, as represented by Eq. 2.1, is adopted to examine the effect of corporate governance monitoring mechanisms on investment efficiency. A dynamic model is employed to take into account the persistent nature of investment

Table 2.1 Summary of predicted relationship between corporate governance monitoring mechanisms and investment efficiency

Variables	Relationship
Board size *(BSIZE)*	Larger boards allow directors to free-ride, which can enable management to pursue a self-serving investment policy (Chen et al., 2016). However, large boards can also provide more robust monitoring (Bzeouich et al., 2019) **H1:** Board size has a significant association with investment efficiency
Board independence *(BIND)*	Independent directors can objectively question investment decisions proposed by the management (Bzeouich et al., 2019; Lu & Wang, 2015) **H2:** Board independence has a positive association with investment efficiency
CEO duality *(CEODUAL)*	CEO duality gives the CEO substantial control, which they may misuse to further their interests (Kor, 2006; Shaikh & Peters, 2018) **H3:** CEO duality has a negative association with investment efficiency
Board gender diversity *(BGD)*	The varied viewpoints and expertise offered by women directors enrich board-room discussions by facilitating the board to analyze a management decision from a broader angle (Farooq et al., 2023; Mirza et al., 2020) **H4:** Board gender diversity has a positive association with investment efficiency
Controlling shareholder *(PROMOTER)*	The sizeable shareholding of the controlling owners can entice them to pursue a self-serving investment policy (Chen & Hsu, 2009). On the contrary, it can also align their interests to adopt a value-maximizing investment strategy (Chau & Gray, 2010) **H5:** Controlling shareholder has a significant association with investment efficiency
Non-controlling large shareholders *(NPD)*	Additional blockholders in India are usually outside investors that do not belong to the controlling or the promoter group[3] (Selarka, 2018), which makes it difficult to coordinate and cooperate (Basu et al., 2017). Hence, a monitoring role of other large owners is predicted **H6:** Non-controlling large shareholders have a positive association with investment efficiency
Auditor independence *(NAF)*	In the presence of a higher proportion of non-audit fees, auditors may become less vigilant and disregard adequate reporting of huge investments in associate entities, which can help detect over-investment behavior (Rahmat et al., 2021). Moreover, excessive non-audit fees result in severe information asymmetry, which can constrain a firm's ability to finance optimal investments at a reasonable cost (Jaehong et al., 2016) **H7:** A higher proportion of non-audit fees has a negative association with investment efficiency

Notes This table presents the hypotheses for examining the linkages between corporate governance and investment efficiency

[3] As per Section 2(69) of the Companies Act, 2013, a promoter is "a person who has control over the affairs of the company, directly or indirectly whether as a shareholder, director or otherwise" (PwC India, 2013).

Table 2.2 Variables used in the expected investment expenditure model

Variables	Measurement	Data Source
Investment	Investment expenditure is calculated by taking the aggregate of capital and research and development (R&D) expenditures. This aggregate investment expenditure is reduced by depreciation and amortization expenditure and cash inflows from selling plant, property, and equipment. The computed investment outlay is then normalized by average total assets	Author's calculation based on the data from Datastream ® and Bloomberg®
Growth opportunities	Tobin's Q	Bloomberg®
Leverage ratio	Total debt to total assets ratio	Datastream ®
Cash holdings	Cash and cash equivalents scaled by total assets	Bloomberg®, Datastream ®
Firm age	Number of years since the firm's inception	Datastream ®
Firm size	Natural logarithm of total assets	Datastream ®
Stock returns	Annual change in the corporation's market capitalization	Datastream ®
Industry effects	Industry dummies based on the Global Industry Classification Standard (GICS)	Datastream ®
Year effects	Year dummies	Author's calculation

Notes This table explains the variables of Richardson's (2006) expected investment model

behavior (Almon, 1965; Coldbeck & Ozkan, 2018). Equation 2.1 is summarized as follows:

$$\begin{aligned} INVEFF_{it} = {} & \beta_0 + \beta_1 INVEFF_{t-1} + \beta_2 BSIZE_{it} \\ & + \beta_3 BIND_{it} + \beta_4 CEODUAL_{it} + \beta_5 BGD_{it} \\ & + \beta_6 PROMOTER_{it} + \beta_7 NPD_{it} + \beta_8 NAF_{it} \\ & + \sum_{j=9}^{N} \beta_j CONTROLS_{it} + Industryeffects_i \\ & + Yeareffects_t + \varepsilon_{it} \end{aligned} \quad (2.1)$$

where, *INVEFF* denotes efficient investment expenditure. The main explanatory variables include governance mechanisms of the board of directors, degree of concentrated ownership, and auditor independence. The monitoring effectiveness of the board is determined by its size (*BSIZE*), independence (*BIND*), diversity (*BGD*), and the presence of a dual CEO (*CEODUAL*). The effect of ownership concentration is indicated by the percentage shareholding of the controlling owner (*PROMOTER*) and the presence of a non-controlling blockholder (*NPD*). The independence of the auditor is gauged by the ratio of non-audit fees to audit fees (*NAF*).

CONTROLS constitute the control variables that have been observed to affect investment efficiency. These firm-level control variables proxy for a varied degree of information asymmetry and agency issues that can distort investment decisions. For instance, large-sized companies are better positioned to implement all the optimal investments since they have comfortable access to a large stock of retained funds and financial markets (Boubaker et al., 2022; Kadapakkam et al., 1998). However, an inordinate supply of funds can exaggerate over-investment tendencies in such corporations (Denis, 2011; Jensen, 1986). Therefore, we control for the effect of firm size (*FSIZE*) on *INVEFF*. Further, firm age (*FAGE*) is incorporated into the econometric model to take into account the inefficiency in capital allocation in younger entities as they are relatively constrained in acquiring external financing (Arslan et al., 2006; Mulier et al., 2016). Inefficiency in investment outlays can also arise due to growing corporations' inability to raise cheaper funds for the lack of information symmetry about the true value of growth prospects (Myers & Majluf, 1984; Vanacker & Manigart, 2010). Hence, the influence of growth opportunities (*GROWTH*) is also considered in the model.

The effect of cash holdings (*CASH*) is also addressed as these reserves can mitigate under-investment while bolstering over-investment at the same time (Arslan et al., 2006; Bhuiyan & Hooks, 2019). Additionally, the critical influence of cash flows (*CFO*) on *INVEFF* is also dealt with since the surplus flow of cash can tempt corporate insiders to waste it on self-serving and negative NPV projects (Stulz, 1990). Cash flow volatility (*CFOVOL*) is also included in the regression model as unpredictable cash flows can exaggerate the issue of under-investment (Huang & Tarkom, 2022). The impact of leverage (*LEV*) on efficient investment expenditures is also examined because indebtedness can curtail over-investment of free cash flows but make under-investment severe (Aivazian et al., 2005; Pour & Khansalar, 2015). Moreover, the role of asset tangibility (*TANG*) in augmenting a firm's ability to borrow required financing for implementing all profitable projects is also contemplated (Alanis & Quijano, 2019; Boasiako et al., 2022).

The impact of financial distress (*ZSCORE*) on a corporation's ability to finance all efficient projects is also considered (López-Gutiérrez et al., 2015). In addition, the current profitability situation of a firm is also addressed in the empirical investigation by introducing an economic loss dummy variable (*LOSS*) in the model. Loss occurrence in a year lowers cash flows available at the disposal of corporate insiders for engaging in empire-building, leading to efficient investment expenditures (Lo & Shiah-Hou, 2022). Alternatively, inadequate cash flows can limit the financing required for implementing all positive NPV projects (Guizani, 2017).

Financial reporting quality (*FRQ*) has also been observed to enhance transparency about a firm's operations, which can mitigate information asymmetry and agency problems afflicting investment decisions (Biddle et al., 2009; Cheng et al., 2013). Therefore, the impact of *FRQ* on *INVEFF* is examined. The effect of dividends (*DIVIDEND*) is addressed as these payouts lower the free cash flow that the corporate insiders could have squandered through investment into unprofitable projects (Jensen, 1986; Rozeff, 1982). Further, the effect of managerial agency costs (*AGENCYC*) on *INVEFF* is also studied. Managerial agency costs encompass selling, general, and administrative expenditures under managers' discretionary control (Anderson et al., 2007; Tekin & Polat, 2021). Consequently, greater spending on such expenditures by self-interested managers can divert away required financing for optimal investment projects. Lastly, industry and year effects are also taken into account to address the impact of heterogeneous industrial conditions and macroeconomic conditions on *INVEFF* (Mullins & Holmes, 2018).

The detailed definition of each control variable has been elaborated in Table 2.3.

Research methodology

Equation 2.1 presents a dynamic panel data model that gives regard to the path-dependent nature of investment expenditure (Almon, 1965; Coldbeck & Ozkan, 2018). As a result, this model poses the problem of autocorrelation and endogeneity (O'Connor & Rafferty, 2012). Endogeneity concerns can also arise because of reverse causality, omitted variable bias, and measurement error (Arellano & Bond, 1991; Blundell & Bond, 2000). For instance, companies afflicted with under-investment owing to severe information asymmetry may use more independent directors to establish a reputation in the financial markets. There could also be an underlying unobserved effect, such as quality workforce, that affects both corporate investments and governance variables, resulting in a correlation between corporate governance and the error term. In addition, although the variables are measured in consonance with the prior literature, any measurement error could lead to endogenous covariates.

In order to address the concerns of autocorrelation and endogeneity, system GMM is employed to estimate Eq. 2.1 (Suman & Singh, 2022). Further, the issue of heteroskedasticity is minimized by using a two-step estimator since it is more efficient than a one-step estimator (Blundell & Bond, 2000). Lastly, Hansen J and AR (2) tests are conducted post the estimation to evaluate the suitability of system GMM.

Before undertaking the empirical investigation, financial variables are subjected to winsorization at 1% to mitigate the effect of extreme observation (Mendiratta et al., 2023).

Descriptive statistics

Table 2.4 depicts the summary statistics of the variables that have been utilized in the empirical investigation. The mean investment efficiency *(INVEFF)* is −0.0336, indicating that irrespective of excessive or under-investment, sampled firms exhibit an average deviation of 3.36%[4] in absolute values from the optimal investment level. Further, the minimum value of *INVEFF* signifies that a company has been able to operate close to its target investment amount in a given year during the periods examined.

In respect of the corporate governance variables of the study, the board size (*BSIZE*) is about 10 directors on average and ranges from 3 to 22 board members. This observation is in conformance with Somvanshi (2019), who reports that Indian

[4] Since investment outlay is scaled by average total assets following Richardson (2006), investment efficiency is expressed as a percentage of mean total assets.

Table 2.3 Summary of control variables used in examining the impact of corporate governance monitoring mechanisms on investment efficiency

Variables	Measurement	Data Source
Firm size *(FSIZE)*	Natural logarithm of total assets (Ward et al., 2020)	Datastream ®
Firm age *(FAGE)*	Number of years since the firm's inception (Chen et al., 2011, 2020)	Datastream ®
Growth opportunities *(GROWTH)*	Tobin's Q (Chen et al., 2020)	Bloomberg®
Cash holdings *(CASH)*	Cash and cash equivalents scaled by total assets (Chen et al., 2011)	Bloomberg®, Datastream ®
Cash flows *(CFO)*	Net operating cash flows to total assets ratio (Chen et al., 2020; Rajkovic, 2020)	Datastream ®
Cash flow volatility *(CFOVOL)*	Standard deviation of the operating cash flows to total assets ratio for the past five years (Rajkovic, 2020)	Datastream ®
Leverage ratio *(LEV)*	Total debt to total assets ratio	Datastream ®
Asset tangibility *(TANG)*	Net plant, property, and equipment divided by total assets (Chen et al., 2011)	Datastream ®
Financial distress *(ZSCORE)*	Altman-Z score (Rajkovic, 2020)	Datastream ®
Economic loss dummy *(LOSS)*	A binary variable that takes the value of one if net income is negative and zero otherwise (Chen et al., 2020)	Datastream ®
Financial reporting quality *(FRQ)*	Financial reporting quality (FRQ) is obtained by multiplying the absolute values of the discretionary revenues by minus one. Discretionary revenues allude to the extent by which earnings have been managed due to early recognition of sales. They are estimated from the earnings management model of Stubben (2010). A higher FRQ suggests better reporting quality	Author's calculation based on the data from Datastream ®
Dividend payouts *(DIVIDEND)*	Cash dividends to total assets ratio (Rajkovic, 2020)	Datastream ®
Agency costs *(AGENCYC)*	Ratio of a firm's selling, general, and administrative (SGA) expenses to its annual sales (Anderson et al., 2007; Chen et al., 2020)	Datastream ®

Notes This table describes the control variables employed in the empirical model to examine the impact of corporate governance mechanisms on investment efficiency

Table 2.4 Summary statistics of investment efficiency, corporate governance monitoring mechanisms, and other firm-level variables

Variables	Mean	Standard deviation	Minimum	Maximum
INVEFF	−0.0336	0.0326	−0.1879	−0.0000102
BSIZE	9.6232	2.6114	3	22
BIND	51.7133	11.1935	0	100
CEODUAL	0.2957	0.4564	0	1
BGD	9.5837	8.1438	0	42.857
PROMOTER	55.7309	16.7186	8.2	90
NPD	0.1166	0.321	0	1
NAF	0.379	0.4562	0	2.6496
FSIZE	20.4918	1.4729	16.856	24.306
FAGE	40.2097	23.4545	3.7917	155
GROWTH	2.6923	2.4074	0.6562	13.779
CASH	0.0752	0.1054	0.0008	0.6016
CFO	0.0993	0.0818	−0.1673	0.3407
CFOVOL	0.0561	0.0382	0.0085	0.2782
LEV	0.2243	0.1898	0	0.7268
TANG	0.3293	0.2009	0.0059	0.8044
ZSCORE	5.9158	6.031	0.1494	35.7928
LOSS	0.0747	0.2629	0	1
FRQ	−0.0257	0.0302	−0.1663	−0.0002
DIVIDEND	0.0251	0.0404	0	0.2439
AGENCYC	0.2396	0.1736	0.0075	0.9615

Notes This table presents the descriptive statistics of variables employed in the study

corporations have relatively larger boards. The average percentage of independent directors (*BIND*) is 51.71%, demonstrating that sampled companies have a relatively balanced composition of executive and outside directors. The lowest value of zero independent directors points out that few corporations have still not complied with corporate governance provisions of the Companies Act. Regarding the power of CEOs, the sample shows that they hold the position of Chairmen (*CEODUAL*) in about 29.57% of firm-year observations. It is also noted that corporate boards in India are not gender-balanced since the mean representation of women directors (*BGD*) is barely 9.58%. The reported participation is well below the average woman director percentage of 14% in European countries (Haque & Jones, 2020) and 15.5% in China. The mean shareholding by the controlling owner (*PROMOTER*) is about 55.73% and can go up to a maximum value of 90%. Thus, it can be inferred that there is a substantial concentration of ownership in the hands of the promoter, which can give rise to the expropriation concerns of minority shareholders. Contestability from non-controlling large shareholders (*NPD*) is comparatively lower because they are present in only 11.66 firm-year observations. Lastly, it can also be observed that sampled companies rely significantly on services other than audit from their assurance providers, as non-audit fees (*NAF*) constitute about 37.9% of audit fees.

Pair-wise correlation is also checked between the variables under investigation. The correlation matrix[5] renders preliminary support to the purported hypotheses. In addition, the use of various firm-level control variables is also validated as they exhibit a significant correlation with *INVEFF*.

Multivariate Regression Analysis

Table 2.5 demonstrates the findings from the empirical estimation of Eq. 2.1, which examines the dynamic association between corporate governance and efficient investment outlay. Column 1 depicts that the equity ownership by the controlling shareholder (*PROMOTER*) has a negative impact on *INVEFF*. This finding provides reasonable support for H5 and evinces assertions that the considerable voting rights conferred by substantial ownership may entice promoters to implement a self-serving investment policy at the cost of minority shareholders' interests (Faccio & Lang, 2002; La Porta et al., 1999). They may build empires to enhance their status and reputation or over-invest in pet projects to extract private benefits (Boubaker et al., 2017). Alternatively, the risk of losing their undiversified wealth or preference for a quiet life may persuade them to avoid value-enhancing complex and risky projects (Bertrand & Mullainathan, 2003; Caixe et al., 2019). Thus, the controlling owner discourages efficient investment expenditure. With regard to other monitoring mechanisms of corporate governance, the empirical investigation does not find a corresponding statistically significant effect on *INVEFF*.

The results in relation to control variables are consistent with the prior literature. Investment efficiency decreases with firm size (*FSIZE*) as large corporations are usually endowed with excess cash flows that can be misused to invest in sub-optimal projects, making over-investment severe (Denis, 2011; Jensen, 1986). It is also noted that high-growth firms (*GROWTH*) tend to make lesser efficient investment decisions. They are more prone to the problem of information asymmetry, which constrains them from raising requisite financing for all their positive NPV projects, leading to under-investment (Myers & Majluf, 1984; Vanacker & Manigart, 2010). Conversely, they can be plagued by performance concerns, thereby forcing the management to over-invest to indicate remarkable expansion in the company's operations (Chen & Liang, 2016; Jain & Shao, 2014). Further, investment efficiency also reduces with an increment in cash holdings (*CASH*) since it enables management to invest in negative NPV projects to extract private benefits (Arslan et al., 2006; Bhuiyan & Hooks, 2019). Finally, it is also inferred that firms with highly volatile cash flows (*CFOVOL*) make inefficient investment expenditures. These companies are restricted in their ability to implement all profitable projects owing to inadequate internal cash flows and availability of external financing at a higher risk premium only (Huang & Tarkom, 2022). However, the management of such companies can also be incentivized to enlarge current investment spending in response to looming cash flow uncertainty to

[5] The detailed correlation matrix is available upon requests to the authors.

Table 2.5 Corporate governance monitoring mechanisms and investment efficiency: Main regression analysis

Dependent variable: *INVEFF*	Overall sample (2010–2019)	Pre-reform period (2010–2014)	Post-reform period (2015–2019)
Variables	(1)	(3)	(4)
L.INVEFF	0.329***	0.379**	0.260**
	(0.115)	(0.172)	(0.103)
BSIZE	0.00177	−0.00101	0.000556
	(0.00109)	(0.00357)	(0.000766)
BIND	−0.000260	−0.000130	−0.000136
	(0.000228)	(0.000296)	(0.000140)
CEODUAL	−0.00412	0.00761	−0.0113**
	(0.00652)	(0.0157)	(0.00526)
BGD	−0.000305	−0.000284	0.000232
	(0.000292)	(0.000415)	(0.000175)
PROMOTER	−0.000592**	−0.00113**	0.000185
	(0.000297)	(0.000575)	(0.000148)
NPD	0.00539	0.00379	0.00237
	(0.00365)	(0.00930)	(0.00353)
NAF	0.00426	0.0269	−0.00244
	(0.00772)	(0.0187)	(0.00322)
FSIZE	−0.00768**	−0.00299	−0.00250
	(0.00350)	(0.00593)	(0.00268)
FAGE	9.13e−06	−0.000183	4.91e-05
	(7.23e-05)	(0.000156)	(6.08e-05)
GROWTH	−0.00410**	−0.00637	−0.00306**
	(0.00198)	(0.00389)	(0.00153)
CASH	−0.0438*	−0.0972**	−0.0342*
	(0.0247)	(0.0468)	(0.0193)
CFO	−0.00610	−0.00833	−0.0105
	(0.0165)	(0.0319)	(0.0158)
CFOVOL	−0.0650*	−0.0778	−0.0496
	(0.0365)	(0.0636)	(0.0420)
LEV	−0.0103	−0.0475*	−0.00135
	(0.0168)	(0.0286)	(0.0173)
TANG	−0.0260	−0.0399	−0.0181
	(0.0276)	(0.0472)	(0.0158)
ZSCORE	0.000419	0.000130	0.000125
	(0.000662)	(0.00125)	(0.000472)

(continued)

Table 2.5 (continued)

Dependent variable: *INVEFF*	Overall sample (2010–2019)	Pre-reform period (2010–2014)	Post-reform period (2015–2019)
Variables	(1)	(3)	(4)
LOSS	−0.00232	0.0162	−0.00318
	(0.00322)	(0.0158)	(0.00298)
FRQ	0.00810	0.407*	0.0821
	(0.0328)	(0.217)	(0.0700)
DIVIDEND	0.0949	0.316**	0.0288
	(0.0676)	(0.153)	(0.0507)
AGENCYC	0.0125	0.0334	0.0224
	(0.0177)	(0.0392)	(0.0155)
Constant	0.200**	0.179	0.0473
	(0.0896)	(0.142)	(0.0614)
Industry &Year FE	Yes	Yes	Yes
Wald F (*p*-value)	26.86 (0.000)	21.52 (0.000)	39.81 (0.000)
AR2 (*p*-value)	0.589 (0.556)	-0.544 (0.586)	0.307 (0.759)
Hansen J (*p*-value)	99.42 (0.305)	48.58 (0.294)	121.2 (0.477)

Notes This table shows the results of the two-step system GMM estimation of Eq. 2.1. Column 1 reports the results of the analysis undertaken on the entire sample from FY 2010 to FY 2019. Column 2 depicts findings for the period before the Companies Act, 2013 came into effect (Pre-reform period). Column 3 presents the results when the empirical investigation is done for years once the Companies Act, 2013 has become applicable (Post-reform period). Windmeijer's (2005) corrected-robust standard errors are indicated in parentheses. ***, **, and * denote significance at 1, 5, and 10% levels, respectively

avoid costly external financing in the future (Boyle & Guthrie, 2003). Thus, various firm-level financial control variables also affect efficient investment outlay.

The empirical investigation is also augmented to consider the passage of the Companies Act, 2013, which brought about sweeping reforms in corporate governance regulations in India (PwC India, 2013). In order to analyze how the effect of corporate governance monitoring mechanisms varies after the implementation of the new act, firm-year observations are segregated into the pre-reform and post-reform periods. The new Companies Act was instituted in the middle of FY 2014 on August 30, 2013 (Jhunjhunwala & Deepa, 2013; Selarka and Sarkar, 2021). Therefore, following Selarka and Sarkar 2021, the pre-reform period is extended up to the end of FY 2014. Thus, the post-reform period consists of years from FY 2015–2019, when the new act is in enforcement.

Columns 2 and 3 of Table 2.5 present the findings for pre-reform and post-reform periods, respectively. It can be concluded from comparing the results of the two periods that the negative impact of promoter ownership (*PROMOTER*) on investment efficiency (*INVEFF*) is prominent only in the pre-reform period. Its effect diminishes and becomes insignificant once the significant corporate governance changes are ushered in by the Companies Act, 2013. Interestingly, it is also observed that CEO duality (*CEODUAL*) lessens efficient investment expenditure in the post-reform period. This finding evinces the assertions of H3, which state that the additional authority entitled to CEOs when they assume the Chairman position may heighten their opportunistic behavior (Kor, 2006). They may pursue empire-building by over-investing in sub-optimal projects to enhance their reputation and expand the corporate resources under their discretionary control (Lu & Wang, 2015; Shleifer & Vishny, 1989). On the other hand, dual CEOs can also under-invest in complex and risky R&D investments as they can be guided by their career concerns, short-term performance pressures, or simply a choice of leading a quiet life (Bertrand & Mullainathan, 2003; Block, 2012; Stein, 1989).

Table 2.5 also corroborates the suitability of system-GMM for all the reported cases as demonstrated by the diagnostic tests of AR (2) and Hansen J. The AR (2) test is not significant, indicating the absence of second-order autocorrelation. The Hansen J statistic is also insignificant for all the models, which validates the null hypothesis that the system GMM-generated instruments are exogenous.

2.3 Additional Analyses

2.3.1 Over-Investment and Under-Investment

In the previously discussed empirical analyses, it is inferred that the percentage ownership of controlling shareholders (*PROMOTER*) deteriorates investment efficiency. It is also noted that in the post-reform period, efficient investment spending is adversely affected by a joint CEO-Chair (*CEODUAL*). In order to uncover whether *PROMOTER* and *CEODUAL* reduce efficient investments by intensifying either over-investment, under-investment, or both, a distinction between these two sub-optimal expenditures is made.

As specified earlier, the positive and negative differences between actual and optimal investment levels indicate over-investment and under-investment, respectively (Chen et al., 2011; Rajkovic, 2020). Hence, observations with positive deviations are classified into the over-investment category and those with negative residuals are grouped into the under-investment sample. Further, since this additional analysis focuses on inefficient long-term outlays, the dependent variable is re-defined to reflect abnormal investments. The absolute value of differences between actual and target investment spending represents sub-optimal investment and is taken as the dependent variable.

Columns 1 and 2 of Table 2.6 show the results from the empirical estimation for the over-investment and under-investment groups, respectively. It is observed that the dominant owner (*PROMOTER*) lowers investment efficiency by encouraging both over-investment and under-investment. Thus, promoters invest excessively in negative NPV projects to build empires and extract private benefits (Oswald et al., 2009). However, their risk-averse behavior owing to their undiversified wealth limits them from undertaking highly variable investments (Caixe et al., 2019; Chen & Hsu, 2009). Further, the findings demonstrate that dual CEOs (*CEODUAL*) make inefficient investment decisions by exacerbating over-investment in pet projects that maximize their interests. On the contrary, they have a diametrically opposite effect on under-investment. This observed impact contravenes the arguments underlying H3 and can be expounded by understanding the benefits of CEO duality as highlighted by the stewardship theory (Davis et al., 1997; Donaldson & Davis, 1991). A combined CEO and Chairman position provides a strong and unified leadership that can overcome the quiet life of the management by expediting board decisions and implementing value-enhancing investments (Finkelstein & D'aveni, 1994). In addition, CEO duality enables individuals to possess superior firm- and industry-specific knowledge, which may give them the confidence to execute risky but profitable projects (Hirshleifer et al., 2012; Yang & Zhao, 2014). Thus, when CEOs hold the post of Chairman, they tend to lessen under-investment.

2.3.2 Role of CEO Tenure

According to Aguilera et al. (2008), the efficacy of corporate governance devices is dependent upon the circumstances and environment a company faces. Therefore, the empirical investigation is supplemented to understand the contingent effects of various governance attributes on investment efficiency. The first contextual factor that is taken into account is the tenure that the incumbent CEO has completed in their office.

As per Zona (2016), the influence of the CEO over corporate decisions varies according to the length of their tenure. Newly-appointed CEOs are under constant scrutiny of the board and shareholders and have to work according to the mandate provided for which they have been hired. Further, CEOs in the early stage of their tenure have inadequate firm- or job-specific experience and expertise to undertake optimal investment decisions (Miller & Shamsie, 2001). In contrast, a longer tenure allows CEOs to gather substantial company- and job-specific knowledge, resulting in an enhanced ability to evaluate, select, and execute profitable investment projects (Simsek, 2007). Moreover, such CEOs enjoy overwhelming support from the board owing to their past successes (Lorsch & MacIver, 1989). Board approval is also a consequence of building close ties with the sitting directors over the years (Goyal & Park, 2002). As a result, a lengthy tenure can entrench CEOs, leading them to prioritize their interests. Long-tenured CEOs may prefer to pursue a quiet life by avoiding complex and strategic investments or sticking with previously successful investment policies that may no longer be optimal (Hambrick & Fukutomi, 1991; Miller, 1991). In addition, a considerable tenure aggravates risk-aversion, due to which a CEO may turn down R&D projects for fear of losing their jobs if the project fails (Caliskan &

Table 2.6 Over-investment and under-investment

Dependent variable: Inefficient investment	Over-Investment	Under-Investment
Variables	(1)	(2)
L.Inefficient investment	0.558***	0.0824*
	(0.143)	(0.0462)
BSIZE	0.00197	−0.000133
	(0.00175)	(0.000664)
BIND	0.000453	-5.50e-05
	(0.000455)	(5.92e-05)
CEODUAL	0.0212**	−0.00600*
	(0.00856)	(0.00347)
BGD	9.26e-05	-1.57e-05
	(0.000324)	(9.10e-05)
PROMOTER	0.000983***	0.000111**
	(0.000366)	(5.19e-05)
NPD	−0.0139	−0.000713
	(0.00860)	(0.00348)
NAF	−0.00147	−0.00106
	(0.00580)	(0.00193)
FSIZE	0.00129	−0.000818
	(0.00454)	(0.00198)
FAGE	0.000182*	-2.18e-05
	(0.000102)	(4.60e-05)
GROWTH	0.00549*	0.00192*
	(0.00292)	(0.00113)
CASH	0.101*	−0.0161
	(0.0600)	(0.0165)
CFO	0.0203	−0.0244**
	(0.0297)	(0.0124)
CFOVOL	0.132*	0.0190
	(0.0762)	(0.0317)
LEV	0.0481	−0.00288
	(0.0296)	(0.0139)
TANG	0.0416	−0.00285
	(0.0439)	(0.00719)
ZSCORE	−0.00112	−0.000125
	(0.000990)	(0.000378)
LOSS	−0.0171*	0.000987
	(0.00935)	(0.00328)

(continued)

Table 2.6 (continued)

Dependent variable: Inefficient investment	Over-Investment	Under-Investment
Variables	(1)	(2)
FRQ	−0.0957	−0.0803
	(0.0648)	(0.0705)
DIVIDEND	−0.109	0.0188
	(0.145)	(0.0479)
AGENCYC	0.00240	−0.00273
	(0.0336)	(0.00589)
Constant	−0.173*	0.0449
	(0.104)	(0.0377)
Industry &Year FE	Yes	Yes
Wald F (*p*-value)	22.25 (0.000)	65.13 (0.000)
AR (2) (*p*-value)	1.345 (0.179)	−1.097 (0.273)
Hansen J (*p*-value)	103.5 (0.333)	213.4 (0.201)

Notes This table depicts the empirical estimation results for the over-investment and under-investment groups. Firm-year observations with positive deviations (negative) from the target investment spending are classified into over-investment (under-investment) sub-samples. The dependent variable in this analysis is inefficient investment expenditure, which is the absolute value of differences between actual and optimal investment levels. Windmeijer's (2005) corrected-robust standard errors are reported in parentheses. ***, **, and * denote significance at 1, 5, and 10% levels, respectively

Doukas, 2015). Thus, investment efficiency can also be distorted in the late stages of CEO tenure.

In line with the preceding discussion, it can be concluded that a CEO's power and the severity of agency conflicts differ as per the tenure of the CEO. Hence, the observed effects of promoter ownership and CEO duality can also be expected to be stronger or weaker according to the different stages of a CEO's tenure. For the purpose of testing this prediction, the sample is segregated based on the quartile values of CEO tenure into the following groups: short-tenured, medium-tenured, and long-tenured CEOs. CEO tenure is measured as the number of years since a particular individual has assumed the CEO position in the firm (Goyal & Park, 2002).

Table 2.7 summarizes the findings when the sample is partitioned on the basis of quartile values of CEO tenure and the dependent variable is investment efficiency. The results depict that the negative impact of controlling shareholders (*PROMOTER)* on efficient investment outlay is prominent only when CEOs are in the early stages of their tenure (Column 1). In their initial years in the office, CEOs are under continuous evaluation by the board (Shen and Cannella, 2002; Berns & Klarner, 2017), whose members are often the representatives of the controlling group (Kuo, 2017; Sarkar et al., 2008). The substantial voting rights also entitle promoters to a significant say in matters relating to the CEO's performance (Faccio & Lang, 2002). Consequently, early in their tenure, CEOs are required to work according to the directives of the board and the dominant owner (Abernethy et al., 2019; Zona, 2016). Therefore, to secure legitimacy and jobs, such CEOs may implement investment decisions aligning with a controlling owner's interests. Hence, when the CEOs are relatively new to the office, promoters can drive their choice of investments that support their empire-building pursuits and minimize the risk.

Table 2.7 also demonstrates that the effect of CEO duality does not vary with the stages of CEO tenure. However, Column 3 shows that larger boards stimulate investment efficiency when the CEOs are in the late stages of their tenure. A longer tenure extends considerable power to CEOs over capital allocation decisions (Zona, 2016). Consequently, long-tenured CEOs may push for lower risky innovations and over-investment in previous successful projects. In such a scenario, an oversized board can provide strengthened monitoring and reduce sub-optimal investment expenditure by long-term CEOs (Bzeouich et al., 2019). When boards have a larger number of members, it is difficult for powerful CEOs to gather blinding support from all (Haynes et al., 2019). Moreover, large boards enhance the possibility of a CEO's investment decision being questioned by any one of the directors (Cheng, 2008; Upadhyay & Sriram, 2011). Furthermore, these boards bring a broad and rich experience that assists in making efficient investment outlay (Pfeffer, 1972). Therefore, when CEO entrenchment becomes severe due to their lengthy tenures, the benefits of larger boards can become dominant. This result somewhat aligns with the contentions underlying H1 that emphasize the advantages of oversized boards.

2.3.3 *Role of Firm Size*

The scope of investment opportunity set is likely to differ between large and small corporations. Smaller firms are usually characterized by higher growth prospects than larger ones (Fama & French, 2001). The realization of growth opportunities is expected to be affected by the information environment surrounding the companies (Myers & Majluf, 1984). Compared to their large counterparts, smaller business enterprises are relatively lesser known and have a lower analyst following, making them more prone to agency issues (Ben-Nasr, 2015; Shamsabadi & Chung, 2016). Hence, the implications of corporate governance monitoring mechanisms on efficient investment outlay are predicted to vary according to the corporation's size. In order to examine this assertion, the sample is divided into small-sized, medium-sized, and large-sized sub-groups using the quartile values of firm size (Prakash et al., 2024). The results from the empirical investigation undertaken for corporations with different ranges of firm size are summarized in Table 2.8.

Column 1 indicates that controlling ownership (*PROMOTER*) deteriorates investment efficiency (*INVEFF*) only in small-sized corporations. Since a smaller company has more scope for growth (Kuo, 2017), promoters may over-invest in pursuit of

Table 2.7 Corporate governance monitoring mechanisms and investment efficiency: Role of CEO tenure

Dependent variable: *INVEFF*	Short-tenured CEOs	Medium-tenured CEOs	Long-tenured CEOs
Variables	(1)	(2)	(3)
L.INVEFF	0.105*	0.193***	0.249***
	(0.0575)	(0.0503)	(0.0655)
BSIZE	−0.00244	0.00120	0.00240**
	(0.00155)	(0.00139)	(0.00120)
BIND	0.000106	4.93e-05	−0.000209
	(0.000150)	(0.000155)	(0.000160)
CEODUAL	0.0168	−0.00611	0.00666
	(0.0107)	(0.00847)	(0.00592)
BGD	−0.000246	6.54e-05	−0.000324
	(0.000443)	(0.000278)	(0.000423)
PROMOTER	−0.000247**	5.77e-05	-1.41e-05
	(0.000116)	(0.000226)	(0.000122)
NPD	0.000367	0.000641	−0.00214
	(0.00952)	(0.00589)	(0.0127)
NAF	0.00340	−0.000156	0.00518
	(0.00420)	(0.00773)	(0.00547)
FSIZE	0.00100	−0.000867	0.000285
	(0.00382)	(0.00379)	(0.00367)
FAGE	1.89e-05	3.24e-05	−0.000138
	(8.64e-05)	(5.92e-05)	(0.000104)
GROWTH	−0.00101	−0.00120	−0.00521*
	(0.00213)	(0.00240)	(0.00277)
CASH	−0.0177	−0.0275	−0.0221
	(0.0270)	(0.0399)	(0.0345)
CFO	−0.00557	0.00424	−0.0432*
	(0.0448)	(0.0232)	(0.0258)
CFOVOL	−0.0899	−0.0638	−0.0202
	(0.0845)	(0.0418)	(0.0586)
LEV	−0.0103	−0.0171	−0.0254
	(0.0270)	(0.0209)	(0.0248)
TANG	−0.0155	−0.0198*	−0.0361
	(0.0228)	(0.0118)	(0.0255)
ZSCORE	0.000631	−0.000917	0.000765
	(0.000945)	(0.000776)	(0.000692)

(continued)

Table 2.7 (continued)

Dependent variable: *INVEFF*	Short-tenured CEOs	Medium-tenured CEOs	Long-tenured CEOs
Variables	(1)	(2)	(3)
LOSS	−0.00578	−0.00854*	0.00821
	(0.00491)	(0.00447)	(0.00515)
FRQ	0.00663	0.0690	0.00443
	(0.0871)	(0.0475)	(0.0540)
DIVIDEND	−0.0476	0.0753	0.0185
	(0.0849)	(0.125)	(0.0765)
AGENCYC	0.0152	0.0245	0.00215
	(0.0250)	(0.0175)	(0.0248)
Constant	−0.00402	0.000263	−0.0223
	(0.0811)	(0.0794)	(0.0900)
Industry & Year FE	Yes	Yes	Yes
Wald F (*p*-value)	22.98 (0.000)	35.71 (0.000)	24.35 (0.000)
AR (2) (*p*-value)	0.0906 (0.928)	0.145 (0.885)	−0.275 (0.783)
Hansen J (*p*-value)	92.08 (0.362)	74.89 (0.109)	116 (0.378)

Notes This table summarizes the findings when the sample is classified based on the criteria of CEO tenure. Short-tenured CEOs encompass years of CEO tenure within the lowest quartile (CEO tenure < 2.5 years). Years of CEO tenure in the upper quartile are classified as long-tenured CEOs (CEO tenure > 19.66667 years). Observations in the middle two quartiles constitute medium-tenured CEOs (CEO tenure from 2.5 to 19.66667 years). Windmeijer's (2005) corrected-robust standard errors are shown in parentheses. ***, **, and * denote significance at 1, 5, and 10% levels, respectively

empire-building (Boubaker et al., 2017). They may expand their firms beyond the optimal size to reap the benefits of enhanced power and reputation associated with huge firms (Lu & Wang, 2015; Stulz, 1990). In addition, over-investment can assist the dominant shareholders in demonstrating remarkable expansion of corporate operations to the external capital providers (Chen & Liang, 2016). It is also noted from Column 1 that board independence (*BIND*) lowers *INVEFF* in smaller companies. This observation opposes the assertions of H2 and casts doubt about the effectiveness of independent directors. Promoters in small firms usually have substantial ownership, due to which they have an undue influence on the board (Mishra & Kapil, 2017), including its independent directors (Saini & Singhania, 2018; Singla & Singh, 2019). Further, these corporations may find it difficult to attract qualified independent directors with requisite industry-specific knowledge due to their lower reputation than larger firms (Ben-Nasr, 2015; Subramanian, 2022). Hence, the absence of true independence and required expertise can cause independent directors to ratify inefficient investments in small-sized companies.

Table 2.8 Corporate governance monitoring mechanisms and investment efficiency: Role of firm size

Dependent variable: *INVEFF*	Small-sized firms	Medium-sized firms	Large-sized firms
Variables	(1)	(2)	(3)
L.INVEFF	0.109*	0.320***	0.233***
	(0.0601)	(0.0869)	(0.0646)
BSIZE	0.00232	0.000333	0.000446
	(0.00301)	(0.00124)	(0.00171)
BIND	−0.00112**	0.000197	3.57e-05
	(0.000543)	(0.000299)	(0.000301)
CEODUAL	−0.000861	−0.00338	0.00791
	(0.0112)	(0.00611)	(0.00903)
BGD	−0.000550	1.50e-05	−0.000190
	(0.000689)	(0.000262)	(0.000287)
PROMOTER	−0.000409**	−0.000116	-5.96e-05
	(0.000178)	(0.000239)	(0.000122)
NPD	0.00394	−0.000708	0.00514
	(0.00908)	(0.0120)	(0.00542)
NAF	0.0132	0.00150	0.00158
	(0.0129)	(0.00433)	(0.00474)
FSIZE	−0.00696	0.00146	0.000529
	(0.00615)	(0.00314)	(0.00407)
FAGE	3.73e-05	2.67e-05	0.000102
	(0.000135)	(6.64e-05)	(8.39e-05)
GROWTH	0.00147	−0.00316	−0.00127
	(0.00265)	(0.00239)	(0.00433)
CASH	−0.0470	−0.0495*	0.0288
	(0.0561)	(0.0289)	(0.0408)
CFO	−0.00624	−0.000304	0.0294
	(0.0242)	(0.0157)	(0.0362)
CFOVOL	−0.0187	−0.0435	−0.0127
	(0.0631)	(0.0516)	(0.0810)
LEV	−0.0558*	−0.0300	0.0452*
	(0.0326)	(0.0195)	(0.0244)
TANG	−0.0296	−0.0300	−0.0229
	(0.0369)	(0.0229)	(0.0215)
ZSCORE	−0.000991	0.000154	0.000351
	(0.000735)	(0.00113)	(0.00121)

(continued)

Table 2.8 (continued)

Dependent variable: *INVEFF*	Small-sized firms	Medium-sized firms	Large-sized firms
Variables	(1)	(2)	(3)
LOSS	−0.00508	0.00555	0.00795
	(0.0148)	(0.00929)	(0.00879)
FRQ	0.113	0.140	0.00858
	(0.0837)	(0.0859)	(0.0537)
DIVIDEND	−0.0698	0.0358	0.100
	(0.0532)	(0.0491)	(0.105)
AGENCYC	0.00222	0.00320	0.00840
	(0.0279)	(0.0259)	(0.0196)
Constant	0.183	−0.0286	−0.0637
	(0.133)	(0.0683)	(0.103)
Industry & Year FE	Yes	Yes	Yes
Wald F (*p*-value)	43.69 (0.000)	36.11 (0.000)	45.09 (0.000)
AR (2) (*p*-value)	−0.999 (0.318)	0.0552 (0.956)	0.0662 (0.947)
Hansen J (*p*-value)	77.24 (0.439)	119.8 (0.412)	65.36 (0.464)

Notes This table depicts the results from the empirical estimation of Eq. 2.1 when the sample is segregated based on the quartile values of firm size. The bottom quartile observations are termed as small-sized firms (firm size < 19.47032). Values of firm size in the top quartile are classified as large-sized firms (firm size > 21.33156). The remaining firm-year observations in the middle two quartiles are grouped as medium-sized firms (firm size from 19.47032 to 21.33156). Parentheses indicate Windmeijer's (2005) corrected-robust standard errors. ***, **, and * denote significance at 1, 5, and 10% levels, respectively

2.3.4 Role of Firm Age

Older companies, as compared to younger firms, are endowed with larger internal funds (Saravia, 2014). They can also acquire external financing at a reasonable cost due to better credit and performance histories (Arslan et al., 2006; Mulier et al., 2016). Despite having comfortable access to capital, corporations in the late stages of their lifecycle may not undertake value-enhancing innovative projects. Aged firms tend to be susceptible to organizational inertia, whereby their management is encumbered by entrenched corporate practices and a previously acquired knowledge base (Petruzzelli et al., 2018; Teofilus et al., 2022). Consequently, they are inhibited in their ability to identify and execute profitable R&D investments. Thus, old enterprises may pursue a quiet life by avoiding complex projects and continuing with long-standing resource allocation patterns.

Corollary to the preceding discussion, it is analyzed if the impact of corporate governance attributes on investment efficiency is more prominent in older corporations. In order to undertake the purported empirical examination, sampled firms are split based on quartile values of firm age into the following categories: younger, middle-aged, and older firms. Table 2.9 provides the findings for firms in different stages of their lifecycle.

It can be inferred from Column 3 that CEO duality (*CEODUAL*) enhances efficient investment outlay (*INVEFF*) in older corporations. A joint CEO-Chairman position grants an organization with a powerful and united leadership that facilitates swift decision-making in response to current business and environmental conditions (Finkelstein & D'aveni, 1994). Thus, CEO duality can ameliorate organizational inertia in old-aged firms as they have the authority to enforce innovative projects that are in line with a business' growth opportunities (Boyd, 1995). Further, a dual CEO has superior firm- and industry-specific knowledge that can aid in identifying and executing complex positive NPV investments (Hirshleifer et al., 2012; Yang & Zhao, 2014). Hence, a combined post of CEO and Chairman can benefit older companies as it can restrain the quiet life of the executives.

2.3.5 *Role of Firm Growth Opportunities*

The value of the intangible investment opportunity set of growth firms is difficult to be ascertained by outside investors (Myers & Majluf, 1984; Vanacker & Manigart, 2010). As a result of higher information asymmetry, managerial entrenchment can be exacerbated in growing corporations. On the other hand, low-growth business entities with excess cash flows are more prone to the over-investment problem (La Porta et al., 2000; Shamsabadi et al., 2016). The empirical investigation is undertaken again to uncover the role of corporate governance on efficient investment expenditure for firms in different growth stages. In order to perform this extended analysis, firm-year observations are disaggregated using the quartile values of Tobin's Q, which proxies a company's growth prospects. Firms are grouped into low-growth, moderate-growth, and high-growth firms. Table 2.10 presents the findings of the stated empirical examination.

Column 3 indicates that a combined CEO-Chairman position (*CEODUAL*) lowers investment efficiency (*INVEFF*) only in high-growth corporations. As companies with significant growth prospects have an extensive capacity to expand, dual CEOs may be tempted to grow their firms rapidly by investing in all the available projects to reap the benefits of a huge empire (Jensen, 1986; Richardson, 2006). An expanded firm can provide the CEO with enhanced prestige and compensation (Lu & Wang, 2015). In addition, over-investment can help a joint CEO-Chairman portray impressive growth to outside investors (Chen & Liang, 2016; Jain & Shao, 2014). Consequently, when CEOs assume the post of Chairman in growing companies, they may abuse their strengthened power by engaging in empire-building.

Table 2.9 Corporate governance monitoring mechanisms and investment efficiency: Role of firm age

Dependent variable: *INVEFF*	Younger firms	Middle-aged firms	Older firms
Variables	(1)	(2)	(3)
L.INVEFF	0.368***	0.173***	0.149*
	(0.128)	(0.0356)	(0.0782)
BSIZE	0.000630	−0.000233	−0.000385
	(0.00180)	(0.00169)	(0.00127)
BIND	−0.000803	−0.000113	-6.44e-05
	(0.000627)	(0.000251)	(0.000256)
CEODUAL	−0.00356	0.00127	0.0164**
	(0.00515)	(0.00738)	(0.00823)
BGD	0.000208	−0.000312	−0.000555
	(0.000629)	(0.000332)	(0.000528)
PROMOTER	-2.74e-05	−0.000241	−0.000358
	(0.000531)	(0.000253)	(0.000311)
NPD	0.00270	0.00288	0.00269
	(0.0119)	(0.00562)	(0.0134)
NAF	−0.0127	0.00167	0.00416
	(0.0130)	(0.00309)	(0.00509)
FSIZE	0.000464	−0.00272	−0.00316
	(0.00678)	(0.00462)	(0.00402)
FAGE	0.000107	4.64e-05	3.23e-05
	(0.000466)	(0.000138)	(0.000125)
GROWTH	−0.00192	−0.000435	−0.00420
	(0.00638)	(0.00158)	(0.00301)
CASH	−0.0786	−0.0224	−0.0340
	(0.0940)	(0.0239)	(0.0278)
CFO	−0.000176	−0.00820	−0.000508
	(0.0300)	(0.0188)	(0.0322)
CFOVOL	−0.0486	−0.0606	−0.0382
	(0.0903)	(0.0432)	(0.0653)
LEV	−0.0129	−0.0193	0.0488*
	(0.0462)	(0.0243)	(0.0279)
TANG	−0.00761	−0.0664**	−0.0259
	(0.0282)	(0.0269)	(0.0280)
ZSCORE	−0.00101	−0.000832	0.00214
	(0.00247)	(0.000710)	(0.00155)

(continued)

Table 2.9 (continued)

Dependent variable: *INVEFF*	Younger firms	Middle-aged firms	Older firms
Variables	(1)	(2)	(3)
LOSS	0.00649	0.0199**	−0.00248
	(0.0212)	(0.00832)	(0.00508)
FRQ	0.0368	0.0870	0.0553
	(0.168)	(0.112)	(0.0588)
DIVIDEND	0.0193	0.0616	0.0711
	(0.0700)	(0.0490)	(0.0683)
AGENCYC	0.0238	0.0191	0.0495
	(0.0216)	(0.0228)	(0.0371)
Constant	0.0178	0.101	0.0488
	(0.160)	(0.0964)	(0.0941)
Industry & Year FE	Yes	Yes	Yes
Wald F (*p*-value)	26.27 (0.000)	22.11 (0.000)	27.85 (0.000)
AR (2) (*p*-value)	−1.607 (0.108)	−1.096 (0.273)	1.505 (0.132)
Hansen J (*p*-value)	40.59 (0.357)	132.7 (0.138)	52.44 (0.496)

Notes This table shows the results from the empirical estimation of Eq. 2.1 when the sample is partitioned based on firm age. Firm-year observations falling below quartile one are assigned as younger firms (firm age < 23 years). Observations beyond quartile three constitute the sample of older firms (firm age > 54.79 years). The remaining values of firm age ranging from the first to third quartile are classified as middle-aged firms (firm age from 23 to 54.79 years). Parentheses show Windmeijer's (2005) corrected-robust standard errors. ***, **, and * indicate significance at 1, 5, and 10% levels, respectively

2.3.6 *Role of Firm Financial Condition*

A company's financial condition plays an important role in determining the efficiency of capital allocation. A highly distressed firm is constrained in its ability to undertake all the positive NPV investments due to the availability of costly external financing (López-Gutiérrez et al., 2015). As the risk of default is high for such corporations, external capital suppliers are expected to provide funds at a higher premium only (De Jong et al., 2012; Gupta & Mahakud, 2022). Therefore, financially weaker companies are forced to undercut expenditures on profitable projects. On the contrary, financially sound organizations are better positioned to implement all the optimal investments since they have comfortable access to a large stock of retained funds and financial markets (Marchica & Mura, 2010). However, an inordinate supply of funds can exaggerate over-investment tendencies in financially healthy corporations (Cheng et al., 2013; Denis, 2011). Thus, the nature of agency conflicts distorting investment efficiency differs according to a company's financial situation.

Table 2.10 Corporate governance monitoring mechanisms and investment efficiency: Role of firm growth opportunities

Dependent variable: *INVEFF*	Low-growth firms	Moderate-growth firms	High-growth firms
Variables	(1)	(2)	(3)
L.INVEFF	0.388***	0.184***	0.150***
	(0.131)	(0.0441)	(0.0494)
BSIZE	−0.00253	0.000348	−0.000217
	(0.00204)	(0.00116)	(0.00110)
BIND	4.52e-05	−9.87e-05	2.67e-05
	(0.000143)	(0.000169)	(0.000228)
CEODUAL	0.00523	−0.000652	−0.00770**
	(0.00402)	(0.00693)	(0.00382)
BGD	−0.000223	−8.99e-05	0.000272
	(0.000322)	(0.000234)	(0.000223)
PROMOTER	−0.000121	-1.15e-05	0.000231
	(0.000113)	(8.11e-05)	(0.000290)
NPD	−0.00405	0.00406	0.0191
	(0.00606)	(0.00625)	(0.0166)
NAF	−0.00493	0.00191	0.00708
	(0.00340)	(0.00244)	(0.0110)
FSIZE	0.00520	−0.000257	−0.00242
	(0.00332)	(0.00277)	(0.00343)
FAGE	1.72e-05	-7.47e-07	0.000100
	(6.11e-05)	(4.53e-05)	(9.13e-05)
GROWTH	0.00111	0.00354	−0.00338**
	(0.00395)	(0.00268)	(0.00167)
CASH	−0.0529	−0.0151	−0.0121
	(0.0517)	(0.0304)	(0.0360)
CFO	−0.0182	−0.00839	−0.0654
	(0.0705)	(0.0189)	(0.0474)
CFOVOL	−0.0289	−0.0309	−0.150*
	(0.0422)	(0.0552)	(0.0891)
LEV	−0.0102	−0.0107	0.0110
	(0.0258)	(0.0215)	(0.0322)
TANG	−0.0194	−0.0351***	0.00362
	(0.0162)	(0.00952)	(0.0278)
ZSCORE	−0.00169**	−0.00189	0.000832
	(0.000828)	(0.00122)	(0.000777)

(continued)

Table 2.10 (continued)

Dependent variable: *INVEFF*	Low-growth firms	Moderate-growth firms	High-growth firms
Variables	(1)	(2)	(3)
LOSS	−0.00655	0.000229	−0.00648
	(0.00968)	(0.0109)	(0.0142)
FRQ	0.00611	0.169	0.268*
	(0.0604)	(0.105)	(0.143)
DIVIDEND	0.194	−0.0477	0.0991**
	(0.246)	(0.0434)	(0.0484)
AGENCYC	0.0315	0.00340	0.0128
	(0.0230)	(0.00710)	(0.0251)
Constant	−0.0835	0.00616	0.0314
	(0.0820)	(0.0625)	(0.0731)
Industry & Year FE	Yes	Yes	Yes
Wald F (*p*-value)	39.92 (0.000)	41.95 (0.000)	60.13 (0.000)
AR(2) (*p*-value)	0.225 (0.822)	−0.0354 (0.972)	0.0406 (0.968)
Hansen J (*p*-value)	78.19 (0.378)	87.41 (0.467)	125 (0.433)

Notes This table depicts the findings from the empirical estimation of Eq. 2.1, undertaken for firms in different stages of growth. Growth opportunities are proxied by Tobin's Q. Hence, all the firm-year observations within the lowest quartile value of Tobin's Q are grouped as low-growth firms (Tobin's Q < 1.1532). The sample of high-growth firms consists of observations whose values are above the upper quartile of the Q ratio (Tobin's Q > 3.2513). The remaining values in the middle two quartiles are categorized as moderate-growth firms (Tobin's Q from 1.1532 to 3.2513). Windmeijer's (2005) corrected-robust standard errors are shown in parentheses. ***, **, and * represent significance at 1, 5, and 10% levels, respectively

In line with the preceding discussion, it can be expected that the influence of corporate governance attributes is heterogeneous as per the firm's financial condition. For examining this prediction, firm-year observations are disaggregated based on the Altman-Z score, which is an indicator of a company's financial health. A higher Altman-Z score alludes to a lower risk of bankruptcy and financial distress (Habib et al., 2020). Hence, sampled corporations are grouped into three categories: firms in financial distress, firms with moderate financial conditions, and firms with financially sound conditions. The results from the empirical estimation of Eq. 2.1 for companies facing varying levels of default risk are reported in Table 2.11.

It can be noted from Column 3 of Table 2.11 that the negative impact of controlling owners (*PROMOTER*) on efficient investment expenditure (*INVEFF*) is prominent only in firms with sound financial conditions. Such companies have better availability of economic resources to execute their strategies. However, substantial funds at the disposal of corporate insiders can bolster over-investment behavior (Denis, 2011). Dominant shareholders can be enticed to utilize the power conferred to them by their concentrated holdings to push for the investment of excess cash flows in pet projects

Table 2.11 Corporate governance monitoring mechanisms and investment efficiency: Role of firm financial condition

Dependent Variable: *INVEFF*	Financial distress conditions (Low Altman-Z scores)	Moderate financial conditions (Medium range Altman-Z scores)	Financially sound conditions (High Altman-Z scores)
Variables	(1)	(2)	(3)
L.INVEFF	0.533***	0.208**	0.145**
	(0.148)	(0.104)	(0.0698)
BSIZE	0.000267	−0.000137	−0.000689
	(0.00151)	(0.000676)	(0.00147)
BIND	−0.000149	−9.77e-05	−0.000593
	(0.000359)	(0.000118)	(0.000486)
CEODUAL	0.00593	−0.00800	0.00423
	(0.0128)	(0.00717)	(0.00487)
BGD	−0.000605	−0.000371	0.000253
	(0.000407)	(0.000285)	(0.000310)
PROMOTER	7.62e-05	−8.24e-05	−0.00104*
	(0.000122)	(0.000250)	(0.000573)
NPD	0.000443	0.00197	0.0180*
	(0.00753)	(0.00448)	(0.0102)
NAF	−0.0124	0.00591	0.00595
	(0.00873)	(0.00625)	(0.00488)
FSIZE	0.000800	4.74e-05	−0.00293
	(0.00222)	(0.00296)	(0.00478)
FAGE	5.74e-06	−2.50e-05	−0.000108
	(5.55e-05)	(6.04e-05)	(0.000112)
GROWTH	−0.00548	−0.00800**	0.00186
	(0.00683)	(0.00311)	(0.00145)
CASH	−0.0837	−0.0229	−0.0234
	(0.0534)	(0.0237)	(0.0338)
CFO	−0.0190	−0.00413	−0.0718*
	(0.0298)	(0.0162)	(0.0385)
CFOVOL	−0.0430	−0.112**	−0.105*
	(0.0677)	(0.0516)	(0.0580)
LEV	−0.0150	0.0132	−0.00545
	(0.0294)	(0.0180)	(0.0625)
TANG	−0.0422	−0.0266	−0.0178
	(0.0258)	(0.0189)	(0.0271)
ZSCORE	0.00111	0.00165	−0.000735

(continued)

Table 2.11 (continued)

Dependent Variable: *INVEFF*	Financial distress conditions (Low Altman-Z scores)	Moderate financial conditions (Medium range Altman-Z scores)	Financially sound conditions (High Altman-Z scores)
Variables	(1)	(2)	(3)
	(0.00372)	(0.00124)	(0.000552)
LOSS	0.000820	0.00277	−0.0527**
	(0.00792)	(0.00529)	(0.0225)
FRQ	0.000254	0.0339	0.0597
	(0.0762)	(0.0424)	(0.0839)
DIVIDEND	−0.541	0.0208	0.0514
	(0.435)	(0.0687)	(0.0839)
AGENCYC	0.0186	0.00623	−0.00625
	(0.0129)	(0.0195)	(0.0151)
Constant	0.0186	0.0144	0.138
	(0.0583)	(0.0714)	(0.0877)
Industry & Year FE	Yes	Yes	Yes
Wald F (*p*-value)	31.30 (0.000)	29.95 (0.000)	1714.40 (0.000)
AR (2) (*p*-value)	0.807 (0.420)	−0.219 (0.827)	0.268 (0.789)
Hansen J (*p*-value)	69.59 (0.457)	119.3 (0.278)	57.68 (0.487)

Notes This table specifies the results from the empirical estimation of Eq. 2.1 when the sample is divided using the Altman Z-scores. Altman Z-score is an indicator of a firm's financial condition. A higher score signifies lower default risk (Habib et al., 2020). Hence, observations in the bottom quartile are classified as firms in financial distress conditions (Z score < 2.0393). Values of Z scores in the top quartile make up the sample of firms with financially sound conditions (Z score > 7.674983). The firm-year observations in the middle two quartiles are labeled as firms with moderate financial conditions (Z score from 2.0393 to 7.674983). Parentheses denote Windmeijer's (2005) corrected-robust standard errors. ***, **, and * show significance at 1, 5, and 10% levels, respectively

to derive private benefits (Boubaker et al., 2017). In addition, they can spend overly on sub-optimal investments in pursuit of empire-building, which would also expand the reserve of assets under their discretionary control (Chen & Hsu, 2009; Oswald et al., 2009). Contrastingly, Column 3 also depicts that the presence of non-controlling large owners (*NPD*) results in higher investment efficiency for financially healthy corporations. This observed effect is consistent with their monitoring role, which has been underscored while formulating H6. The large equity ownership of additional blockholders incentivizes them to scrutinize business decisions to keep opportunism by management and promoters under check (Attig et al., 2013; Maury & Pajuste, 2005). Hence, they can limit the misuse of excess funds in financially strong entities by disputing the inefficient investments being undertaken by corporate insiders (Boubaker et al., 2017).

2.3.7 Role of Industry Concentration

The dominance of few competing firms in highly concentrated industries results in gravely low competition in the given industry (Ali et al., 2014; Azar et al., 2022). The absence of adequate competitive forces can foster managerial slack, leading to inefficient operations (Schmidt, 1997; Shleifer & Vishny, 1997). In addition, the limited number of competitors can constrain the ability of outside investors to evaluate a company's performance compared to its peers. Consequently, corporate insiders of firms in concentrated industries can overinvest in sub-optimal projects or pursue a quiet life by shunning risky and complex investments (Giroud & Mueller, 2011; Hicks, 1935). On the other hand, competition makes inefficiencies costly and disciplines the management by forcing them to abandon their expropriation activities. Failure to do so can depress a firm's profits and make it incompetent, thereby magnifying the likelihood of an organization's liquidation (Schmidt, 1997). Thus, intense competition reduces the discretion of corporate insiders and encourages them to improve their efficiency (Srivastava et al., 2023). However, the literature also suggests that performance pressures induced by competition can drive corporate insiders to engage in opportunistic behavior (El Diri et al., 2020; Scharfstein, 1988).

In essence, the level of competition, as determined by the industry structure, influences the degree of accompanying agency conflicts. Correspondingly, the ramifications of corporate governance monitoring mechanisms on efficient investment outlay are likely to differ depending on the extent of industry concentration. Hence, the sample is partitioned using the quartile values of the Herfindahl–Hirschman Index (HHI), which indicates the severity of concentration in a specific market (El Diri et al., 2020). Firm-year observations are classified into low-concentrated, medium-concentrated, and highly-concentrated industries according to the quartile values of HHI. The findings from the empirical estimation undertaken for each of the stated sub-samples are summarized in Table 2.12.

Column 2 yields that the shareholding%age of the controlling owner (*PROMOTER*) diminishes investment efficiency (*INVEFF*) only in medium-concentrated industries. This result aligns with those reported by Akdoğu and MacKay (2008) and Park et al. (2017), which state that companies in medium-concentrated industries implement strategic investments aggressively to raise the entry barriers for new entrants and fend off existing rivals. Since such firms do not hold significant market power, promoters may attempt to consolidate the business' position by investing excessively in production and distribution facilities to deter new corporations from entering the market. Further, they may also try to entrench the firm by taking on unprofitable predatory investments to minimize competition from incumbent players (Bayer, 2007; Pittman, 1984). Hence, consistent with Scharfstein's (1988) argument that competitive forces intensify managerial opportunism, it

Table 2.12 Corporate governance monitoring mechanisms and investment efficiency: Role of industry concentration

Dependent Variable: *INVEFF*	Low-concentrated industries	Medium-concentrated industries	Highly-concentrated industries
Variables	(1)	(2)	(3)
L.INVEFF	0.284**	0.135***	0.202***
	(0.117)	(0.0314)	(0.0549)
BSIZE	0.00109	−0.000195	8.57e-05
	(0.00130)	(0.00100)	(0.000808)
BIND	0.000249	−0.000424	−0.000378
	(0.000342)	(0.000441)	(0.000250)
CEODUAL	−0.00149	0.00978	−0.00886***
	(0.00786)	(0.00644)	(0.00335)
BGD	−0.000496	−0.000158	0.000547
	(0.000457)	(0.000315)	(0.000409)
PROMOTER	-2.68e-05	−0.000837***	0.000295
	(0.000147)	(0.000270)	(0.000196)
NPD	−0.0112	0.00379	0.00838*
	(0.0137)	(0.00702)	(0.00442)
NAF	−0.000888	0.00502	−0.00351
	(0.00419)	(0.00845)	(0.00387)
FSIZE	0.00185	−0.00422	−0.000879
	(0.00424)	(0.00322)	(0.00303)
FAGE	6.55e-05	−0.000111	6.31e-05
	(8.47e-05)	(0.000103)	(7.77e-05)
GROWTH	−0.000520	−0.00249	−0.00212
	(0.00381)	(0.00159)	(0.00208)
CASH	−0.00575	−0.0274	−0.0123
	(0.0309)	(0.0241)	(0.0200)
CFO	−0.0147	−0.00561	−0.00651
	(0.0697)	(0.0193)	(0.0187)
CFOVOL	−0.0680	−0.119***	−0.0205
	(0.0802)	(0.0420)	(0.0525)
LEV	−0.0129	−0.0174	−0.0210
	(0.0322)	(0.0196)	(0.0160)
TANG	−0.0235*	−0.0547***	−0.0396**
	(0.0140)	(0.0181)	(0.0193)
ZSCORE	0.000132	−0.000687	−0.000909
	(0.00123)	(0.000532)	(0.000688)

(continued)

Table 2.12 (continued)

Dependent Variable: *INVEFF*	Low-concentrated industries	Medium-concentrated industries	Highly-concentrated industries
Variables	(1)	(2)	(3)
LOSS	0.000610	−0.00536	−0.00888
	(0.00470)	(0.00430)	(0.00702)
FRQ	0.0327	0.0827	0.0737
	(0.0879)	(0.0600)	(0.0622)
DIVIDEND	−0.0221	0.164*	0.0259
	(0.0473)	(0.0880)	(0.0384)
AGENCYC	0.00210	0.0220	0.0113
	(0.0189)	(0.0198)	(0.0166)
Constant	−0.0630	0.165**	0.0310
	(0.0941)	(0.0664)	(0.0692)
Industry & Year FE	Yes	Yes	Yes
Wald F (*p*-value)	32.05 (0.000)	27.32 (0.000)	31.36 (0.000)
AR (2) (*p*-value)	0.734 (0.463)	−1.020 (0.308)	−0.0409 (0.967)
Hansen J (*p*-value)	75.80 (0.485)	121.6 (0.493)	94.16 (0.447)

Notes This table demonstrates the results from the empirical examination of Eq. 2.1 when the sample is segregated based on the degree of industry concentration. HHI is employed to measure the severity of concentration in a given market and is estimated as the summation of the squares of all the firms' market shares in a given industry (Sheikh, 2020). Therefore, firm-year observations that are less than the value of quartile one of HHI are assigned as low-concentrated industries (HHI < 0.0329862). Sample values exceeding quartile three are classified as highly-concentrated industries (HHI > 0.0771521). The observations ranging from quartiles one to three are clubbed as medium-concentrated industries (HHI from 0.0329862 to 0.0771521). Parentheses report Windmeijer's (2005) corrected-robust standard errors. ***, **, and * denote significance at 1, 5, and 10% levels, respectively

is concluded that dominant shareholders of entities operating medium-concentrated industries invest in sub-optimal projects to fortify their market position.

It is also observed from Column 3 that the negative effect of a combined CEO-Chairman post (*CEODUAL*) on *INVEFF* is pronounced in highly concentrated markets. The absence of adequate competitive pressures can tempt a dual CEO to exploit their magnified power to tunnel resources by way of over-investment in pet projects (Richardson, 2006; Srivastava et al., 2024). In addition, it is inferred that a non-controlling large owner (*NPD*) substitutes for the disciplinary role of competition as it enhances efficient investment spending in concentrated industries. Since managerial discretion intensifies without the forces of competition, outside blockholders can use their significant voting rights to monitor and question management's decisions, which ensures that only value-maximizing investments are undertaken (Attig et al., 2013; Maury & Pajuste, 2005).

2.4 Summary and Concluding Observations

The current chapter analyzes and discusses the ramifications of corporate governance monitoring mechanisms on the efficiency of investment expenditure. The allocation of capital to long-term projects can be affected by the agency issue of empire-building, which results in the over-investment of free cash flows (Jensen, 1986; Richardson, 2006). Alternatively, a firm's investment decisions may also be dictated by corporate insiders' risk aversion (Chen & Hsu, 2009), preference for a quiet life (Bertrand & Mullainathan, 2003), or focus on short-term performance (Bushee, 1998; Stein, 1989), all leading to under-investment. Under-investment can also be an outcome of the availability of external financing at a higher risk premium owing to information disparity between the management and outside investors (Myers & Majluf, 1984). Corporate governance mechanisms have been established to regulate agency conflicts and information asymmetry that distort investment outlay (Shleifer & Vishny, 1997). Hence, the governance role of the board, large shareholders, and auditor independence is investigated in determining the efficiency of investment decisions using a sample of non-financial firms listed on the NIFTY 500 from FY 2010 to FY 2019.

The key results from the empirical analyses are presented in Table 2.13. Collectively, they highlight that the impact of corporate governance monitoring mechanisms is contingent upon organizational circumstances.

The subsequent chapter supplements the present analysis by inspecting the implications of corporate governance monitoring mechanisms on short-term investment decisions concerning the level of cash holdings.

Table 2.13 Summary of results from empirical investigation of corporate governance monitoring mechanisms on investment efficiency

Variables	Analyses	Results
Board size	Main effect	• No significant main effect
	Contingent effect	*CEO Tenure* • Positive impact in the late stages of a CEO's tenure *Other contingency factors* • No significant effect
Board independence	Main effect	• No significant main effect
	Contingent effect	*Firm size* • Negative impact in the case of smaller firms *Other contingency factors* • No significant effect
CEO duality	Main effect	• Negative impact in the post-reform period • Increases over-investment, reduces under-investment
	Contingent effect	*Firm age* • Positive impact in the case of older firms *Firm growth opportunities* • Negative impact in the case of high-growth firms *Industry concentration* • Negative impact in the case of highly-concentrated industries *Other contingency factors* • No significant effect
Board gender diversity	Main effect	• No significant main effect
	Contingent effect	• No significant contingent effect
Controlling shareholder	Main effect	• Negative impact, present in the pre-reform period • Increases over-investment and under-investment

(continued)

Table 2.13 (continued)

Variables	Analyses	Results
	Contingent effect	*CEO tenure* • Negative impact in the early stages of a CEO tenure *Firm size* • Negative impact in the case of smaller firms *Firm financial condition* • Negative impact in the case of financially sound firms *Industry concentration* • Negative impact in the case of medium-concentrated industries *Other contingency factors* • No significant effect
Non-controlling large shareholders	Main effect	• No significant main effect
	Contingent effect	*Firm financial condition* • Positive impact in the case of financially sound firms *Industry concentration* • Positive impact in the case of highly-concentrated industries
Auditor independence	Main effect	• No significant main effect
	Contingent effect	• No significant contingent effect

Notes This table briefly summarizes the results obtained from the current empirical examination

References

Abernethy, M. A., Kuang, Y. F., & Qin, B. (2019). The relation between strategy, CEO selection, and firm performance. *Contemporary Accounting Research, 36*(3), 1575–1606.

Aguilera, R. V., Filatotchev, I., Gospel, H., & Jackson, G. (2008). An organizational approach to comparative corporate governance: Costs, contingencies, and complementarities. *Organization Science, 19*(3), 475–492.

Aivazian, V. A., Ge, Y., & Qiu, J. (2005). The impact of leverage on firm investment: Canadian evidence. *Journal of Corporate Finance, 11*(1–2), 277–291.

Akdoğu, E., & MacKay, P. (2008). Investment and competition. *Journal of Financial and Quantitative Analysis, 43*(2), 299–330.

Alanis, E., & Quijano, M. (2019). Investment-cash flow sensitivity and the Bankruptcy Reform Act of 1978. *The North American Journal of Economics and Finance, 48*, 746–756.

Ali, A., Klasa, S., & Yeung, E. (2014). Industry concentration and corporate disclosure policy. *Journal of Accounting and Economics, 58*(2–3), 240–264.

Almon, S. (1965). The distributed lag between capital appropriations and expenditures. *Econometrica: Journal of the Econometric Society, 33*(1), 178–196.

Amihud, Y., & Lev, B. (1981). Risk reduction as a managerial motive for conglomerate mergers. *The Bell Journal of Economics*, 605–617.

Anderson, M., Banker, R., Huang, R., & Janakiraman, S. (2007). Cost behavior and fundamental analysis of SG&A costs. *Journal of Accounting, Auditing & Finance, 22*(1), 1–28.

Arellano, M., & Bond, S. (1991). Some tests of specification for panel data: Monte Carlo evidence and an application to employment equations. *The Review of Economic Studies, 58*(2), 277–297.

Arslan, Ö., Florackis, C., & Ozkan, A. (2006). The role of cash holdings in reducing investment–cash flow sensitivity: Evidence from a financial crisis period in an emerging market. *Emerging Markets Review, 7*(4), 320–338.

Attig, N., El Ghoul, S., Guedhami, O., & Rizeanu, S. (2013). The governance role of multiple large shareholders: Evidence from the valuation of cash holdings. *Journal of Management & Governance, 17*(2), 419–451.

Azar, J., Marinescu, I., & Steinbaum, M. (2022). Labor market concentration. *Journal of Human Resources, 57*(S), S167–S199.

Basu, N., Paeglis, I., & Toffanin, M. (2017). Reading between the blocks. *Journal of Corporate Finance, 45*, 294–317.

Bayer, C. (2007). Investment timing and predatory behavior in a duopoly with endogenous exit. *Journal of Economic Dynamics and Control, 31*(9), 3069–3109.

Benlemlih, M., & Bitar, M. (2018). Corporate social responsibility and investment efficiency. *Journal of Business Ethics, 148*(3), 647–671.

Ben-Nasr, H. (2015). Government ownership and dividend policy: Evidence from newly privatized firms. *Journal of Business Finance & Accounting, 42*(5–6), 665–704.

Berns, K. V., & Klarner, P. (2017). A review of the CEO succession literature and a future research program. *Academy of Management Perspectives, 31*(2), 83–108.

Bertrand, M., & Mullainathan, S. (2003). Enjoying the quiet life? Corporate governance and managerial preferences. *Journal of Political Economy, 111*(5), 1043–1075.

Bhuiyan, M. B. U., & Hooks, J. (2019). Cash holding and over-investment behavior in firms with problem directors. *International Review of Economics & Finance, 61*, 35–51.

Biddle, G. C., Hilary, G., & Verdi, R. S. (2009). How does financial reporting quality relate to investment efficiency? *Journal of Accounting and Economics, 48*(2–3), 112–131.

Block, J. H. (2012). R&D investments in family and founder firms: An agency perspective. *Journal of Business Venturing, 27*(2), 248–265.

Blundell, R., & Bond, S. (2000). GMM estimation with persistent panel data: An application to production functions. *Econometric Reviews, 19*(3), 321–340.

Boasiako, K. A., Manu, S. A., & Antwi-Darko, N. Y. (2022). Does financing influence the sensitivity of cash and investment to asset tangibility? *International Review of Financial Analysis, 80*, Article 102055.

Boyd, B. K. (1995). CEO duality and firm performance: A contingency model. *Strategic Management Journal, 16*(4), 301–312.

Boyle, G. W., & Guthrie, G. A. (2003). Investment, uncertainty, and liquidity. *The Journal of Finance, 58*(5), 2143–2166.

Boubaker, S., Dang, V. A., & Sassi, S. (2022). Competitive pressure and firm investment efficiency: Evidence from corporate employment decisions. *European Financial Management, 28*(1), 113–161.

Boubaker, S., Rouatbi, W., & Saffar, W. (2017). The role of multiple large shareholders in the choice of debt source. *Financial Management, 46*(1), 241–274.

Bushee, B. J. (1998). The influence of institutional investors on myopic R&D investment behavior. *Accounting Review*, 305–333.

Bzeouich, B., Lakhal, F., & Dammak, N. (2019). Earnings management and corporate investment efficiency: Does the board of directors matter? *Journal of Financial Reporting and Accounting, 17*(4), 650–670.

Caixe, D. F., Kalatzis, A. E. G., & de Castro, L. R. K. (2019). Controlling shareholders and investment-risk sensitivity in an emerging economy. *Emerging Markets Review, 39*, 133–153.

Caliskan, D., & Doukas, J. A. (2015). CEO risk preferences and dividend policy decisions. *Journal of Corporate Finance, 35*, 18–42.

Chau, G., & Gray, S. J. (2010). Family ownership, board independence and voluntary disclosure: Evidence from Hong Kong. *Journal of International Accounting, Auditing and Taxation, 19*(2), 93–109.
Chen, F., Hope, O. K., Li, Q., & Wang, X. (2011). Financial reporting quality and investment efficiency of private firms in emerging markets. *The Accounting Review, 86*(4), 1255–1288.
Chen, H. L., & Hsu, W. T. (2009). Family ownership, board independence, and R&D investment. *Family Business Reviewr, 22*(4), 347–362.
Chen, H. K., & Liang, W. L. (2016). Do venture capitalists improve the operating performance of IPOs? *International Review of Economics & Finance, 44*, 291–304.
Chen, X., Sun, Y., & Xu, X. (2016). Free cash flow, over-investment and corporate governance in China. *Pacific-Basin Finance Journal, 37*, 81–103.
Chen, Y., Cui, C., Yang, T., & Zhang, X. (2020). Political favouritism and investment efficiency. *Pacific-Basin Finance Journal, 61*, Article 101058.
Cheng, M., Dhaliwal, D., & Zhang, Y. (2013). Does investment efficiency improve after the disclosure of material weaknesses in internal control over financial reporting? *Journal of Accounting and Economics, 56*(1), 1–18.
Cheng, S. (2008). Board size and the variability of corporate performance. *Journal of Financial Economics, 87*(1), 157–176.
Coldbeck, B., & Ozkan, A. (2018). Comparison of adjustment speeds in target research and development and capital investment: What did the financial crisis of 2007 change? *Journal of Business Research, 84*, 1–10.
Dahiya, M., Singh, S., & Chaudhry, N. (2024). Unveiling the role of corporate social responsibility on the efficiency of capital investments and their speed of adjustment: Insights from India. *Asia Pacific Journal of Management, 41*, 1963–1988.
Davis, J. H., Schoorman, F. D., & Donaldson, L. (1997). Toward a stewardship theory of management. *Academy of Management Review, 22*(1), 20–47.
De Jong, A., Verbeek, M., & Verwijmeren, P. (2012). Does financial flexibility reduce investment distortions? *Journal of Financial Research, 35*(2), 243–259.
Denis, D. J. (2011). Financial flexibility and corporate liquidity. *Journal of Corporate Finance, 17*(3), 667–674.
Donaldson, L., & Davis, J. H. (1991). Stewardship theory or agency theory: CEO governance and shareholder returns. *Australian Journal of Management, 16*(1), 49–64.
El Diri, M., Lambrinoudakis, C., & Alhadab, M. (2020). Corporate governance and earnings management in concentrated markets. *Journal of Business Research, 108*, 291–306.
Faccio, M., & Lang, L. H. (2002). The ultimate ownership of Western European corporations. *Journal of Financial Economics, 65*(3), 365–395.
Fama, E. F., & French, K. R. (2001). Disappearing dividends: Changing firm characteristics or lower propensity to pay? *Journal of Financial Economics, 60*, 3–43.
Farooq, S., Gan, C., & Nadeem, M. (2023). Boardroom gender diversity and investment inefficiency: New evidence from the United Kingdom. *Corporate Governance: An International Review, 31*(1), 2–32.
Finkelstein, S., & D'aveni, R. A. (1994). CEO duality as a double-edged sword: How boards of directors balance entrenchment avoidance and unity of command. *Academy of Management Journal, 37*(5), 1079–1108.
García-Sánchez, I. M., & García-Meca, E. (2018). Do talented managers invest more efficiently? The moderating role of corporate governance mechanisms. *Corporate Governance: An International Review, 26*(4), 238–254.
Giroud, X., & Mueller, H. M. (2011). Corporate governance, product market competition, and equity prices. *The Journal of Finance, 66*(2), 563–600.
Goyal, V. K., & Park, C. W. (2002). Board leadership structure and CEO turnover. *Journal of Corporate Finance, 8*(1), 49–66.
Guizani, M. (2017). The financial determinants of corporate cash holdings in an oil rich country: Evidence from Kingdom of Saudi Arabia. *Borsa Istanbul Review, 17*(3), 133–143.

Gupta, G., & Mahakud, J. (2022). Impact of financial distress on investment-cash flow sensitivity: Evidence from emerging economy. *International Journal of Managerial Finance, 19*(4), 713–743.

Habib, A., Costa, M. D., Huang, H. J., Bhuiyan, M. B. U., & Sun, L. (2020). Determinants and consequences of financial distress: Review of the empirical literature. *Accounting & Finance, 60*, 1023–1075.

Hambrick, D. C., & Fukutomi, G. D. (1991). The seasons of a CEO's tenure. *Academy of Management Review, 16*(4), 719–742.

Haque, F., & Jones, M. J. (2020). European firms' corporate biodiversity disclosures and board gender diversity from 2002 to 2016. *The British Accounting Review, 52*(2), Article 100893.

Haynes, K. T., Zattoni, A., Boyd, B. K., & Minichilli, A. (2019). Figureheads or potentates? CEO power and board oversight in the context of Sarbanes Oxley. *Corporate Governance: An International Review, 27*(6), 402–426.

He, W. (2012). Agency problems, product market competition and dividend policies in Japan. *Accounting & Finance, 52*(3), 873–901.

Hicks, J. R. (1935). Annual survey of economic theory: the theory of monopoly. *Econometrica: Journal of the Econometric Society*, 1–20.

Hirshleifer, D., Low, A., & Teoh, S. H. (2012). Are overconfident CEOs better innovators? *The Journal of Finance, 67*(4), 1457–1498.

Huang, X., & Tarkom, A. (2022). Labor investment efficiency and cash flow volatility. *Finance Research Letters, 50*, Article 103227.

Jaehong, L., Eunjung, C., & Hyunjung, C. (2016). The effect of internal control weakness on investment efficiency. *Journal of Applied Business Research, 32*(3), 649–662.

Jain, B. A., & Shao, Y. (2014). Family involvement and post-IPO investment policy. *Family Business Review, 27*(4), 287–306.

Jensen, M. C. (1986). Agency costs of free cash flow, corporate finance, and takeovers. *The American Economic Review, 76*(2), 323–329.

Jhunjhunwala, S., & Deepa, B. (2013). Corporate Governance Law in India: An update comparative analysis of Companies Act 2013 and Companies Act 1956. *Indian Journal of Corporate Governance, 6*(2), 52–114.

Kadapakkam, P. R., Kumar, P. C., & Riddick, L. A. (1998). The impact of cash flows and firm size on investment: The international evidence. *Journal of Banking & Finance, 22*(3), 293–320.

Kim, J. B., Lee, J. J., & Park, J. C. (2015). Audit quality and the market value of cash holdings: The case of office-level auditor industry specialization. *Auditing: A Journal of Practice & Theory, 34*(2), 27–57.

Kor, Y. Y. (2006). Direct and interaction effects of top management team and board compositions on R&D investment strategy. *Strategic Management Journal, 27*(11), 1081–1099.

Kuo, L. W. (2017). Reputation as a governance mechanism? Evidence from payout policy of insider-controlled firms in Taiwan. *Journal of Business Finance & Accounting, 44*(9–10), 1443–1476.

La Porta, R., Lopez-de-Silanes, F., & Shleifer, A. (1999). Corporate ownership around the world. *The Journal of Finance, 54*(2), 471–517.

La Porta, R., Lopez-de-Silanes, F., Shleifer, A., & Vishny, R. W. (2000). Agency problems and dividend policies around the world. *The Journal of Finance, 55*(1), 1–33.

Lee, P. M., & O'Neill, H. M. (2003). Ownership structures and R&D investments of US and Japanese firms: Agency and stewardship perspectives. *Academy of Management Journal, 46*(2), 212–225.

Lo, H. C., & Shiah-Hou, S. R. (2022). The effect of CEO power on overinvestment. *Review of Quantitative Finance and Accounting, 59*, 23–63.

López-Gutiérrez, C., Sanfilippo-Azofra, S., & Torre-Olmo, B. (2015). Investment decisions of companies in financial distress. *BRQ Business Research Quarterly, 18*(3), 174–187.

Lorsch, J. W., & MacIver, E. (1989). *Pawns or potentates: The reality of America's corporate boards*. Harvard Business School Press.

Lu, J., & Wang, W. (2015). Board independence and corporate investments. *Review of Financial Economics, 24*, 52–64.

Mangesti Rahayu, S. (2019). Mediation effects financial performance toward influences of corporate growth and assets utilization. *International Journal of Productivity and Performance Management, 68*(5), 981–996.
Marchica, M. T., & Mura, R. (2010). Financial flexibility, investment ability, and firm value: Evidence from firms with spare debt capacity. *Financial Management, 39*(4), 1339–1365.
Maury, B., & Pajuste, A. (2005). Multiple large shareholders and firm value. *Journal of Banking & Finance, 29*(7), 1813–1834.
Mendiratta, A., Singh, S., Yadav, S. S., & Mahajan, A. (2023). When do ESG controversies reduce firm value in India? *Global Finance Journal, 55*, Article 100809.
Miller, D. (1991). Stale in the saddle: CEO tenure and the match between organization and environment. *Management Science, 37*(1), 34–52.
Miller, D., & Shamsie, J. (2001). Learning across the life cycle: Experimentation and performance among the Hollywood studio heads. *Strategic Management Journal, 22*(8), 725–745.
Mirza, S. S., Majeed, M. A., & Ahsan, T. (2020). Board gender diversity, competitive pressure and investment efficiency in Chinese private firms. *Eurasian Business Review, 10*, 417–440.
Mishra, R., & Kapil, S. (2017). Effect of ownership structure and board structure on firm value: Evidence from India. *Corporate Governance: The International Journal of Business in Society, 17*(4), 700–726.
Mulier, K., Schoors, K., & Merlevede, B. (2016). Investment-cash flow sensitivity and financial constraints: Evidence from unquoted European SMEs. *Journal of Banking & Finance, 73*, 182–197.
Mullins, F., & Holmes, J. (2018). Balancing board? The effects of board independence and capital on firms offering work-family benefits. *Human Resource Management, 57*(2), 457–469.
Myers, S. C., & Majluf, N. S. (1984). Corporate financing and investment decisions when firms have information that investors do not have. *Journal of Financial Economics, 13*(2), 187–221.
Naeem, K., & Li, M. C. (2019). Corporate investment efficiency: The role of financial development in firms with financing constraints and agency issues in OECD non-financial firms. *International Review of Financial Analysis, 62*, 53–68.
Nguyen, T., Nguyen, H. G., & Yin, X. (2015). Corporate Governance and Corporate Financing and Investment during the 2007–2008 Financial Crisis. *Financial Management, 44*(1), 115–146.
O'Connor, M., & Rafferty, M. (2012). Corporate governance and innovation. *Journal of Financial and Quantitative Analysis, 47*(2), 397–413.
O'Toole, C. M., Morgenroth, E. L., & Ha, T. T. (2016). Investment efficiency, state-owned enterprises and privatisation: Evidence from Viet Nam in Transition. *Journal of Corporate Finance, 37*, 93–108.
Oehmichen, J. (2018). East meets west—Corporate governance in Asian emerging markets: A literature review and research agenda. *International Business Review, 27*(2), 465–480.
Oswald, S. L., Muse, L. A., & Rutherford, M. W. (2009). The influence of large stake family control on performance: Is it agency or entrenchment? *Journal of Small Business Management, 47*(1), 116–135.
Park, K., Yang, I., & Yang, T. (2017). The peer-firm effect on firm's investment decisions. *The North American Journal of Economics and Finance, 40*, 178–199.
Petruzzelli, A. M., Ardito, L., & Savino, T. (2018). Maturity of knowledge inputs and innovation value: The moderating effect of firm age and size. *Journal of Business Research, 86*, 190–201.
Pfeffer, J. (1972). Size and composition of corporate boards of directors: The organization and its environment. *Administrative Science Quarterly*, 218–228.
Pindado, J., Requejo, I., & De La Torre, C. (2011). Family control and investment–cash flow sensitivity: Empirical evidence from the Euro zone. *Journal of Corporate Finance, 17*(5), 1389–1409.
Pittman, R. W. (1984). Predatory investment US vs IBM. *International Journal of Industrial Organization, 2*(4), 341–365.
Pour, E. K., & Khansalar, E. (2015). Does debt capacity matter in the choice of debt in reducing the underinvestment problem? *Research in International Business and Finance, 34*, 251–264.

Prakash, N., Singh, S., & Sharma, S. (2024). Technological diffusion, bank performance, and Solow's paradox: Insights from an emerging economy. *Journal of the Knowledge Economy*. Advanced online publication. https://doi.org/10.1007/s13132-024-02347-4.

PwC India. (2013). *Companies Act, 2013 Key Highlights and analysis*. Retrieved January 4, 2025 from companies-act-2013-key-highlights-and-analysis.pdf (pwc.in).

Rahmat, M. M., Ali, S. H. A., & Saleh, N. M. (2021). Auditor-client relationship and related party transactions disclosure: The role of family controlling shareholders from a network perspective. *Managerial Auditing Journal, 36*(4), 591–615.

Rajkovic, T. (2020). Lead independent directors and investment efficiency. *Journal of Corporate Finance, 64*, Article 101690.

Richardson, S. (2006). Over-investment of free cash flow. *Review of Accounting Studies, 11*(2), 159–189.

Rozeff, M. S. (1982). Growth, beta and agency costs as determinants of dividend payout ratios. *Journal of Financial Research, 5*(3), 249–259.

Saini, N., & Singhania, M. (2018). Corporate governance, globalization and firm performance in emerging economies: Evidence from India. *International Journal of Productivity and Performance Management, 67*(8), 1310–1333.

Sarkar, J., & Selarka, E. (2021). Women on board and performance of family firms: Evidence from India. *Emerging Markets Review, 46*, Article 100770.

Sarkar, J., Sarkar, S., & Sen, K. (2008). Board of directors and opportunistic earnings management: Evidence from India. *Journal of Accounting, Auditing & Finance, 23*(4), 517–551.

Scharfstein, D. (1988). Product-market competition and managerial slack. *The RAND Journal of Economics*, 147–155.

Schmidt, K. M. (1997). Managerial incentives and product market competition. *The Review of Economic Studies, 64*(2), 191–213.

Selarka, E. (2018). *Corporate Governance practices in India*. Retrieved January 4, 2025 from http://www.mse.ac.in/wp-content/uploads/2018/08/Working-Paper-173.pdf

Shaikh, I. A., & Peters, L. (2018). The value of board monitoring in promoting R&D: A test of agency-theory in the US context. *Journal of Management and Governance, 22*, 339–363.

Shamsabadi, H. A., Min, B. S., & Chung, R. (2016). Corporate governance and dividend strategy: Lessons from Australia. *International Journal of Managerial Finance, 12*(5), 583–610.

Shen, W., & Cannella, A. A. (2002). Power dynamics within top management and their impacts 865 on CEO dismissal followed by inside succession. *Academy of Management Journal, 45*(6), 1195–1206.

Shleifer, A., & Vishny, R. W. (1989). Management entrenchment: The case of manager-specific investments. *Journal of Financial Economics, 25*(1), 123–139.

Shleifer, A., & Vishny, R. W. (1997). A survey of corporate governance. *The Journal of Finance, 52*(2), 737–783.

Simsek, Z. (2007). CEO tenure and organizational performance: An intervening model. *Strategic Management Journal, 28*(6), 653–662.

Singh, S., Jain, P. K., & Yadav, S. S. (2012). Capital budgeting decisions: Evidence from India. *Journal of Advances in Management Research, 9*(1), 96–112.

Singla, M., & Singh, S. (2019). Board monitoring, product market competition and firm performance. *International Journal of Organizational Analysis, 27*(4), 1036–1052.

Somvanshi, K. K. (2019). *India Inc boards bigger, more independent than 5 years ago*. Retrieved January 4, 2025 from https://economictimes.indiatimes.com/markets/stocks/news/india-inc-boards-bigger-more-independent-than-5-years-ago/articleshow/72286398.cms?utm_source=contentofinterest&utm_medium=text&utm_campaign=cppst

Srivastava, B., Singh, S., & Jain, S. (2023). Bank competition, risk-taking and financial stability: Insights from an emerging economy. *Competitiveness Review: An International Business Journal, 33*(5), 959–992.

Srivastava, B., Singh, S., & Jain, S. (2024). A frontier-based parametric framework for exploring the competition–efficiency nexus in commercial banking: Insights from an emerging economy. *Managerial Finance, 50*(5), 854–889.
Stein, J. C. (1989). Efficient capital markets, inefficient firms: A model of myopic corporate behavior. *The Quarterly Journal of Economics, 104*, 655–669.
Stubben, S. R. (2010). Discretionary revenues as a measure of earnings management. *The Accounting Review, 85*(2), 695–717.
Stulz, R. (1990). Managerial discretion and optimal financing policies. *Journal of Financial Economics, 26*(1), 3–27.
Subramanian, S. (2022). *Strengthening the role of independent directors in a company*. Retrieved January 4, 2025 from https://economictimes.indiatimes.com/small-biz/legal/strengthening-the-role-of-independent-directorsin%20%20company/articleshow/90455204.cms?utm_source=contentofinterest&utm_medium=text&utm_campaign=cppst
Suman, S., & Singh, S. (2022). The role of multiple large shareholders in dividend payouts: Evidence from India. *American Business Review, 25*(1), 120–151.
Tekin, H., & Polat, A. Y. (2021). Do market differences matter on dividend policy? *Borsa Istanbul Review, 21*(2), 197–208.
Teofilus, T., Ardyan, E., Sutrisno, T., Sabar, S., & Sutanto, V. (2022). Managing organizational inertia: Indonesian family business perspective. *Frontiers in Psychology, 13*, Article 839266.
Upadhyay, A., & Sriram, R. (2011). Board size, corporate information environment and cost of capital. *Journal of Business Finance & Accounting, 38*(9–10), 1238–1261.
Vanacker, T. R., & Manigart, S. (2010). Pecking order and debt capacity considerations for high-growth companies seeking financing. *Small Business Economics, 35*(1), 53–69.
Ward, C., Yin, C., & Zeng, Y. (2020). Motivated monitoring by institutional investors and firm investment efficiency. *European Financial Management, 26*(2), 348–385.
Windmeijer, F. (2005). A finite sample correction for the variance of linear efficient two-step GMM estimators. *Journal of Econometrics, 126*(1), 25–51.
Yang, T., & Zhao, S. (2014). CEO duality and firm performance: Evidence from an exogenous shock to the competitive environment. *Journal of Banking & Finance, 49*, 534–552.
Zona, F. (2016). Agency models in different stages of CEO tenure: The effects of stock options and board independence on R&D investment. *Research Policy, 45*(2), 560–575.

Chapter 3
Corporate Governance and Cash Holdings

The previous chapter delineated the effects of corporate governance monitoring devices on the efficiency of long-term investment decisions. The current chapter adds to the former empirical framework by focusing on the ramifications of corporate governance on short-term investment decisions that concern the quantum of cash reserves. Cash holdings assist in satisfying operational and investment requirements and extend a liquidity buffer for meeting unexpected contingencies (La Rocca et al., 2019). The safeguard extended by these liquid assets particularly assumes prominence when the information asymmetry is high (Chauhan et al., 2018; Opler et al., 1999). However, accumulated cash stock under the discretionary control of corporate insiders[1] can be easily expropriated to extract private gains by carrying out their opportunistic activities of over-investment and tunneling (Atif et al., 2019; Chen et al., 2014). Considering that cash reserves are vulnerable to agency conflicts, corporate governance mechanisms can affect the buildup of these liquid funds. In order to examine the purported relationship, the impact of the board of directors' attributes, large shareholders, and auditor independence on cash holdings is checked for non-financial NIFTY 500 firms. The analysis, which is undertaken from FY 2010 to FY 2019, is also extended to investigate how the influence of various governance mechanisms varies post the implementation of the Companies Act, 2013. Further, the conditional effects of corporate governance are also determined by segregating the sample based on select CEO-, firm-, and industry-level contextual factors.

The layout of the chapter is elaborated in the following manner. Section 3.1 introduces the research problem. Section 3.2 describes the empirical results. The contingent effects uncovered from the additional analyses have been shown and explained in Sect. 3.3. Finally, Sect. 3.4 proffers concluding observations.

---

[1] Corporate insiders include the controlling owner and managers.

S. Singh and S. Suman, *Corporate Governance Monitoring Mechanisms and Corporate Performance and Valuation*, India Studies in Business and Economics,
https://doi.org/10.1007/978-981-96-9736-6_3

3.1 Introduction

A reservoir of cash confers flexibility to management by extending readily accessible financial slack to execute business decisions (Kuan et al., 2011; La Rocca et al., 2019). Further, when severe information asymmetry raises the risk premium on outside funds, cash holdings provide a reasonable source of financing (Chauhan et al., 2018; Myers & Majluf, 1984). Consequently, these reserves obviate the need to liquidate non-cash assets to raise funds and minimize the cost of acquiring external capital (Miller & Orr, 1966). They also provide a cushion against unexpected exigencies, thereby ensuring that positive NPV investments are not left underfunded (Chang et al., 2017; Opler et al., 1999). On the contrary, a massive stock of cash at the disposal of corporate insiders can magnify agency costs (Atif et al., 2019; Chen et al., 2014). Since cash can be easily deployed to pursue self-interests, controlling shareholders and executives can expropriate these liquid assets (Dittmar & Mahrt-Smith, 2007; Pinkowitz et al., 2006). Management may prefer to retain excess cash to enhance its perquisites consumption, carry out its empire-building aspirations, and engage in tunneling or outright theft of these corporate resources (Jensen, 1986). Moreover, surplus cash averts the circumstances of going to a financial market to procure financing, which avoids the external scrutiny of corporate insiders' misdeeds (John et al., 2017; Seifert & Gonenc, 2018). Lastly, accumulated cash can also be employed as a mechanism to foil takeover bids by repurchasing the firm's stock or buying the bidder's stock to consolidate control over the business (Faleye, 2004; Harford et al., 2008).

In summary, when corporate insiders are self-serving, they can stockpile cash to extract private benefits. Since corporate governance monitoring mechanisms have been put in place to manage agency conflicts, they are also expected to affect build up and dissipation of cash holdings. The formulation of hypotheses that state the relationship between distinct corporate governance attributes and the level of accumulated cash has been summarized in Table 3.1.

3.2 Main Empirical Analysis and Discussion

Sample description

The initial sample of the empirical investigation is NIFTY 500 entities, which are analyzed from FY 2010–FY 2019. However, after excluding the financial entities and considering available data on all the variables utilized in the study, the analysis is undertaken on 3469 firm-year observations.

Regression model and variables

Equation 3.1 is utilized to examine the dynamic relationship between corporate governance monitoring devices and the level of cash holdings. It recognizes that

Table 3.1 Summary of the predicted relationship between corporate governance monitoring mechanisms and cash holdings

Variables	Relationship
Board size *(BSIZE)*	Oversized boards augment board monitoring and a corporation's ability to obtain outside financing, thereby reducing the propensity to hold cash (Ezeani et al., 2023). However, these boards are prone to structural issues inherent to large groups, which can allow management to dominate board decision-making (Lee & Lee, 2009) **H1:** Board size has a significant association with the cash holdings level
Board independence *(BIND)*	Independent directors can supervise managerial actions strictly to ensure that only value-maximizing cash retention strategies are implemented (Boubaker et al., 2015; Ezeani et al., 2023) **H2:** Board independence has a negative association with cash holdings level
CEO duality *(CEODUAL)*	A joint CEO-Chair can abuse their power to push for cash accumulation to extract private benefits (Boubaker et al., 2015; Kuan et al., 2011) **H3:** CEO duality has a negative association with cash holdings level
Board gender diversity *(BGD)*	The enhanced board independence upon the inclusion of female directors can ensure that only well-deliberated value-maximizing cash management strategies are adopted (Cambrea et al., 2020; Ezeani et al., 2023) **H4:** Board gender diversity has a positive association with cash holdings level
Controlling shareholder *(PROMOTER)*	The significant blockholding of the controlling owners can either entrench them to hoard cash for tunneling or align their interests in holding lower cash reserves to reduce expropriation concerns (Gupta & Bedi, 2020; Liu et al., 2015) **H5:** Controlling shareholder has a significant association with cash holdings level
Non-controlling large shareholders *(NPD)*	As additional blockholders in India are non-promoters[2] (Selarka, 2018), they can pressure management to lower the spare cash by disbursing it through payouts (Attig et al., 2013) **H6:** Non-controlling large shareholders have a positive association with cash holdings level
Auditor independence *(NAF)*	When the payment for non-audit services is exorbitantly high, the quality of financial reporting can be hampered since auditors may hesitate to raise concerns for fear of losing a significant income stream (Mitra, 2007). Consequently, the monitoring by external governance mechanisms will also be weakened as they will fail to detect managerial misappropriations of amassed cash from the distorted statements (Smith et al., 2021). Thus, a large ratio of the non-audit services fees can facilitate cash accumulation **H7:** A higher proportion of non-audit fees has a negative association with cash holdings level

Notes This table describes the hypotheses for investigating the relationship between corporate governance and cash holdings

[2] Promoters are considered as controlling owners in the context of Indian corporations (Gupta & Bedi, 2020).

contemporary cash values depend upon the previous year's cash levels as corporations partially adjust their cash reserves toward an optimal amount (Batuman et al., 2022; Jiang & Lie, 2016). It is represented as follows:

$$\begin{aligned} CASH_{it} = & \beta_0 + \beta_1 CASH_{t-1} + \beta_2 BSIZE_{it} + \beta_3 BIND_{it} \\ & + \beta_4 CEODUAL_{it} + \beta_5 BGD_{it} + \beta_6 PROMOTER_{it} \\ & + \beta_7 NPD_{it} + \beta_8 NAF_{it} + \sum_{j=9}^{N} \beta_j CONTROLS_{it} \\ & + Industryeffects_i + Yeareffects_t + \varepsilon_{it}. \end{aligned} \tag{3.1}$$

where *CASH* denotes the dependent variable of the empirical analysis and is measured by the cash-to-total assets ratio. The data for cash holdings is retrieved from Bloomberg®. The main variables of interest in the study include the attributes that indicate the board of directors' effectiveness, namely, board size (*BSIZE*), board independence (*BIND*), the existence of a combined CEO-Chair post (*CEODUAL*), and board gender diversity (*BGD*). The influence of large shareholders is also addressed by considering a controlling owners' equity stakeholding (*PROMOTER*) and the participation of additional blockholders in the ownership structure (*NPD*). Lastly, the effect of auditor independence is also ascertained by taking non-audit fees as a fraction of audit fees (*NAF*). The discussion on their measurement is undertaken in Chapter 1.

CONTROLS encompasses several control variables that have been documented in the literature to affect the level of cash holdings. The influence of firm size *(FSIZE)* and firm age *(FAGE)* is considered, as larger and older firms typically require less cash due to their relatively easier access to external capital financing (Mulier et al., 2016; Ozkan & Ozkan, 2004). Growth opportunities (*GROWTH*) are also included as a control since high-growth firms are likely to favor the retention of cash to finance all their profitable projects (Guizani, 2017). Alternatively, corporate insiders of low-growth firms may hoard cash to extract private benefits (Batuman et al., 2022; Jensen, 1986). Therefore, a negative linkage between growth opportunities and cash holdings can also arise in the presence of severe agency conflicts.

The effect of net working capital *(NWC)* is addressed because it can be easily and reasonably liquidated to generate much-needed financing for corporations, thereby minimizing the need to pile up cash (D'Mello et al., 2008; Diaw, 2021). As internally generated cash flows (*CFO*) can add to the liquidity stock, their impact is also taken into account in the empirical investigation (Bao et al., 2012; Batuman et al., 2022). In addition, cash flow volatility (*CFOVOL*) is also considered in the research model since unpredictable cash flows raise the need to amass cash to prevent circumstances of cash deficit (Guizani, 2017; Wasiuzzaman, 2014). The disciplinary role of debt *(LEV)* and dividends (*DIVIDEND)* is also reckoned as these payments decrease the excess cash at the disposal of corporate insiders (Jensen, 1986). Companies with a greater degree of asset tangibility (*TANG*) are also predicted to keep lower cash levels as fixed assets can be deployed to support borrowings at a reasonable cost

(Shah & Shah, 2016). The risk of financial distress *(ZSCORE)* in influencing the build-up of cash buffer is also analyzed in the empirical analysis (García-Teruel & Martínez-Solano, 2008).

Variables proxying capital *(CAPEX)* and research and development expenditures *(RD)* are also incorporated in the econometric model as higher investment expenses reduce the stock of cash (Opler et al., 1999). The empirical analysis also controls for managerial agency costs, which cover expenses under the discretionary control of management, such as salaries and fringe benefits (Li & Luo, 2020; Tekin & Polat, 2021). Therefore, when managerial entrenchment is high, executives are predicted to hoard cash to inflate their compensation and perks consumption (Nikolov & Whited, 2014). Conversely, the outlay on discretionary expenses can lower the amount of retained funds (Nagasawa & Nagasawa, 2021).

In line with previous empirical analysis undertaken in Chapter 2, the current research study also includes industry and year effects in the baseline regression model to deal with variations in cash holdings arising from changes in industrial and macroeconomic situations (Chen et al., 2014). The definition of each control variable used in the study has been elaborated in Table 3.2.

Research methodology

The dynamic nature of the proposed regression model, as indicated by Eq. 3.1, gives rise to autocorrelation and endogeneity problems (O'Connor & Rafferty, 2012). There can also be endogeneity issues on account of corporate governance and control variables. For example, an unobserved effect like managerial conservatism may impact certain governance mechanisms and cash-hoarding behavior, leading to a correlation between the explanatory variables and the error term. Furthermore, there could also be the possibility that additional large owners are attracted to companies with an efficient cash management policy, which produces causation concerns. Therefore, a two-step system GMM estimation approach is utilized to mitigate the highlighted issues of autocorrelation and endogeneity (Suman & Singh, 2022). After the estimation, the diagnostic tests of Hansen J and AR (2) are also conducted to validate the appropriateness of the system GMM estimator. The empirical study also winsorizes financial variables at 1% to remove the effect of outliers (Mendiratta et al., 2023).

Descriptive statistics

Table 3.3 presents the summary statistics of all the variables employed in the current research study. The mean cash-to-total assets (*CASH*) percentage of 7.81% is well below the average liquidity levels of corporations based in other countries (Goodell et al., 2021; Gupta & Bedi, 2020). The reported percentage is fairly lower than the average cash holdings level of 19%, as noted in the case of listed Chinese entities (Zhang et al., 2020). The observations concerning the descriptive statistics of the corporate governance variables that are under the scope of the empirical investigation are similar to those reported in Chapter 2.

Table 3.2 Summary of control variables used in examining the impact of corporate governance monitoring mechanisms on the level of cash holdings

Variables	Measurement	Data Source
Firm size *(FSIZE)*	Natural logarithm of total assets (Atif et al., 2019; Seifert & Gonenc, 2018)	Datastream®
Firm age *(FAGE)*	Number of years since the firm's inception (Kusnadi et al., 2015; La Rocca et al., 2019)	Datastream®
Growth opportunities *(GROWTH)*	Tobin's Q (Bao et al., 2012; Chauhan et al., 2018)	Bloomberg®
Adjusted net working capital *(NWC)*	Adjusted net working capital is calculated by deducting cash holdings from the net working capital (NWC). The non-cash component of NWC is scaled by total assets. NWC is current assets less current liabilities (Chauhan et al., 2018; Harford et al., 2008)	Bloomberg® and Datastream®
Cash flows *(CFO)*	Net operating cash flows to total assets ratio (Cambrea et al., 2020; Liu et al., 2015)	Datastream®
Cash flow volatility *(CFOVOL)*	Standard deviation of the operating cash flows to total assets ratio for the past five years (Boubaker et al., 2015; Gupta & Bedi, 2020)	Datastream®
Leverage ratio *(LEV)*	Total debt to total assets ratio (Batuman et al., 2022; Chauhan et al., 2018)	Datastream®
Asset tangibility *(TANG)*	Net plant, property, and equipment divided by total assets (Cambrea et al., 2020; Shah & Shah, 2016)	Datastream®
Financial distress *(ZSCORE)*	Altman-Z score (Martínez-Sola et al., 2018)	Datastream®
Capital expenditures *(CAPEX)*	Capital expenditure to total assets ratio (Batuman et al., 2022; Chen et al., 2014)	Datastream®
Research and development (R&D) expenditures *(RD)*	R&D expenditures to total assets ratio (Boubaker et al., 2015; Zhang et al., 2020)	Datastream®
Dividend payouts *(DIVIDEND)*	Cash dividends to total assets ratio (Atif et al., 2019; Ozkan & Ozkan, 2004)	Datastream®
Agency costs *(AGENCYC)*	Ratio of a firm's SGA expenses to its annual sales (Li & Luo, 2020; Tekin & Polat, 2021)	Datastream®

Notes This table expounds on the definitions of the control variables utilized in the empirical model for analyzing the impact of corporate governance monitoring mechanisms on the cash holdings level

Table 3.3 Summary statistics of cash holdings, corporate governance monitoring mechanisms, and other firm-level variables

Variables	Mean	Standard deviation	Minimum	Maximum
CASH	0.0781	0.1097	0.0008	0.6016
BSIZE	9.5316	2.6241	3	22
BIND	51.5759	11.1395	0	100
CEODUAL	0.2981	0.4575	0	1
BGD	9.6045	8.1661	0	42.857
PROMOTER	56.648	16.9652	8.2	90
NPD	0.1188	0.3236	0	1
NAF	0.3797	0.4624	0	2.6496
FSIZE	20.4345	1.4719	16.856	24.306
FAGE	38.6344	23.4591	1.7917	155
GROWTH	2.7322	2.4285	0.6562	13.779
NWC	0.0412	0.1569	−0.5178	0.4379
CFO	0.0994	0.0838	−0.1673	0.3407
CFOVOL	0.058	0.0411	0.0085	0.2782
LEV	0.2216	0.1895	0	0.7268
TANG	0.3281	0.2043	0.0059	0.8044
ZSCORE	6.0054	6.1934	0.1494	35.7928
CAPEX	0.0644	0.0541	0.0004	0.2844
RD	0.0046	0.0112	0	0.0702
DIVIDEND	0.0245	0.0397	0	0.2439
AGENCYC	0.2427	0.1802	0.0075	0.9615

Notes This table summarizes the descriptive statistics of variables utilized in the study

The testing of correlation[3] between cash holdings and corporate governance also yields initial evidence in favor of the proposed hypotheses.

Multivariate regression analysis

Table 3.4 presents the results from the empirical estimation of Eq. 3.1. It is inferred from Column 1 that board independence (*BIND*) has a significant and negative influence on the level of cash holdings (*CASH*). This finding corroborates H2 and provides evidence in favor of the monitoring role of independent directors. Guided by the incentives to preserve their reputation in the labor markets, independent directors bring objective and firm supervision over the corporate insiders' decisions to prevent misuse of corporate cash (Beasley, 1996; Fama & Jensen, 1983). Since excess cash reserves can be easily converted into private benefits, there is a higher likelihood that management can squander the holdings through over-investment in negative

[3] Detailed correlation matrix is available upon request.

NPV projects, lavish expenditure on perks, or tunneling to related entities (Boubaker et al., 2015; Jensen, 1986). Moreover, amassed cash can evade the scrutiny of financial market participants as it minimizes external financing requirements (John et al., 2017; Seifert & Gonenc, 2018). Consequently, independent directors prefer low-cash retention strategies to assuage expropriation concerns.

Column 1 of Table 3.4 also vouches for the governance role of non-controlling large shareholders (*NPD*) as it is observed that their presence in the ownership structure has a significantly negative effect on *CASH.* The substantial stake empowers additional blockholders to press for the reduction of substantial reserves at the disposal of controlling owners and executives to minimize the scope of their value-diminishing activities (Dittmar & Mahrt-Smith, 2007; Opler et al., 1999). Thus, this result supports H6. Furthermore, it is also noted that the size and diversity of the board, CEO duality, dominant ownership, and auditor independence do not affect the cash stock level in the entire investigated sample.

As far as the control variables are concerned, the results align with those reported by previous studies. It can be reckoned that a higher amount of non-cash net working capital (*NWC*) lowers the need to accumulate cash. Net working capital can substitute for cash provision as it can be easily liquidated to meet corporate financing requirements (D'Mello et al., 2008; Diaw, 2021). In addition, it is inferred that cash holdings rise with an increase in operating cash flows (*CFO*). Internally generated cash flows that exceed the current operational and investment demand augment the precautionary cash reserves (Bao et al., 2012; Batuman et al., 2022). Lastly, the findings also demonstrate that cash levels decrease with growing capital expenditure (*CAPEX*). Capital expenditures represent the utilization of liquid holdings leading to a depletion in amassed cash (Diaw, 2021; Opler et al., 1999).

The empirical investigation is also extended to understand how the effectiveness of governance attributes has changed post the introduction of the Companies Act, 2013. For this purpose, the sample is divided into pre-reform and post-reform periods. The pre-reform period ranges from FY 2010 to FY 2014, encompassing years before the implementation of the new Companies Act. Years post FY 2014[4] reflect the era of improved corporate governance regulations and constitute the post-reform period. The relevant results have been presented in Columns 2 and 3 of Table 3.4. They demonstrate that the diminishing influence of non-controlling large shareholders (*NPD*) and board independence (*BIND*) on discretionary cash (*CASH*) is pronounced only in the post-reform period. On the contrary, no significant association between corporate governance mechanisms and the level of accumulated cash is detected in the pre-reform period. Hence, it can be concluded that the robust governance regime brought in by the Companies Act, 2013 extends a bolstering force to the monitoring role of additional large owners and independent directors in relation to cash management practices.

[4] As specified in Chapter 2, the Companies Act, 2013 was enacted on August 30, 2013. Since it was instituted in the middle of FY 2014, following Sarkar and Selarka (2021), the post-reform period consists of years only after FY 2014.

Table 3.4 Corporate governance monitoring mechanisms and cash holdings: Main regression analysis

Dependent variable: *CASH*	Overall sample (2010–2019)	Pre-reform period (2010–2014)	Post-reform period (2015–2019)
Variables	(1)	(2)	(3)
L.CASH	0.791***	0.661***	0.753***
	(0.0718)	(0.0802)	(0.0958)
BSIZE	−0.000192	−0.00114	−0.000685
	(0.00119)	(0.00171)	(0.00161)
BIND	−0.000447*	−0.000299	−0.000681**
	(0.000228)	(0.000574)	(0.000329)
CEODUAL	0.0124	−0.00337	0.000618
	(0.0145)	(0.0226)	(0.0141)
BGD	7.98e-06	0.000217	0.000485
	(0.000238)	(0.000479)	(0.000549)
PROMOTER	0.000448	0.000197	0.000136
	(0.000311)	(0.000610)	(0.000389)
NPD	−0.0166**	−0.00562	−0.0218**
	(0.00763)	(0.00815)	(0.0109)
NAF	0.00411	0.00973	−0.0106
	(0.00432)	(0.00627)	(0.0136)
FSIZE	−0.00548	−0.00276	0.00590
	(0.00411)	(0.00639)	(0.00613)
FAGE	0.000165	-2.71e-05	0.000115
	(0.000107)	(0.000154)	(0.000109)
GROWTH	−0.00199	−0.00249	−0.000792
	(0.00381)	(0.00475)	(0.00403)
NWC	−0.0739**	−0.0688*	−0.0350
	(0.0344)	(0.0407)	(0.0279)
CFO	0.155*	0.102**	0.151***
	(0.0911)	(0.0449)	(0.0391)
CFOVOL	0.00581	0.0281	0.0603
	(0.0546)	(0.114)	(0.0798)
LEV	−0.00586	−0.0410	−0.000707
	(0.0333)	(0.0391)	(0.0327)
TANG	−0.0187	−0.0234	−0.0367
	(0.0288)	(0.0478)	(0.0302)
ZSCORE	0.00158	0.00219	0.000710
	(0.00153)	(0.00169)	(0.00178)

(continued)

Table 3.4 (continued)

Dependent variable: *CASH*	Overall sample (2010–2019)	Pre-reform period (2010–2014)	Post-reform period (2015–2019)
Variables	(1)	(2)	(3)
CAPEX	−0.105*	−0.0876*	−0.0656
	(0.0562)	(0.0486)	(0.0618)
RD	−0.0215	−0.270	−0.109
	(0.262)	(0.549)	(0.252)
DIVIDEND	−0.279	−0.0437	−0.214
	(0.182)	(0.158)	(0.166)
AGENCYC	−0.0273	−0.0107	0.0535*
	(0.0251)	(0.0445)	(0.0310)
Constant	0.148	0.132	−0.0995
	(0.101)	(0.155)	(0.143)
Industry & Year FE	Yes	Yes	Yes
Wald F (*p*-value)	78.41 (0.000)	59.07 (0.000)	69.57 (0.000)
AR2 (*p*-value)	0.543 (0.587)	−0.869 (0.385)	0.338 (0.735)
Hansen J (*p*-value)	74.23 (0.255)	57.85 (0.181)	103 (0.164)

Notes This table depicts the findings from the estimation of Eq. 3.1 using the two-step system GMM approach. Column 1 presents the results when the empirical investigation is carried out for the whole sample from FY 2010-FY 2019. Column 2 shows findings for the period before the implementation of the Companies Act, 2013 (Pre-reform period). Column 3 reports the results when the analysis is undertaken for years after the commencement of the Companies Act, 2013 (Post-reform period). Windmeijer's (2005) corrected-robust standard errors are shown in parentheses. ***, **, and * indicate significance at 1, 5, and 10% levels, respectively

Columns 1 to 3 also report the findings from the diagnostic tests, which affirm the appropriateness of system GMM. Across all empirical analyses undertaken, the observed Hansen J statistic is insignificant, thereby indicating that the instruments employed by the system GMM estimator are strictly exogenous. Furthermore, the second-order autocorrelation is not present as the AR (2) test is statistically insignificant. Moreover, the Wald F test evinces the joint significance of variables. Lastly, the primary assumption of system GMM is also satisfied as it is noted that current cash levels depend upon the previous year's values of cash reserves.

3.3 Additional Analyses

3.3.1 Role of CEO Tenure

The research study is augmented with additional analyses to understand how the effectiveness of corporate governance devices differs when the organizational environments are heterogeneous. The first contextual variable that is considered is the tenure a CEO has completed in their current position.

CEOs in the initial stages of their tenure are under the constant watch and evaluation of the board. They are bound to comply with the requirements and expectations for which they were appointed in their current position in order to secure their jobs (Shen & Cannella, 2002; Zona, 2016). As a result, the exploitation of corporate resources to attain private benefits is expected to be minimal during the early stages of the CEO's tenure. Contrastingly, when the CEOs have been in the office for a long time, they become closely familiar with board members and other top management team executives (Lewellyn & Muller-Kahle, 2012). Further, their past performance track record also enables such CEOs to retain the board's firm confidence in their authority, due to which their decisions may not be subjected to continuous scrutiny (Lorsch & MacIver, 1989; Shen, 2003). Hence, long-tenured CEOs enjoy substantial power, which they can misuse by advocating for substantial cash retention for deriving private benefits (Zona, 2016).

Consistent with the previous discourse, it can be anticipated that the effect of additional blockholders and independent directors varies as per the length of a CEO's tenure. Following the approach adopted in the last chapter, firm-year observations are segregated based on the quartile values of a CEO's tenure into short-tenured, medium-tenured, and long-tenured CEOs. The findings from the empirical estimation of Eq. 3.1 for each sub-group are provided in Table 3.5.

The results demonstrate that the negative impact of board independence (*BIND*) on the level of cash holdings (*CASH*) is pronounced only in the case of medium-tenured and long-tenured CEOs. As the duration of a CEO's tenure increases, their latitude over corporate matters rises (Shen, 2003; Zona, 2016). Considering the growing influence of CEOs with each successive year in the office, independent directors can play a valuable monitoring role (Walters et al., 2007). Non-affiliated outside directors can exercise strict vigilance over managerial opportunism by encouraging the disbursement of surplus cash at the disposal of entrenched CEOs (Beasley, 1996; Fama & Jensen, 1983). This objective supervision can assume more prominence when CEOs gain inordinate power, as evinced by a relatively stronger negative effect of independent directors on discretionary cash for companies with a long-tenured CEO.

Table 3.5 Corporate governance monitoring mechanisms and cash holdings: Role of CEO tenure

Dependent variable: *CASH*	Short-tenured CEOs	Medium-tenured CEOs	Long-tenured CEOs
Variables	(1)	(2)	(3)
L.CASH	0.827***	0.675***	0.534***
	(0.0630)	(0.0665)	(0.102)
BSIZE	−0.00242	−0.000234	−0.000982
	(0.00165)	(0.00381)	(0.00423)
BIND	2.28e-05	−0.000644*	−0.00105**
	(0.000559)	(0.000381)	(0.000527)
CEODUAL	0.0130	−0.0131	−0.00412
	(0.0118)	(0.0139)	(0.0168)
BGD	0.000714	−0.000201	5.68e-05
	(0.000553)	(0.000413)	(0.000926)
PROMOTER	−0.000104	0.000184	−0.000507
	(0.000338)	(0.000564)	(0.000469)
NPD	−0.0104	−0.0163**	−0.00813
	(0.0127)	(0.00693)	(0.0147)
NAF	−0.00239	0.00769	−0.0317
	(0.0112)	(0.00753)	(0.0238)
FSIZE	−0.00756	0.00310	−0.0210
	(0.00489)	(0.00736)	(0.0159)
FAGE	-1.73e-06	0.000164	0.000212
	(0.000136)	(0.000127)	(0.000279)
GROWTH	−0.00476	−0.000660	−0.00236
	(0.00384)	(0.00411)	(0.00503)
NWC	−0.110**	−0.102**	−0.0478
	(0.0428)	(0.0481)	(0.0836)
CFO	0.0836	0.0594	0.0128
	(0.0547)	(0.0915)	(0.0524)
CFOVOL	0.0340	0.0581	−0.0647
	(0.136)	(0.113)	(0.234)
LEV	−0.0213	−0.0720	0.00855
	(0.0524)	(0.0482)	(0.0503)
TANG	−0.00293	−0.0184	−0.167***
	(0.0360)	(0.0413)	(0.0563)
ZSCORE	0.00281	0.000733	0.00121
	(0.00178)	(0.00209)	(0.00214)

(continued)

Table 3.5 (continued)

Dependent variable: *CASH*	Short-tenured CEOs	Medium-tenured CEOs	Long-tenured CEOs
Variables	(1)	(2)	(3)
CAPEX	−0.312***	−0.0772	−0.0281
	(0.0863)	(0.0608)	(0.0556)
RD	−0.153	−0.175	2.252
	(0.507)	(0.555)	(1.524)
DIVIDEND	−0.311*	−0.256	0.0903
	(0.166)	(0.231)	(0.150)
AGENCYC	0.0113	−0.00436	−0.000967
	(0.0344)	(0.0319)	(0.0644)
Constant	0.259**	0.0338	0.704
	(0.120)	(0.158)	(0.431)
Industry & Year FE	Yes	Yes	Yes
Wald F (*p*-value)	98.30 (0.000)	55.38 (0.000)	8.339 (0.000)
AR (2) (*p*-value)	−0.108 (0.914)	0.252 (0.801)	−0.130 (0.896)
Hansen J (*p*-value)	146.8 (0.443)	93.66 (0.490)	52.65 (0.488)

Notes This table depicts the results when the sample is partitioned on the basis of CEO tenure. Short-tenured CEOs include years of CEO tenure within the bottom quartile (CEO tenure < 2.425 years). Years of CEO tenure in the top quartile are classified as long-tenured CEOs (CEO tenure > 18.88333 years). Sample values in the middle two quartiles constitute medium-tenured CEOs (CEO tenure from 2.425 to 18.88333 years). Windmeijer's (2005) corrected-robust standard errors are indicated in parentheses. ***, **, and * denote significance at 1, 5, and 10% levels, respectively

It is also observed from Table 3.5 that the governance role of non-controlling large owners (*NPD*) becomes notable when CEOs have completed considerable tenure since they negatively influence *CASH* only when the medium-tenured CEOs are at the helm. The significant voting rights arising from their concentrated holdings enable additional blockholders to question the huge liquidity levels and demand for the subsequent reduction of cash (Attig et al., 2013; Opler et al., 1999). However, their effect diminishes when the CEOs have occupied the post for a substantially longer time as it may become difficult to contest and dispute the authority of such iconic CEOs (Orens & Reheul, 2013).

3.3.2 *Role of Firm Size*

The disparity of information between corporate insiders and outside minority shareholders tends to be severe in the case of small-sized firms. As compared to larger corporations, small companies are less reputed and subjected to lower external scrutiny since their analyst and media coverage is relatively limited (Ben-Nasr, 2015; Rickling & Sharma, 2017). Consequently, agency conflicts are likely to be grave in small business enterprises. This inference aligns with the results reported in Chapter 2, which indicate that controlling owners over-invest in the case of smaller firms. Hence, it can be expected that the management of small corporations hoards a large stock of cash to pursue the self-serving activities of empire-building and tunneling.

In line with the preceding discussion, it is investigated if corporate governance mechanisms' ramifications on the accumulated cash levels are stronger for small business entities. The analysis is undertaken by dividing the sample using the quartile values of firm size (Prakash et al, 2024). The findings from the empirical estimation of Eq. 3.1 for small-sized, medium-sized, and large-sized firms are summarized in Table 3.6.

It can be observed from Column 1 that the negative effect of board independence (*BIND*) on the level of cash holdings (*CASH*) is present only in smaller corporations. At the outset, this result seems to suggest impartial monitoring by independent directors. However, caution should be exercised in drawing a conclusion when the previously noted observation in Chapter 2 is considered. It shows that independent directors in small-sized companies encourage excessive investment. Therefore, there could be a possibility that the negative impact of *BIND* in small firms arises on account of the dissipation of cash on value-destroying investments. As emphasized earlier, independent directors in smaller entities can lack true independence because of the undue influence of the controlling shareholders and the absence of the required expertise to make informed decisions (Saini & Singhania, 2018; Subramanian, 2022). Hence, a higher percentage of board independence lowers cash reserves through excessive investments in small corporates. This finding is in line with Harford et al. (2008), who emphasize that poorly-governed companies are endowed with less accumulated cash as they spend on unprofitable mergers and acquisitions and capital expenditure projects.

Column 1 of Table 3.6 also demonstrates that the negative influence of non-controlling large shareholders (*NPD*) on *CASH* is prominent only in small-sized firms. As evinced in Chapter 2, since smaller companies have more scope to grow, the dominant owners of such organizations expand the business operations beyond an optimal level to enjoy the benefits of empire-building (Arko et al., 2014; Boubaker et al., 2015). In light of this scenario, additional blockholders can use their considerable say associated with their large ownership to force the management to decrease the discretionary cash (Attig et al., 2013; Dittmar & Mahrt-Smith, 2007).

3.3.3 *Role of Firm Age*

Different lifecycle stages are characterized by distinctive growth prospects, which affect a corporation's strategic actions and information environment in each phase

Table 3.6 Corporate governance monitoring mechanisms and cash holdings: Role of firm size

Dependent variable: *CASH*	Small-sized firms	Medium-sized firms	Large-sized firms
Variables	(1)	(2)	(3)
L.CASH	0.561***	0.731***	0.677***
	(0.102)	(0.0493)	(0.0929)
BSIZE	−0.00460	−0.00230	0.00326
	(0.00492)	(0.00180)	(0.00407)
BIND	−0.000967*	−0.000194	−0.000322
	(0.000573)	(0.000253)	(0.000493)
CEODUAL	−0.0146	0.00707	−0.00455
	(0.0246)	(0.00837)	(0.0204)
BGD	-6.74e-05	0.000275	0.000896
	(0.000664)	(0.000425)	(0.000669)
PROMOTER	0.000186	0.000102	0.000429
	(0.000422)	(0.000355)	(0.000705)
NPD	−0.0286**	−0.00711	0.00436
	(0.0144)	(0.00735)	(0.0180)
NAF	−0.0117	0.00222	0.00334
	(0.0248)	(0.0180)	(0.00964)
FSIZE	0.0192	−0.00318	0.00356
	(0.0169)	(0.00558)	(0.0114)
FAGE	0.000226	7.21e-05	−0.000242
	(0.000318)	(9.81e-05)	(0.000350)
GROWTH	−0.00119	−0.00136	−0.000629
	(0.00370)	(0.00558)	(0.00829)
NWC	−0.117*	−0.00486	−0.00358
	(0.0657)	(0.0341)	(0.0731)
CFO	0.166**	0.0743**	0.148
	(0.0658)	(0.0335)	(0.140)
CFOVOL	0.143	0.00141	0.0491
	(0.287)	(0.0603)	(0.163)
LEV	−0.0518	−0.00511	−0.0449
	(0.0567)	(0.0289)	(0.0607)
TANG	−0.101	−0.00459	−0.123
	(0.0641)	(0.0389)	(0.0791)
ZSCORE	0.00288	0.00139	−0.00136
	(0.00284)	(0.00207)	(0.00374)

(continued)

Table 3.6 (continued)

Dependent variable: *CASH*	Small-sized firms	Medium-sized firms	Large-sized firms
CAPEX	−0.130*	−0.0996	−0.0500
	(0.0728)	(0.0923)	(0.161)
RD	−0.0913	−0.239	−0.0821
	(0.541)	(0.370)	(0.547)
DIVIDEND	−0.710*	0.0323	−0.0849
	(0.368)	(0.114)	(0.284)
AGENCYC	0.0135	−0.00178	0.0338
	(0.0571)	(0.0439)	(0.139)
Constant	−0.217	0.153	−0.0251
	(0.307)	(0.145)	(0.238)
Industry & Year FE	Yes	Yes	Yes
Wald F (*p*-value)	32.77 (0.000)	71.93 (0.000)	52.41 (0.000)
AR (2) (*p*-value)	1.006 (0.314)	0.0701 (0.944)	−0.825 (0.410)
Hansen J (*p*-value)	47.64 (0.447)	113.5 (0.470)	63.35 (0.115)

Notes This table presents the findings from the empirical estimation of Eq. 3.1 when the sample is segregated based on the quartile values of firm size. The upper quartile observations are categorized as small-sized firms (firm size < 19.4216). Observations in the top quartile are classified as large-sized firms (firm size > 21.26417). The remaining sample values in the middle two quartiles are grouped as medium-sized firms (firm size from 19.4216 to 21.26417). Parentheses show Windmeijer's (2005) corrected-robust standard errors. ***, **, and * depict significance at 1, 5, and 10% levels, respectively

(Filatotchev et al., 2006; Zhao & Xiao, 2019). Companies that are in the initial years of their operation possess substantial growth opportunities (Kuo, 2017). However, the true value of these future growth options is difficult to be determined by external capital providers (Chauhan et al., 2018; Myers & Majluf, 1984). Higher information asymmetry in early-stage firms can thus provide an opportunity for promoters and executives to utilize corporate resources to accomplish private interests.

As the scope of managerial opportunism varies with the extent of expected information transparency in each lifecycle stage, it can be gathered that the role of multiple corporate governance attributes on cash management strategies is contingent upon a firm's age. For uncovering the underlined contextual impact, sampled companies are allocated to sub-samples created using quartiles of firm age. The corresponding results for younger, middle-aged, and older corporations in different lifecycle stages are presented in Table 3.7.

Table 3.7 Corporate governance monitoring mechanisms and cash holdings: Role of firm age

Dependent variable: *CASH*	Younger firms	Middle-aged firms	Older firms
Variables	(1)	(2)	(3)
L.CASH	0.639***	0.666***	0.635***
	(0.0917)	(0.0881)	(0.0944)
BSIZE	−0.00513**	−0.00219	0.000840
	(0.00237)	(0.00201)	(0.00229)
BIND	−0.000328	−0.000287	−0.000338
	(0.000382)	(0.000340)	(0.000636)
CEODUAL	−0.0266	0.00595	0.0350
	(0.0172)	(0.0150)	(0.0237)
BGD	0.000528	0.000904**	−0.000202
	(0.000510)	(0.000382)	(0.000632)
PROMOTER	0.000213	−0.000199	5.50e-05
	(0.000396)	(0.000257)	(0.000465)
NPD	−0.0245**	−0.0177	−0.00386
	(0.0110)	(0.0130)	(0.0133)
NAF	0.0143	−0.00158	0.0145
	(0.0134)	(0.0123)	(0.0159)
FSIZE	0.00151	−0.00139	−0.00406
	(0.00707)	(0.00968)	(0.0120)
FAGE	0.000337	0.000417	−0.000158
	(0.000489)	(0.000397)	(0.000368)
GROWTH	−0.0111*	0.000626	−0.00564
	(0.00584)	(0.00387)	(0.00415)
NWC	−0.0477	−0.0864	−0.0708
	(0.0463)	(0.0601)	(0.0821)
CFO	0.0479	0.126***	0.0166
	(0.0558)	(0.0375)	(0.0850)
CFOVOL	0.212	−0.161	−0.334**
	(0.137)	(0.229)	(0.154)
LEV	−0.00406	−0.0438	−0.0461
	(0.0317)	(0.0366)	(0.0532)
TANG	−0.0204	−0.112**	−0.148***
	(0.0360)	(0.0531)	(0.0472)
ZSCORE	0.00554**	0.000486	0.00234
	(0.00233)	(0.00175)	(0.00267)
CAPEX	−0.116	−0.0919*	−0.126

(continued)

Table 3.7 (continued)

Dependent variable: *CASH*	Younger firms	Middle-aged firms	Older firms
Variables	(1)	(2)	(3)
	(0.153)	(0.0549)	(0.0830)
RD	−0.566	−0.380	−0.192
	(0.736)	(0.365)	(0.945)
DIVIDEND	−0.128	−0.0920	−0.153
	(0.222)	(0.106)	(0.272)
AGENCYC	−0.0514	0.0457	0.0300
	(0.0345)	(0.0379)	(0.0667)
Constant	0.0697	0.172	0.233
	(0.162)	(0.224)	(0.305)
Industry & Year FE	Yes	Yes	Yes
Wald F (*p*-value)	37.57 (0.000)	43.10 (0.000)	23.10 (0.000)
AR (2) (*p*-value)	0.226 (0.821)	0.855 (0.393)	−0.673 (0.501)
Hansen J (*p*-value)	105.2 (0.448)	67.20 (0.273)	67.40 (0.463)

Notes This table demonstrates the results from the empirical estimation of Eq. 3.1 for firms in different age brackets. Firm-year observations, which are less than quartile one, are designated as younger firms (firm age < 21.58055 years). Observations above quartile three are classified as older firms (firm age > 53 years). The remaining sample values that vary from the first to third quartile form the sample of middle-aged firms (firm age from 21.58055 to 53 years). Parentheses report Windmeijer's (2005) corrected-robust standard errors. ***, **, and * show significance at 1, 5, and 10% levels, respectively

Column 1 of Table 3.7 shows that non-controlling large owners (*NPD*) discourage cash accumulation in only younger firms. The information asymmetry inherent in early-stage business enterprises posits the risk of liquidity reserves being misappropriated by corporate insiders (Chauhan et al., 2018). Therefore, additional blockholders can use their authority arising from their concentrated shareholding to impel the management to disburse the surplus cash (Dittmar & Mahrt-Smith, 2007; Opler et al., 1999). Further, it also noted from the findings that board size (*BSIZE*) negatively affects the level of cash holdings (*CASH*) in young companies. This observation is in consonance with H1 and supports the benefits of augmented monitoring supplied by oversized boards. These boards increase the likelihood that at least one of its participating members would dispute the manager's decision to maintain a high cash buffer (Upadhyay & Sriram, 2011). Hence, a large board size ensures a moderate amount of discretionary cash by minimizing the scope of corporate strategies being primarily driven by management judgment.

Interestingly, Column 2 of Table 3.7 also reports that a higher percentage of board gender diversity (*BGD*) is positively associated with *CASH* in middle-aged firms. This result contravenes the assertions of H4 and alludes to the risk aversion trait that is more salient in women directors (Cambrea et al., 2020; Jianakoplos & Bernasek, 1998). Female directors usually exhibit lower risk tolerance and practice conservatism in business and financial decisions (Doan & Iskandar-Datta, 2020; Nadeem et al., 2019). Therefore, gender-diverse boards maintain a greater cash buffer to preserve financial flexibility and safeguard against unexpected contingencies (La Rocca et al., 2019). The need to conserve cash particularly assumes importance for middle-aged corporations that have completed considerable years of operations and are approaching the maturity stage of their lifecycle. As the threat of decline is high for mature companies, women directors may exhort cash hoarding to employ readily available liquidity for quickly grabbing strategic opportunities in order to retain their competitive position (Jiang & Lie, 2016; Sirmon et al., 2011).

3.3.4 Role of Firm Growth Opportunities

As specified in the previous sub-section and Chapter 2, corporate insiders possess more knowledge about the worth of the growth opportunities than the outside minority investors (Chauhan et al., 2018; Myers & Majluf, 1984). This asymmetry of information extends latitude to the management in employing corporate resources as per their will, as affirmed by the additional analysis undertaken in Chapter 2. Its findings demonstrate that a joint CEO-Chair stimulates excessive investment expenditure in high-growth companies to enjoy the benefits associated with a huge empire. Since growth entities have significant opportunities to expand, their managers can accumulate cash to overspend on negative NPV investments.

Corollary to these contentions, it is ascertained if corporate governance's effect on cash holdings is stronger in growing business enterprises. The empirical investigation for the same is carried out by classifying the firm-year observations based on the quartile values of Tobin's Q. The findings from the empirical estimation of Eq. 3.1 for low-growth, moderate-growth, and high-growth are depicted in Table 3.8. Column 3 reports that the negative impact of board independence (*BIND*) and non-controlling blockholders (*NPD*) on the cash stock levels (*CASH)* is more prominent in high-growth firms. As over-investment concerns have been shown to be more serious in growth corporations, independent directors and additional large owners can bring robust outside monitoring on corporate insiders' expropriation activities by requiring lower amassed cash levels (Boubaker et al., 2015; Ezeani et al., 2023).

Table 3.8 Corporate governance monitoring mechanisms and cash holdings: Role of firm growth opportunities

Dependent variable: *CASH*	Low-growth firms	Moderate-growth firms	High-growth firms
Variables	(1)	(2)	(3)
L.CASH	0.626***	0.816***	0.608***
	(0.167)	(0.0379)	(0.0751)
BSIZE	-9.05e-05	−0.00234	−0.000265
	(0.00247)	(0.00165)	(0.00407)
BIND	−0.000488	−0.000466	−0.00133**
	(0.000436)	(0.000285)	(0.000671)
CEODUAL	−0.00905	0.000262	−0.00423
	(0.0184)	(0.00878)	(0.0200)
BGD	0.00123	0.000551	0.00133
	(0.00121)	(0.000350)	(0.000923)
PROMOTER	6.18e-05	−0.000353	0.000447
	(0.000503)	(0.000284)	(0.000659)
NPD	−0.00435	−0.0141	−0.0445**
	(0.0100)	(0.00878)	(0.0224)
NAF	0.00178	−0.00367	−0.00469
	(0.00947)	(0.0111)	(0.0196)
FSIZE	−0.00661	−0.00225	−0.00224
	(0.0107)	(0.00370)	(0.00657)
FAGE	4.19e-05	5.54e-05	0.000346
	(0.000188)	(7.89e-05)	(0.000268)
GROWTH	−0.00403	−0.00599	−0.000999
	(0.00887)	(0.00366)	(0.00328)
NWC	−0.0748	−0.0799***	−0.137***
	(0.0840)	(0.0276)	(0.0409)
CFO	0.138**	0.112***	0.0892
	(0.0537)	(0.0281)	(0.0561)
CFOVOL	−0.166	0.0868	0.0569
	(0.126)	(0.0811)	(0.148)
LEV	−0.000517	−0.0166	−0.0848
	(0.0467)	(0.0278)	(0.0695)
TANG	−0.0785	−0.0210	−0.0115
	(0.0642)	(0.0343)	(0.0658)
ZSCORE	−0.000394	0.00223	3.73e-05
	(0.00205)	(0.00167)	(0.00118)
CAPEX	−0.0154	−0.112**	−0.306***

(continued)

Table 3.8 (continued)

Dependent variable: *CASH*	Low-growth firms	Moderate-growth firms	High-growth firms
Variables	(1)	(2)	(3)
	(0.0622)	(0.0470)	(0.117)
RD	−0.135	−0.328	−0.207
	(2.489)	(0.287)	(0.452)
DIVIDEND	0.151	−0.0452	−0.206
	(0.244)	(0.112)	(0.130)
AGENCYC	−0.0270	0.0283	−0.0346
	(0.0433)	(0.0239)	(0.0451)
Constant	0.225	0.159*	0.161
	(0.259)	(0.0872)	(0.129)
Industry & Year FE	Yes	Yes	Yes
Wald F (*p*-value)	8.334 (0.000)	142.1 (0.000)	74.74 (0.000)
AR (2) (*p*-value)	−0.893 (0.372)	−0.0317 (0.975)	0.121 (0.903)
Hansen J (*p*-value)	25.99 (0.463)	160.8 (0.401)	148 (0.284)

Notes This table shows the results from the empirical estimation of Eq. 3.1, which is undertaken for firms in different stages of growth. Growth opportunities are measured by Tobin's Q. Low-growth firms include all the firm-year observations that lie below the lowest quartile value of Tobin's Q (Tobin's Q < 1.1683). The sample of high-growth firms consists of observations whose values are above the upper quartile of the Q ratio (Tobin's Q > 3.314). The remaining sample values in the middle two quartiles are designated as moderate-growth firms (Tobin's Q from 1.1683 to 3.314). Windmeijer's (2005) corrected-robust standard errors are indicated in parentheses. ***, **, and * represent significance at 1, 5, and 10% levels, respectively

3.3.5 Role of Firm Financial Condition

Financially healthy companies have a comfortable supply of internal financing and superior access to capital markets owing to their sound business operations (Arslan-Ayaydin et al., 2014). However, as discussed and observed in Chapter 2, undue provision of funds can exacerbate the wastage of liquid reserves on value-diminishing activities (Cheng et al., 2013; Denis, 2011). On the other hand, financially distressed firms are restricted in their ability to misspend cash as acquiring external capital is costly for such entities (D' Mello et al., 2008). Hence, precautionary cash reserves are valuable in financially weaker enterprises for carrying out routine business activities and undertaking investment opportunities (Chan et al., 2013).

In congruence with the previous discussion, it can be anticipated that the implications of various corporate governance monitoring devices would depend upon a corporation's financial situation. In order to test this prediction, the sampled observations are disaggregated into separate sub-groups using the criteria of prevailing financial condition, which is determined by the Altman-Z scores. Firm-year observations are classified into three categories: firms in financial distress conditions, firms with moderate financial conditions, and firms with financially sound conditions. The findings from the empirical estimation for each sub-group are illustrated in Table 3.9.

It can be inferred from Column 3 of Table 3.9 that the negative influence of independent directors (*BIND*) and non-controlling large shareholders (*NPD*) on the amount of accumulated cash (*CASH*) is more pronounced in firms with sound financial conditions. These corporations have substantial availability of economic resources at corporate insiders' disposal, which makes them prone to over-investment (Denis, 2011). In this context, non-affiliated outside directors can play a disciplinary role by asserting a reduction in substantial levels of cash (Boubaker et al., 2015). Similarly, external blockholders can use their significant voting rights to minimize inefficient investment by challenging management's decision to retain a huge cash stock (Attig et al., 2013; Dittmar & Mahrt-Smith, 2007).

3.3.6 Role of Industry Concentration

The absence of competitive pressures imparts significant market power to firms in concentrated markets (Azar et al., 2022; Schmidt, 1997). The dominant position incites the management of corporations operating in highly concentrated industries to run the business as per their discretion (Han et al., 2016; Schmidt, 1997). This inference is in consonance with the findings reported in Chapter 2, which state that dual CEOs make sub-optimal investments in firms of highly concentrated industries. In contrast, business entities in markets with low concentration are usually subjected to the disciplinary force of competition, which forces executives to abandon their expropriation activities (Singla & Singh, 2019).

In essence, the intensity of agency conflicts is likely to differ according to the degree of industry concentration. Hence, it is examined if the influence of corporate governance attributes on the level of cash reserves is conditional upon the industry structure. For the underlined objective, the sample is split up on the basis of quartile values of the Herfindahl–Hirschman Index (HHI), which measures the extent of concentration in a given industry (Babar & Habib, 2021; Han et al., 2016). Table 3.10 represents the results from the empirical estimation of Eq. 3.1 conducted for low-concentrated, medium-concentrated, and highly concentrated industries.

It can be observed from Column 3 that external blockholders (*NPD*) decrease accumulated cash (*CASH*) in only highly concentrated industries. The lack of competitive force and information asymmetry in highly concentrated markets allows executives to amass cash to pursue their personal interests (Srivastava et al., 2024; Zhang et al., 2022). In this regard, non-controlling large shareholders can lower inefficient expenditures by exerting the management to bring down the surplus cash.

Table 3.9 Corporate governance monitoring mechanisms and cash holdings: Role of firm financial condition

Dependent Variable: *CASH*	Financial distress conditions (Low Altman-Z scores)	Moderate financial conditions (Medium range Altman-Z scores)	Financially sound conditions (High Altman-Z scores)
Variables	(1)	(2)	(3)
L.CASH	0.616***	0.647***	0.669***
	(0.181)	(0.0826)	(0.101)
BSIZE	−0.00156	−0.00285	−0.00204
	(0.00193)	(0.00269)	(0.00592)
BIND	−0.000278	−0.000314	−0.00189**
	(0.000371)	(0.000388)	(0.000944)
CEODUAL	−0.000958	0.0167	−0.000185
	(0.0110)	(0.0134)	(0.0226)
BGD	−0.000190	0.000383	0.00206
	(0.000713)	(0.000553)	(0.00136)
PROMOTER	7.54e-08	7.35e-05	−0.000734
	(0.000171)	(0.000123)	(0.000456)
NPD	−0.00433	−0.00883	−0.100**
	(0.00852)	(0.00795)	(0.0405)
NAF	0.00650	0.0115	0.0129
	(0.00707)	(0.00901)	(0.0244)
FSIZE	0.00126	0.00432	0.00358
	(0.00505)	(0.00736)	(0.0115)
FAGE	5.52e-05	1.80e-05	0.000193
	(9.31e-05)	(0.000127)	(0.000302)
GROWTH	−0.000462	−0.00325	−0.00293
	(0.00382)	(0.00243)	(0.00545)
NWC	−0.0254	−0.0343	−0.128
	(0.0231)	(0.0337)	(0.0827)
CFO	0.0810	0.119***	0.156
	(0.0648)	(0.0322)	(0.122)
CFOVOL	0.00585	−0.115*	0.399**
	(0.0558)	(0.0694)	(0.182)
LEV	0.0238	−0.0122	−0.0733
	(0.0352)	(0.0341)	(0.102)
TANG	−0.0506	−0.0230	−0.0176
	(0.0339)	(0.0453)	(0.0909)
ZSCORE	0.00497*	0.00157	−0.000249

(continued)

Table 3.9 (continued)

Dependent Variable: *CASH*	Financial distress conditions (Low Altman-Z scores)	Moderate financial conditions (Medium range Altman-Z scores)	Financially sound conditions (High Altman-Z scores)
Variables	(1)	(2)	(3)
	(0.00264)	(0.00125)	(0.00170)
CAPEX	−0.0195	−0.0905**	−0.363***
	(0.0711)	(0.0439)	(0.105)
RD	−1.485	−0.320	−0.966
	(1.012)	(0.538)	(0.690)
DIVIDEND	−0.766*	−0.00719	−0.200
	(0.458)	(0.141)	(0.218)
AGENCYC	0.0113	0.0351	−0.0194
	(0.0479)	(0.0353)	(0.0710)
Constant	0.0635	−0.0258	0.205
	(0.155)	(0.155)	(0.233)
Industry & Year FE	Yes	Yes	Yes
Wald F (*p*-value)	17.73 (0.000)	58.49 (0.000)	41.91 (0.000)
AR (2) (*p*-value)	0.391 (0.696)	0.574 (0.566)	0.448 (0.654)
Hansen J (*p*-value)	52.95 (0.476)	85.20 (0.413)	97.51 (0.409)

Notes This table specifies the results from the empirical estimation of Eq. 3.1 when the sample is divided using the Altman Z-scores. Altman Z-score proxies for a firm's financial condition. A higher score signifies lower bankruptcy risk. Hence, firm-year observations in the bottom quartile are classified as firms in financial distress conditions (Z score < 2.059719). Values of Z scores in the top quartile constitute the sub-sample of firms with financially sound conditions (Z score > 7.741979). The remaining observations in the middle two quartiles are termed firms with moderate financial conditions (Z score from 2.059719 to 7.741979). Parentheses represent Windmeijer's (2005) corrected-robust standard errors. ***, **, and * denote significance at 1, 5, and 10% levels, respectively

3.4 Summary and Concluding Observations

The present chapter attempts to understand the role of corporate governance monitoring mechanisms in determining the quantum of cash reserves. Accumulated cash provides readily accessible liquidity for executing normal business operations and a safeguard against exigencies (Chang et al., 2017; Kuan et al., 2011). It also offers a low-cost financing source when the external capital is expensive due to severe information asymmetry (Chauhan et al., 2018; Myers & Majluf, 1984). However, there are also agency considerations in holding cash. As cash can be easily expropriated, corporate insiders can maintain massive liquid holdings to undertake self-serving activities (Jensen, 1986; Pinkowitz et al., 2006). Further, cash holdings enable a company to evade the scrutiny of capital market participants and defend against takeover attempts

Table 3.10 Corporate governance monitoring mechanisms and cash holdings: Role of industry concentration

Dependent Variable: *CASH*	Low-concentrated industries	Medium-concentrated industries	Highly concentrated industries
Variables	(1)	(2)	(3)
L.CASH	0.784***	0.548***	0.609***
	(0.0560)	(0.0761)	(0.0689)
BSIZE	0.000454	−0.00184	−0.000584
	(0.00150)	(0.00239)	(0.00255)
BIND	−0.000718	−0.000207	−0.000520
	(0.000441)	(0.000297)	(0.000460)
CEODUAL	−0.00224	−0.0144	0.0157
	(0.00835)	(0.0103)	(0.0185)
BGD	0.00122	0.00137	0.00124
	(0.000876)	(0.000991)	(0.00103)
PROMOTER	7.02e-05	6.34e-05	0.000267
	(0.000196)	(0.000236)	(0.000403)
NPD	−0.000404	−0.00590	−0.0271*
	(0.0181)	(0.00880)	(0.0144)
NAF	−0.00277	−0.00400	0.00315
	(0.00647)	(0.0165)	(0.0158)
FSIZE	0.000438	−0.00325	−0.0114
	(0.00665)	(0.00819)	(0.00744)
FAGE	0.000112	0.000100	0.000128
	(0.000123)	(0.000184)	(0.000217)
GROWTH	−0.00197	−0.00513	0.000114
	(0.00350)	(0.00342)	(0.00450)
NWC	−0.0622*	−0.101**	−0.166**
	(0.0360)	(0.0476)	(0.0779)
CFO	0.153***	0.0552	0.0947
	(0.0464)	(0.0403)	(0.0800)
CFOVOL	−0.00535	0.0118	−0.117
	(0.0884)	(0.0673)	(0.133)
LEV	0.00276	−0.0545	0.000697
	(0.0340)	(0.0380)	(0.0517)
TANG	−0.0343	−0.108***	−0.125**
	(0.0220)	(0.0339)	(0.0591)
ZSCORE	0.00176	0.00232	0.00157
	(0.00196)	(0.00163)	(0.00152)

(continued)

Table 3.10 (continued)

Dependent Variable: *CASH*	Low-concentrated industries	Medium-concentrated industries	Highly concentrated industries
Variables	(1)	(2)	(3)
CAPEX	−0.184***	−0.102**	−0.167
	(0.0581)	(0.0505)	(0.119)
RD	−0.528	−0.456	0.356
	(0.488)	(0.365)	(0.752)
DIVIDEND	−0.111	−0.243	0.244
	(0.195)	(0.211)	(0.174)
AGENCYC	0.0295	−0.00595	−0.0127
	(0.0470)	(0.0436)	(0.0366)
Constant	0.0611	0.212	0.368*
	(0.139)	(0.178)	(0.187)
Industry & Year FE	Yes	Yes	Yes
Wald F (*p*-value)	110.3 (0.000)	20.18 (0.000)	46.57 (0.000)
AR(2) (*p*-value)	0.619 (0.536)	0.718 (0.473)	−0.879 (0.380)
Hansen J (*p*-value)	107.3 (0.291)	97.22 (0.475)	107.7 (0.464)

Notes This table summarizes the findings from the empirical investigation of Eq. 3.1 when the sample is segregated based on the degree of industry concentration. HHI is utilized to proxy for the severity of concentration in a given industry. Hence, firm-year observations within quartile one of HHI are designated as low-concentrated industries (HHI < 0.0329862). Sample values exceeding quartile three are classified as highly-concentrated industries (HHI > 0.0771521). The observations ranging from quartiles one to three are taken together as medium-concentrated industries (HHI from 0.0329862 to 0.0771521). Parentheses denote Windmeijer's (2005) corrected-robust standard errors. ***, **, and * represent significance at 1, 5, and 10% levels, respectively

(Harford et al., 2008; John et al., 2017). In light of the expropriation concerns that arise with excess liquidity, the implications of corporate governance on the level of cash stock are uncovered by analyzing non-financial NIFTY 500 entities from FY 2010 to FY 2019. The key findings for the same have been summarized in Table 3.11.

The next chapter augments the empirical study by pivoting the focus to how external capital finances a company's investments and total assets. In this regard, the ramifications of corporate governance on a firm's capital structure composition are examined in the following study.

Table 3.11 Summary of results from empirical investigation of corporate governance monitoring mechanisms on cash holdings level

Variables	Analyses	Results
Board size	Main effect	• No significant main effect
	Contingent effect	*Firm age* • Negative impact in the case of younger firms *Other contingency factors* • No significant effect
Board independence	Main effect	• Negative impact, present in the post-reform period
	Contingent effect	*CEO tenure* • Negative impact in the middle and late stages of a CEO's tenure *Firm size* • Negative impact in the case of smaller firms *Firm growth opportunities* • Negative impact in the case of high-growth firms *Firm financial condition* • Negative impact in the case of financially sound firms *Other contingency factors* • No significant effect
CEO duality	Main effect	• No significant main effect
	Contingent effect	• No significant contingent effect
Board gender diversity	Main effect	• No significant main effect
	Contingent effect	*Firm age* • Positive impact in the case of middle-aged firms *Other contingency factors* • No significant effect
Controlling shareholder	Main effect	• No significant main effect
	Contingent effect	• No significant contingent effect

(continued)

Table 3.11 (continued)

Variables	Analyses	Results
Non-controlling large shareholders	Main effect	• Negative impact, present in the post-reform period
	Contingent effect	*CEO tenure* • Negative impact in the middle stages of a CEO's tenure *Firm size* • Negative impact in the case of smaller firms *Firm age* • Negative impact in the case of younger firms *Firm growth opportunities* • Negative impact in the case of high-growth firms *Firm financial condition* • Negative impact in the case of financially sound firms *Industry concentration* • Negative impact in the case of highly-concentrated industries
Auditor independence	Main effect	• No significant main effect
	Contingent effect	• No significant contingent effect

Notes This table provides a succinct summary of all the findings obtained from the present empirical investigation

References

Arko, A. C., Abor, J., Adjasi, C. K., & Amidu, M. (2014). What influence dividend decisions of firms in Sub-Saharan African? *Journal of Accounting in Emerging Economies, 4*(1), 57–78.

Arslan-Ayaydin, Ö., Florackis, C., & Ozkan, A. (2014). Financial flexibility, corporate investment and performance: Evidence from financial crises. *Review of Quantitative Finance and Accounting, 42*(2), 211–250.

Atif, M., Liu, B., & Huang, A. (2019). Does board gender diversity affect corporate cash holdings? *Journal of Business Finance & Accounting, 46*(7–8), 1003–1029.

Attig, N., El Ghoul, S., Guedhami, O., & Rizeanu, S. (2013). The governance role of multiple large shareholders: Evidence from the valuation of cash holdings. *Journal of Management & Governance, 17*(2), 419–451.

Azar, J., Marinescu, I., & Steinbaum, M. (2022). Labor market concentration. *Journal of Human Resources, 57*(S), S167–S199.

Babar, M., & Habib, A. (2021). Product market competition in accounting, finance, and corporate governance: A review of the literature. *International Review of Financial Analysis, 73*, Article 101607.

Bao, D., Chan, K. C., & Zhang, W. (2012). Asymmetric cash flow sensitivity of cash holdings. *Journal of Corporate Finance, 18*(4), 690–700.

Batuman, B., Yildiz, Y., & Karan, M. B. (2022). The impact of the global financial crisis on corporate cash holdings: Evidence from Eastern European countries. *Borsa Istanbul Review, 22*(4), 678–687.

Beasley, M. S. (1996). An empirical analysis of the relation between the board of director composition and financial statement fraud. *Accounting Review, 71*(4), 443–465.

Ben-Nasr, H. (2015). Government ownership and dividend policy: Evidence from newly privatized firms. *Journal of Business Finance & Accounting, 42*(5–6), 665–704.

Boubaker, S., Derouiche, I., & Nguyen, D. K. (2015). Does the board of directors affect cash holdings? A study of French listed firms. *Journal of Management & Governance, 19*(2), 341–370.

Cambrea, D. R., Tenuta, P., & Vastola, V. (2020). Female directors and corporate cash holdings: Monitoring vs executive roles. *Management Decision, 58*(2), 295–312.

Chan, H. W., Lu, Y., & Zhang, H. F. (2013). The effect of financial constraints, investment policy, product market competition and corporate governance on the value of cash holdings. *Accounting & Finance, 53*(2), 339–366.

Chang, Y., Benson, K., & Faff, R. (2017). Are excess cash holdings more valuable to firms in times of crisis? Financial constraints and governance matters. *Pacific-Basin Finance Journal, 45*, 157–173.

Chauhan, Y., Pathak, R., & Kumar, S. (2018). Do bank-appointed directors affect corporate cash holding? *International Review of Economics & Finance, 53*, 39–56.

Chen, D., Li, S., Xiao, J. Z., & Zou, H. (2014). The effect of government quality on corporate cash holdings. *Journal of Corporate Finance, 27*, 384–400.

Cheng, M., Dhaliwal, D., & Zhang, Y. (2013). Does investment efficiency improve after the disclosure of material weaknesses in internal control over financial reporting? *Journal of Accounting and Economics, 56*(1), 1–18.

Denis, D. J. (2011). Financial flexibility and corporate liquidity. *Journal of Corporate Finance, 17*(3), 667–674.

Diaw, A. (2021). Corporate cash holdings in emerging markets. *Borsa Istanbul Review, 21*(2), 139–148.

Dittmar, A., & Mahrt-Smith, J. (2007). Corporate governance and the value of cash holdings. *Journal of Financial Economics, 83*(3), 599–634.

D'Mello, R., Krishnaswami, S., & Larkin, P. J. (2008). Determinants of corporate cash holdings: Evidence from spin-offs. *Journal of Banking & Finance, 32*(7), 1209–1220.

Doan, T., & Iskandar-Datta, M. (2020). Are female top executives more risk-averse or more ethical? Evidence from corporate cash holdings policy. *Journal of Empirical Finance, 55*, 161–176.

Ezeani, E., Salem, R. I. A., Usman, M., & Kwabi, F. (2023). Board characteristics and corporate cash holding: Evidence from the UK, France and Germany. *International Journal of Accounting & Information Management, 31*(3), 413–439.

Faleye, O. (2004). Cash and corporate control. *The Journal of Finance, 59*(5), 2041–2060.

Fama, E. F., & Jensen, M. C. (1983). Separation of ownership and control. *The Journal of Law and Economics, 26*(2), 301–325.

Filatotchev, I., Toms, S., & Wright, M. (2006). The firm's strategic dynamics and corporate governance life-cycle. *International Journal of Managerial Finance, 2*(4), 256–279.

García-Teruel, P. J., & Martínez-Solano, P. (2008). On the determinants of SME cash holdings: Evidence from Spain. *Journal of Business Finance & Accounting, 35*(1–2), 127–149.

Goodell, J. W., Goyal, A., & Urquhart, A. (2021). Uncertainty of uncertainty and firm cash holdings. *Journal of Financial Stability, 56*, Article 100922.

Guizani, M. (2017). The financial determinants of corporate cash holdings in an oil rich country: Evidence from Kingdom of Saudi Arabia. *Borsa Istanbul Review, 17*(3), 133–143.

Gupta, C. P., & Bedi, P. (2020). Corporate cash holdings and promoter ownership. *Emerging Markets Review, 44*, Article 100718.

Han, S., Nanda, V. K., & Silveri, S. (2016). CEO power and firm performance under pressure. *Financial Management, 45*(2), 369–400.

Harford, J., Mansi, S. A., & Maxwell, W. F. (2008). Corporate governance and firm cash holdings in the US. *Journal of Financial Economics, 87*(3), 535–555.

Jensen, M. C. (1986). Agency costs of free cash flow, corporate finance, and takeovers. *The American Economic Review, 76*(2), 323–329.

Jianakoplos, N. A., & Bernasek, A. (1998). Are women more risk averse? *Economic Inquiry, 36*(4), 620–630.

Jiang, Z., & Lie, E. (2016). Cash holding adjustments and managerial entrenchment. *Journal of Corporate Finance, 36*, 190–205.

John, K., Li, Y., & Pang, J. (2017). Does corporate governance matter more for high financial slack firms? *Management Science, 63*(6), 1872–1891.

Kuan, T. H., Li, C. S., & Chu, S. H. (2011). Cash holdings and corporate governance in family-controlled firms. *Journal of Business Research, 64*(7), 757–764.

Kuo, L. W. (2017). Reputation as a governance mechanism? Evidence from payout policy of insider-controlled firms in Taiwan. *Journal of Business Finance & Accounting, 44*(9–10), 1443–1476.

Kusnadi, Y., Yang, Z., & Zhou, Y. (2015). Institutional development, state ownership, and corporate cash holdings: Evidence from China. *Journal of Business Research, 68*(2), 351–359.

La Rocca, M., La Rocca, T., Staglianó, R., Vecellio, P., & Montalto, F. (2019). Gender diversity, cash holdings and the role of the institutional environment: Empirical evidence in Europe. *Applied Economics, 51*(29), 3137–3152.

Lee, K. W., & Lee, C. F. (2009). Cash holdings, corporate governance structure and firm valuation. *Review of Pacific Basin Financial Markets and Policies, 12*(03), 475–508.

Lewellyn, K. B., & Muller-Kahle, M. I. (2012). CEO power and risk taking: Evidence from the subprime lending industry. *Corporate Governance: An International Review, 20*(3), 289–307.

Li, X., & Luo, D. (2020). Increase in cash holdings of US firms: The role of healthcare and technology industries. *Journal of Business Research, 118*, 286–298.

Liu, Q., Luo, T., & Tian, G. G. (2015). Family control and corporate cash holdings: Evidence from China. *Journal of Corporate Finance, 31*, 220–245.

Lorsch, J. W., & MacIver, E. (1989). *Pawns or potentates: The reality of America's corporate boards*. Harvard Business School Press.

Martínez-Sola, C., García-Teruel, P. J., & Martínez-Solano, P. (2018). Cash holdings in SMEs: Speed of adjustment, growth and financing. *Small Business Economics, 51*, 823–842.

Mendiratta, A., Singh, S., Yadav, S. S., & Mahajan, A. (2023). When do ESG controversies reduce firm value in India? *Global Finance Journal, 55*, Article 100809.

Miller, M. H., & Orr, D. (1966). A model of the demand for money by firms. *The Quarterly Journal of Economics, 80*(3), 413–435.

Mitra, S. (2007). Nonaudit service fees and auditor independence: Empirical evidence from the oil and gas industry. *Journal of Accounting, Auditing & Finance, 22*(1), 85–107.

Mulier, K., Schoors, K., & Merlevede, B. (2016). Investment-cash flow sensitivity and financial constraints: Evidence from unquoted European SMEs. *Journal of Banking & Finance, 73*, 182–197.

Myers, S. C., & Majluf, N. S. (1984). Corporate financing and investment decisions when firms have information that investors do not have. *Journal of Financial Economics, 13*(2), 187–221.

Nadeem, M., Suleman, T., & Ahmed, A. (2019). Women on boards, firm risk and the profitability nexus: Does gender diversity moderate the risk and return relationship? *International Review of Economics & Finance, 64*, 427–442.

Nagasawa, S., & Nagasawa, M. (2021). Free riding, empire building, and cost management prior to and post municipal enterprise mergers in Japan. *Asia-Pacific Journal of Accounting & Economics, 28*(1), 94–116.

Nikolov, B., & Whited, T. M. (2014). Agency conflicts and cash: Estimates from a dynamic model. *The Journal of Finance, 69*(5), 1883–1921.

O'Connor, M., & Rafferty, M. (2012). Corporate governance and innovation. *Journal of Financial and Quantitative Analysis, 47*(2), 397–413.

Opler, T., Pinkowitz, L., Stulz, R., & Williamson, R. (1999). The determinants and implications of corporate cash holdings. *Journal of Financial Economics, 52*(1), 3–46.

Orens, R., & Reheul, A. M. (2013). Do CEO demographics explain cash holdings in SMEs? *European Management Journal, 31*(6), 549–563.

Ozkan, A., & Ozkan, N. (2004). Corporate cash holdings: An empirical investigation of UK companies. *Journal of Banking & Finance, 28*(9), 2103–2134.

Pinkowitz, L., Stulz, R., & Williamson, R. (2006). Does the contribution of corporate cash holdings and dividends to firm value depend on governance? A cross-country analysis. *The Journal of Finance, 61*(6), 2725–2751.

Prakash, N., Singh, S., & Sharma, S. (2024). Technological diffusion, bank performance, and Solow's paradox: Insights from an emerging economy. *Journal of the Knowledge Economy*. Advanced online publication. https://doi.org/10.1007/s13132-024-02347-4

Rickling, M. F., & Sharma, D. S. (2017). Audit committee cash compensation and propensity of firms to beat earnings by a large margin: Conditional effects of CEO power and agency risks. *International Journal of Auditing, 21*(3), 304–323.

Saini, N., & Singhania, M. (2018). Corporate governance, globalization and firm performance in emerging economies: Evidence from India. *International Journal of Productivity and Performance Management, 67*(8), 1310–1333.

Sarkar, J., & Selarka, E. (2021). Women on board and performance of family firms: Evidence from India. *Emerging Markets Review, 46*, Article 100770.

Schmidt, K. M. (1997). Managerial incentives and product market competition. *The Review of Economic Studies, 64*(2), 191–213.

Seifert, B., & Gonenc, H. (2018). The effects of country and firm-level governance on cash management. *Journal of International Financial Markets, Institutions and Money, 52*, 1–16.

Selarka, E. (2018). *Corporate governance practices in India*. Retrieved January 4, 2025 from http://www.mse.ac.in/wp-content/uploads/2018/08/Working-Paper-173.pdf

Shah, H. A., & Shah, A. (2016). The relationship between judicial efficiency and corporate cash holdings: An international study. *Economic Modelling, 59*, 448–462.

Shen, W., & Cannella, A. A. (2002). Power dynamics within top management and their impacts on CEO dismissal followed by inside succession. *Academy of Management Journal, 45*(6), 1195–1206.

Shen, W. (2003). The dynamics of the CEO-board relationship: An evolutionary perspective. *Academy of Management Review, 28*(3), 466–476.

Singla, M., & Singh, S. (2019). Board monitoring, product market competition and firm performance. *International Journal of Organizational Analysis, 27*(4), 1036–1052.

Sirmon, D. G., Hitt, M. A., Ireland, R. D., & Gilbert, B. A. (2011). Resource orchestration to create competitive advantage: Breadth, depth, and life cycle effects. *Journal of Management, 37*(5), 1390–1412.

Smith, D. D., Gleason, K. C., & Kannan, Y. H. (2021). Auditor liability and excess cash holdings: Evidence from audit fees of foreign incorporated firms. *International Review of Financial Analysis, 78*, Article 101947.

Srivastava, B., Singh, S., & Jain, S. (2024). A frontier-based parametric framework for exploring the competition–efficiency nexus in commercial banking: Insights from an emerging economy. *Managerial Finance, 50*(5), 854–889.

Subramanian, S. (2022). *Strengthening the role of independent directors in a company*. Retrieved January 4, 2025 from https://economictimes.indiatimes.com/small-biz/legal/strengthening-the-role-of-independent-directors-in-acompany/articleshow/90455204.cms?utm_source=contentofinterest&utm_medium=text&utm_campaign=cppst

Suman, S., & Singh, S. (2022). The role of multiple large shareholders in dividend payouts: Evidence from India. *American Business Review, 25*(1), 120–151.

Tekin, H., & Polat, A. Y. (2021). Do market differences matter on dividend policy? *Borsa Istanbul Review, 21*(2), 197–208.

Upadhyay, A., & Sriram, R. (2011). Board size, corporate information environment and cost of capital. *Journal of Business Finance & Accounting, 38*(9–10), 1238–1261.

Walters, B. A., Kroll, M. J., & Wright, P. (2007). CEO tenure, boards of directors, and acquisition performance. *Journal of Business Research, 60*(4), 331–338.
Wasiuzzaman, S. (2014). Analysis of corporate cash holdings of firms in Malaysia. *Journal of Asia Business Studies, 8*(2), 118–135.
Windmeijer, F. (2005). A finite sample correction for the variance of linear efficient two-step GMM estimators. *Journal of Econometrics, 126*(1), 25–51.
Zhang, J., Chen, H., Zhang, P., & Jiang, M. (2022). Product market competition and the value of corporate cash: An agency theory explanation. *International Review of Financial Analysis, 84*, Article 102422.
Zhang, X., Zhang, Z., & Zhou, H. (2020). Oil price uncertainty and cash holdings: Evidence from China. *Energy Economics, 87*, Article 104732.
Zhao, T., & Xiao, X. (2019). The impact of corporate social responsibility on financial constraints: Does the life cycle stage of a firm matter? *International Review of Economics & Finance, 63*, 76–93.
Zona, F. (2016). Agency models in different stages of CEO tenure: The effects of stock options and board independence on R&D investment. *Research Policy, 45*(2), 560–575.

Chapter 4
Corporate Governance and Leverage Ratio

The preceding chapter explored the linkages between corporate governance monitoring mechanisms and internal cash reserves. This chapter extends empirical investigation to uncover the role of governance attributes in determining how outside funds finance a firm's assets. Since corporate governance seeks to ensure the safety of and return on investor capital, it can be anticipated that they are likely to affect the proportion of leverage and equity in a firm's capital structure (Haque et al., 2011; Shleifer & Vishny, 1997). While debt renders tax benefits and lowers the discretionary free cash flow (Jensen, 1986; Lee & Kuo, 2014), it increases the bankruptcy risk, which may not align with management's risk appetite (Chakraborty, 2018; Schmid, 2013). Furthermore, debt financing can also be employed as a tool to consolidate control over business decisions by the dominant owners (King & Santor, 2008; Stulz, 1988). In light of diverging implications of leverage for corporate insiders,[1] it becomes imperative to clarify the impact of corporate governance on capital structure composition when there is a misalignment of interests with minority shareholders. The corresponding empirical examination is undertaken by analyzing the effect of the board of directors, concentrated ownership, and auditor independence on the debt-to-total assets ratio for a sample of top-listed non-financial Indian entities from FY 2010 to FY 2019. In addition, the establishment of the new Companies Act during the sample period is also taken into account by checking how the influence of governance mechanisms has changed from the pre-reform to post-reform periods. Lastly, the boundary conditions of various corporate governance attributes are also ascertained by conducting disaggregate analyses using the quartile values of contextual factors of CEO tenure, firm size, firm age and growth opportunities, a corporate's financial condition, and degree of industry concentration.

The rest of the chapter has been organized as follows. Section 4.1 introduces the relationship between corporate governance and leverage ratio. Section 4.2 presents and describes the results from the main empirical analysis. The findings from the

[1] Corporate insiders include the controlling owner and managers.

S. Singh and S. Suman, *Corporate Governance Monitoring Mechanisms and Corporate Performance and Valuation*, India Studies in Business and Economics,
https://doi.org/10.1007/978-981-96-9736-6_4

additional analyses illustrating the contingent effects are summarized and explained in Sect. 4.3. Section 4.4 concludes the study.

4.1 Introduction

Debt capital decreases a corporation's tax liability through tax deductibility of interest payouts (Lee & Kuo, 2014). It also provides a cheaper source of financing when the retained funds are inadequate and information asymmetry is severe (Boateng et al., 2017; Myers & Majluf, 1984). In addition, debt can perform the function of a governance device (Bajaj et al., 2021a). According to Jensen (1986), leverage mitigates the problem of free cash flows since it bonds the management to make periodic payments of interest and principal amount. At the same time, the lender of the funds monitors the management regularly to ensure that the debt is repaid (Chauhan et al., 2018; Jung et al., 1996). Thus, when the governance environment is weaker and corporate insiders are entrenched, they can deliberately avoid capital gearing as it lowers the excess cash flow that could have been over-invested or tunnelled (Lee & Kuo, 2014). Alternatively, the management of such companies where outside shareholders' expropriation concerns are grave may prefer to subject its entities to lender monitoring to build a capital market reputation for accessing financing at a reasonable cost (Jiraporn et al., 2012; La Porta et al., 2000). In essence, it can be concluded that debt can complement or substitute different corporate governance monitoring mechanisms.

Apart from its disciplinary role, the extant literature also espouses the control-enhancing function of leverage. In order to preserve and secure control, dominant shareholders may utilize debt financing to consolidate control and minimize the dilution of voting rights that is likely to occur when going for equity issuances (Ramalho et al., 2018; Schmid, 2013). On the other hand, prior studies also note that the risk preferences of corporate insiders may dominate the decision to gear the firm. The bankruptcy risk emanating from debt usage may lead controlling owners and executives to procure less debt financing (Chakraborty, 2018). The risk of default poses the danger of loss of job and income for the manager (Baysinger et al., 1991; Fama, 1980) and substantial wealth in the case of the promoter (Rossi et al., 2018a, 2018b). Consequently, management may keep the leverage ratio low to ameliorate the likelihood of bankruptcy. Lastly, the literature also documents that companies borrow money in excess to divert funds to related entities (Boateng & Huang, 2017; Paligorova & Xu, 2012).

Consistent with the preceding discourse, it can be gathered that the impact of agency problems on the capital structure composition is obscure. Correspondingly, the related implications of corporate governance mechanisms for the long-term financing structure are unclear. The rising default risk with the increased debt usage limits its deployment as a sole governance device (John et al., 2015). Hence, alternative corporate governance mechanisms can simultaneously employ debt to bind the management to make pre-committed payouts to the debtholders (Benkraiem et al.,

2018; Flavin et al., 2021). Corporate governance can also stimulate capital gearing when the risk aversion of corporate insiders influences financing choices to reap the tax savings benefit associated with borrowed funds (Kieschnick & Moussawi, 2018). In contrast, when the dominant shareholders deliberately overleverage the firm to enhance their control or engage in tunneling, effective governance attributes can lower debt capital to ameliorate the risk of financial distress situations (Boateng & Huang, 2017; Ramalho et al., 2018). As the positive or negative impact of multiple corporate governance attributes on the leverage ratio is equally likely in the milieu of Indian corporates, only a significant linkage is purported between the main variables of interest. A brief discussion of each governance mechanism is presented in Table 4.1 to understand how they affect the proportion of debt in the capital structure.

4.2 Main Empirical Analysis and Discussion

Sample description

The non-financial corporations that are listed on the NIFTY 500 have been selected as the sample for the empirical investigation. The sampled firm's capital structure is analyzed from FY 2010 to FY 2019. However, certain observations are eliminated from the sample on account of missing data. In totality, 3494 observations are subjected to empirical examination, which represent 403 firms.

Regression model and variables

The empirical model for the study is given by Eq. 4.1, which represents the dynamic relationship between the corporate governance monitoring mechanisms and the leverage ratio. A dynamic regression model addresses the practice of capital structure adjustment done over time by companies in pursuit of attaining optimal debt ratio (Bajaj et al., 2024; Ezeani et al., 2022). As a consequence of partially bridging the deviation from the target levels, the leverage ratio of the current year relies on its past year's values (Erkan et al., 2016). Equation 4.1 is depicted in the following manner:

$$\begin{aligned} LEV_{it} &= \beta_0 + \beta_1 LEV_{t-1} + \beta_2 BSIZE_{it} + \beta_3 BIND_{it} \\ &+ \beta_4 CEODUAL_{it} + \beta_5 BGD_{it} + \beta_6 PROMOTER_{it} \\ &+ \beta_7 NPD_{it} + \beta_8 NAF_{it} + \sum_{j=9}^{N} \beta_j CONTROLS_{it} \\ &+ Industryeffects_i + Yeareffects_t + \varepsilon_{it} \end{aligned} \tag{4.1}$$

where *LEV* indicates the leverage ratio, which is computed by scaling the total debt amount with the book value of total assets (Mendiratta et al., 2024). The ratio is computed by acquiring data from Datastream®. The main explanatory variables

Table 4.1 Summary of the predicted relationship between corporate governance monitoring mechanisms and leverage ratio

Variables	Relationship
Board size *(BSIZE)*	CEOs on large boards can easily take control of corporate decision-making to implement a self-interested leverage policy as these boards can be prone to free-riding and communication issues (Abor & Biekpe, 2006). Contrastingly, oversized boards can provide the benefit of enhanced monitoring, thereby pushing management to implement a value-maximizing capital structure (Ezeani et al., 2022) **H1:** Board size has a significant association with the leverage ratio
Board independence *(BIND)*	Independent directors can perform a valuable monitoring function by urging risk-averse managers to utilize cheaper debt financing (Boateng et al., 2017). Conversely, when capital gearing is being deployed as a tool to consolidate control or misappropriate borrowed funds, outside directors can cause corporate insiders to reduce the leverage ratio (Kieschnick & Moussawi, 2018) **H2:** Board independence has a significant association with the leverage ratio
CEO duality *(CEODUAL)*	When CEOs also occupy the post of Chairman, they retain significant authority over various corporate matters. Correspondingly, the joint CEO-Chairman can misuse their authority to impose a capital structure of their choice (Dimitropoulos, 2014; Kyriazopoulos, 2017) **H3:** CEO duality has a significant association with the leverage ratio
Board gender diversity *(BGD)*	The diverse perspectives brought by female directors can aid in a comprehensive and protracted evaluation of all possible alternatives, which facilitates the adoption of value-enhancing decisions (López-Delgado & Diéguez-Soto, 2020; Rossi et al., 2018a, 2018b). Consequently, the participation of female directors can lead to the maintenance of an appropriate amount of debt in the capital structure **H4:** Board gender diversity has a significant association with the leverage ratio
Controlling shareholder *(PROMOTER)*	Controlling owners can use their significant voting rights to overleverage the firm to maintain control or tunnel corporate funds (Boateng & Huang, 2017; Ramalho et al., 2018). Alternatively, they can reduce leverage to avoid the bonding mechanism of debt or risk of bankruptcy (González et al., 2013; Schmid, 2013) **H5:** Controlling shareholder has a significant association with the leverage ratio
Non-controlling large shareholders *(NPD)*	As additional large owners are usually outside shareholders in the case of Indian business entities (Sethiya & Thenmozhi, 2020), they can deploy their consequential rights to urge the management to institute an appropriate capital structure (Boateng & Huang, 2017; Boubaker et al., 2017) **H6:** Non-controlling large shareholders have a significant association with the leverage ratio

(continued)

Table 4.1 (continued)

Variables	Relationship
Auditor independence *(NAF)*	Auditors may be unwilling to report any financial misstatements when non-audit fees are high (Ashbaugh et al., 2003). As a result, it can become difficult for governance mechanisms to accurately ascertain the corporation's liquidity position from such audited financials that are afflicted by the auditor's biases (Bley et al., 2019). Thus, non-audit services can decrease information transparency and extend the scope to corporate insiders to maintain debt levels according to their preferences **H7:** A higher proportion of non-audit fees has a significant association with the leverage ratio

Notes This table describes the hypotheses for examining the relationship between corporate governance and leverage ratio

encompass the corporate governance mechanisms of the board of directors, large ownership, and auditors. These governance attributes have been detailed in Chapter 1.

CONTROLS considers the effect of multiple control variables that have been shown in the extant literature to affect the debt ratio. The effect of firm size *(FSIZE)* is considered as large-sized corporations are expected to have higher leverage since they are in a better position to withstand bankruptcy risk (Chakraborty, 2018; Matemilola et al., 2019). In addition, the impact of firm age *(FAGE)* is also addressed as mature firms are endowed with considerable internal funds retained over the course of their operations, which minimizes the need for outside financing (Cole, 2013; La Rocca et al., 2011). Mature organizations may also have lower debt levels as they have an established capital market reputation, which facilitates undertaking a sizeable issue of equity (Goyal et al., 2011). Furthermore, growing firms are conjectured to resort to cheaper debt financing to realize their growth opportunities (Chakraborty, 2018; Ezeani et al., 2022). Therefore, the empirical investigation also includes growth opportunities *(GROWTH)*. The analysis also controls for non-debt tax shields (*NDTS*) as the presence of other expenses that can economize a firm's tax liability would diminish the desirability of tax benefits provided by debt instruments (Boateng et al., 2017).

The empirical analysis also incorporates profitability *(PROFIT)* as a control variable. Higher profitability enlarges a corporation's retained earnings, which can obviate the need to procure external debt financing (Chakraborty, 2018; Cole, 2013). Furthermore, unpredictable profits and financial distress situations can constrain a firm's ability to honour debt obligations (Al-Najjar, 2011). Hence, the influence of business risk *(BRISK)* and financial distress (*ZSCORE*) on the leverage ratio is also taken into account. In addition, tangible assets (*TANG*) can serve as collateral, which can enable a company to borrow funds at a reasonable cost (Boateng et al., 2017; Chakraborty, 2018). An entity's liquidity position *(LIQUIDP)* is also considered in the empirical examination since firms with large quantum of liquid assets can rely on their internal reserves to finance their operational and investment requirements (Al-Najjar & Taylor, 2008; Pathak & Chandani, 2023). The role of dividends

(DIVIDEND) in strengthening a corporation's ability to access debt financing is also addressed as these payouts can assure its lenders about its good earnings prospects and financial condition (Matemilola et al., 2019). The impact of managerial agency costs *(AGENCYC)* as proxied by discretionary selling, general, and administrative *(SGA)* expenditures is also investigated (Floackis, 2008; Tekin & Polat, 2021). Since executives may be tempted to expend internal funds on the disbursement of exorbitant compensation, reckless consumption of perks, and expensive advertisement budgets, they may try to evade the bonding mechanism of debt (Liu & Tian, 2012).

The empirical analysis also considers the industry and year effects in the empirical model to address the impact of heterogeneous industrial conditions and macroeconomic variables (La Rocca et al., 2011). The definition of each control variable has been expounded in Table 4.2.

Research methodology

The issues of endogeneity and autocorrelation become prominent when capital structure dynamics, as modeled by Eq. 4.1, are taken into account (Bajaj et al., 2021b; Guney et al., 2011). At the same time, there can also be endogeneity concerns relating to corporate governance variables. An unobserved effect, such as risk aversion, that influences both the debt levels and governance attributes can cause the independent variables and error term to be correlated. The correlation between explanatory variables and the error term may also arise because of the inaccurate measurement of the former (Arellano & Bond, 1991). In addition, the problem of reverse causality can also give rise to endogenous covariates (Blundell & Blond, 2000; Matemilola et al., 2019). For instance, it can also happen that women directors choose to participate on the boards of companies that are not heavily indebted.

In light of the underlined issues, Eq. 4.1 is estimated by employing the two-step system GMM estimator (Suman & Singh, 2022). In addition, diagnostic tests are also performed to check the validity of the system GMM technique for the stated model. Lastly, financial variables are also winsorized at 1 and 99% to alleviate the influence of extreme observations.

Descriptive statistics

Table 4.3 provides summary statistics of all the variables under the purview of the current empirical examination. It is observed that about 22% of the total assets, on average, are financed by debt capital (*LEV*). The observed level is higher than the leverage ratio of 20 and 18.2% noted for German and Japanese bank-based economies, respectively, by Ezeani et al. (2022) for a similar period. Further, the related inferences concerning corporate governance variables align with those reported in Chapter 2.

The correlation matrix[2] demonstrates significant pair-wise correlation between various corporate governance devices and the *LEV*, which extends preliminary support to the formulated hypotheses.

[2] Correlation matrix is available upon requests.

Table 4.2 Summary of control variables used in examining the impact of corporate governance monitoring mechanisms on the leverage ratio

Variables	Measurement	Data Source
Firm size *(FSIZE)*	Natural logarithm of total assets (Haque et al., 2011; Kang & Kim, 2006)	Datastream®
Firm age *(FAGE)*	Number of years since the firm's inception (Ramalho et al., 2018; Schmid, 2013)	Datastream®
Growth opportunities *(GROWTH)*	Tobin's Q (Kieschnick & Moussawi, 2018; Rossi et al., 2018a, 2018b)	Bloomberg®
Non-debt tax shields *(NDTS)*	Depreciation expense divided by the book value of total assets (Matemilola et al., 2019; Pathak & Chandani, 2023)	Datastream®
Profitability *(PROFIT)*	Ratio of net income to total assets (Haque et al., 2011; Liu & Tian, 2012)	Datastream®
Business risk *(BRISK)*	Standard deviation of the profitability (*PROFIT*) over the last five years (Kang & Kim, 2006)	Datastream®
Asset tangibility *(TANG)*	Net plant, property, and equipment divided by total assets (Chakraborty, 2018; Jiraporn et al., 2012)	Datastream®
Financial distress *(ZSCORE)*	Altman-Z score (Boubaker et al., 2017; Chao et al., 2017)	Datastream®
Liquidity position *(LIQUIDP)*	Current assets to the current liabilities ratio (Al-Najjar, 2011; Pathak & Chandani, 2023)	Datastream®
Dividend payouts *(DIVIDEND)*	Cash dividends to total assets ratio (Al-Najjar, 2011; Matemilola et al., 2019)	Datastream®
Agency costs *(AGENCYC)*	Ratio of a firm's SGA expenses to its annual sales (Tarus & Ayabei, 2016; Tekin & Polat, 2021)	Datastream®

Notes This table details the construction of the control variables used in the regression model to estimate the effect of corporate governance monitoring mechanisms on the leverage ratio

Table 4.3 Summary statistics of the leverage ratio, corporate governance monitoring mechanisms, and other firm-level variables

Variables	Mean	Standard deviation	Minimum	Maximum
LEV	0.2215	0.1893	0	0.7268
BSIZE	9.5215	2.6246	3	22
BIND	51.5715	11.176	0	100
CEODUAL	0.2977	0.4573	0	1
BGD	9.5883	8.1593	0	42.857
PROMOTER	56.7009	16.9849	8.2	90
NPD	0.1188	0.3236	0	1
NAF	0.3794	0.4614	0	2.6496
FSIZE	20.4296	1.4713	16.856	24.306
FAGE	38.5415	23.4918	1	155
GROWTH	2.7293	2.4245	0.6562	13.779
NDTS	0.0295	0.0181	0.0006	0.1003
PROFIT	0.0814	0.0707	−0.1345	0.2623
BRISK	0.0349	0.0384	0.0027	0.2893
TANG	0.3283	0.2045	0.0059	0.8044
ZSCORE	5.994	6.1793	0.1494	35.7928
LIQUIDP	1.8448	1.3009	0.3146	8.4871
DIVIDEND	0.0244	0.0395	0	0.2439
AGENCYC	0.2423	0.1798	0.0084	0.9615

Notes This table presents the descriptive statistics of variables employed in the current study

Multivariate regression analysis

The results from the two-step system GMM estimation of Eq. 4.1 are depicted in Table 4.4. The capital structure dynamics modeled by Eq. 4.1 are evinced by the positively significant coefficients of the lagged leverage ratio across all the specifications. In addition, the insignificant Hansen J statistic in all the columns demonstrates that the instruments generated by system GMM are exogenous. The absence of second-order autocorrelation is also confirmed as the AR (2) test is not significant. Lastly, the Walf F tests have p-values below 5%, which suggests that the variables are jointly significant.

Column 1 shows that the controlling shareholder's equity ownership (*PROMOTER*) has a negative and statistically significant impact on the leverage ratio (*LEV*). This observation supports H5 and alludes to the dominance of risk aversion among promoter owners. Promoters[3] may prefer to lower their risk exposure as they have substantial undiversified wealth tied up in the corporation (Chakraborty, 2018;

[3] According to Sect. 2(69) of the Companies Act, 2013, a promoter is "a person who has control over the affairs of the company, directly or indirectly whether as a shareholder, director or otherwise" (PwC India, 2013).

Table 4.4 Corporate governance monitoring mechanisms and the leverage ratio: Main regression analysis

Dependent variable: *LEV*	Overall sample (2010–2019)	Pre-reform period (2010–2014)	Post-reform period (2015–2019)
Variables	(1)	(2)	(3)
L.LEV	0.719***	0.517***	0.783***
	(0.0400)	(0.0874)	(0.0479)
BSIZE	0.000906	0.00797	0.00479
	(0.00320)	(0.00887)	(0.00326)
BIND	2.41e−05	−0.000676	0.000989**
	(0.000613)	(0.00112)	(0.000497)
CEODUAL	−0.00269	−0.0105	0.000749
	(0.0122)	(0.0235)	(0.0107)
BGD	0.000565	−0.000771	0.00143
	(0.00148)	(0.000773)	(0.000905)
PROMOTER	−0.00103**	−0.00270***	8.86e−05
	(0.000489)	(0.000973)	(0.000205)
NPD	−0.0159	−0.00664	−0.00329
	(0.0101)	(0.0197)	(0.0117)
NAF	−0.00617	−0.00978	0.00308
	(0.00935)	(0.0403)	(0.00779)
FSIZE	0.000725	0.00393	0.00153
	(0.00640)	(0.0206)	(0.00791)
FAGE	−0.000325*	−0.000944**	−8.06e−05
	(0.000173)	(0.000389)	(0.000163)
GROWTH	0.00945*	0.0184*	0.00630
	(0.00500)	(0.0111)	(0.00808)
NDTS	−1.241***	−1.714	−0.822*
	(0.317)	(1.161)	(0.442)
PROFIT	−0.789***	−0.756***	−0.520***
	(0.0891)	(0.247)	(0.116)
BRISK	0.0255	0.0448	−0.0857
	(0.0901)	(0.161)	(0.200)
TANG	0.0707	0.266***	0.0395
	(0.0486)	(0.0955)	(0.0297)
ZSCORE	−0.000663	−0.00626	−0.000218
	(0.00198)	(0.00477)	(0.00267)
LIQUIDP	−0.0119***	−0.00795	−0.00805
	(0.00438)	(0.00707)	(0.00820)

(continued)

Table 4.4 (continued)

Dependent variable: *LEV*	Overall sample (2010–2019)	Pre-reform period (2010–2014)	Post-reform period (2015–2019)
Variables	(1)	(2)	(3)
DIVIDEND	0.305**	0.613**	0.0679
	(0.146)	(0.292)	(0.101)
AGENCYC	−0.174***	−0.301*	−0.0649
	(0.0575)	(0.160)	(0.0481)
Constant	0.204	0.211	−0.0460
	(0.161)	(0.450)	(0.171)
Industry & Year FE	Yes	Yes	Yes
Wald F (p-value)	319.7 (0.000)	101.9 (0.000)	381.9 (0.000)
AR2 (p-value)	0.0828 (0.934)	−0.332 (0.740)	0.519 (0.604)
Hansen J (p-value)	96.04 (0.155)	45.92 (0.434)	87.39 (0.408)

Notes This table presents the findings of the two-step system GMM estimation of Eq. 4.1. Column 1 reports results when the empirical examination is conducted from FY 2010-FY 2019. Column 2 depicts findings for the period before the institution of the Companies Act, 2013 (Pre-reform period). Column 3 shows the results for years when the Companies Act, 2013 is in operation (Post-reform period). Windmeijer's (2005) corrected-robust standard errors are represented in parentheses. ***, **, and * depict significance at 1, 5, and 10% levels, respectively

González et al., 2013). Considering the intensified risk of bankruptcy due to heavy debt usage, controlling owners are likely to keep the leverage ratio down to shield against the loss of wealth and control from financial distress situations (Mishra & McConaughy, 1999; Rossi et al., 2018a, 2018b). Dominant shareholders may also exert downward pressure on the leverage ratio to avoid the disciplinary role of debt (Jiraporn et al., 2012; Schmid, 2013). Borrowed funds reduce the discretionary cash flow by binding the management to periodic interest payments, thereby imposing a constraint on its expropriation activities (Jensen, 1986). Hence, a negative association between controlling ownership and debt ratio is noted. As far as other governance mechanisms are concerned, it is observed that the attributes of the board of directors, the presence of MLS in a firm's ownership structure, and auditor independence have an insignificant effect on capital gearing levels in the overall sample.

Regarding the control variables, the findings indicate that firms in the mature stages of their lifecycle (*FAGE*) have lower leverage ratios (*LEV*). These corporations can have minimal debt financing requirements as they are expected to accumulate large amounts of internal funds during their multiple years of operation (Cole, 2013; La Rocca et al., 2011). Alternatively, a considerable history of their performance can enhance information transparency, which can assist aged companies in easily undertaking large-scale equity issuances (Goyal et al., 2011; Pathak and Chandani, 2023). Equity offerings by mature entities are likely to subsequently bring down their debt ratio. Furthermore, it also inferred that *LEV* increases with an increment in growth opportunities (*GROWTH*). Equity financing for growth firms can be relatively costly as they face severe information asymmetry with respect to the value of their investment opportunities (Feng et al., 2007; Matemilola et al., 2019). In light of inadequate retained earnings, growing corporations can make use of the security with lower information risk, i.e., debt, to fund their growth prospects.

It is also observed from the results that non-debt tax shields (*NDTS*) have a negative effect on *LEV*. Non-debt tax shields can serve as a substitute for debt in relation to saving tax on a corporation's net earnings (Boateng et al., 2017). Hence, the desirability of debt for their tax benefits is reduced when sizeable non-debt tax shields exist. Additionally, debt ratios (*LEV*) decrease with profitability (*PROFIT*). Higher profits enhance the availability of internal funds, which diminishes the necessity to acquire external capital (Chakraborty, 2018; Myers & Majluf, 1984). Companies with a good liquidity position (*LIQUIDP*) are also noted to be relatively less levered. According to Al-Najjar and Taylor (2008), such business enterprises avoid issuing new debt and prefer using their stock of liquid assets to pay off their operational and investment needs. Furthermore, dividends (*DIVIDEND*) stimulate debt levels as they may be perceived favorably by lenders. The payment of dividends can be taken as a signal of high earnings potential by lenders, due to which they may be willing to supply funds at a reasonable rate (Matemilola et al., 2019). Lastly, it is also shown that managerial agency costs (*AGENCYC*) curtail the leverage ratio (*LEV*). Since debt reduces the free cash flow that could be used for discretionary selling, general, and administrative (SGA) expenses such as perquisite consumption, self-interested managers prefer to avoid borrowed capital (Kang & Kim, 2006; Liu & Tian, 2012).

An extension to the empirical study is also made to analyze if there has been any change in the impact of corporate governance monitoring mechanisms post the introduction of the Companies Act, 2013. In order to investigate the underlined objective, firm-year observations are categorized into pre-reform and post-reform periods. The pre-reform period consists of years until FY 2014.[4] The post-reform period includes years when the new corporate governance regulations are applicable. The results from the empirical estimation of Eq. 4.1 undertaken separately for pre-reform and post-reform periods are summarized in Columns 2 and 3, respectively.

It is noted that the negative effect of the controlling owner's shareholding (*PROMOTER*) on the leverage ratio (*LEV*) is pronounced only in the pre-reform period. Its impact turns negligible in the post-reform period when a more robust corporate governance framework is in place. It is also inferred that board independence (*BIND*) positively influences *LEV* in the post-reform period. This finding conforms to H2 and points to the monitoring role of independent directors. Guided by the incentives to maintain their labor market reputation, independent directors can bring an impartial judgment and varied expertise to the board (Rashid, 2015; Solomon, 2007). Therefore, they are able to supervise and advise the management to deploy less expensive loan financing that also renders tax savings on a corporation's earnings. In addition, they may also encourage the use of debt as it moderates the free

[4] The Companies Act, 2013 was launched on August 30, 2013. Since the Act was introduced in the middle of FY 2014, the pre-reform period is extended to the end of the year (Sarkar and Selarka, 2021).

cash flow at the disposal of corporate insiders by binding the firm to make regular interest payouts (Jensen, 1986; Jiraporn et al., 2012).

4.3 Additional Analyses

4.3.1 Role of CEO Tenure

The empirical investigation is further augmented to uncover if there are any contingent effects of corporate governance monitoring mechanisms on the capital structure composition. The contextual impact is identified by first focusing on the number of years a CEO has completed in their current position. A lengthy tenure entrenches a CEO since it equips them to establish a close-knit relationship with board members (Chen et al., 2012; Goyal & Park, 2002). In addition, they have secured legitimacy and considerable support from the top management team owing to their long record of prior accomplishments (Lorsch & MacIver, 1989; Shen, 2003). Consequently, long-tenured CEOs tend to have a significant influence on corporate matters. They can exploit this acquired power to satisfy their interests at the cost of the corporation's value. Hence, CEOs in the late stages of tenure can sway capital gearing levels by avoiding the bonding mechanism of debt. Since leverage ameliorates the free cash flow problem, powerful CEOs are likely to steer away from borrowed funds (Chao et al., 2017). Furthermore, the preference for lower loan financing can arise from the risk aversion of long-tenured CEOs (Caliskan & Doukas, 2015). When debt levels become untenable, these CEOs risk losing their undiversified human capital build up over the course of their tenure (Baysinger et al., 1991; Simsek, 2007). Moreover, CEOs in their advanced career stages exhibit low task interest and are expected to underlever the firm to minimize the performance pressures associated with debt capital (Berger et al., 1997; Zona, 2016). In contrast, CEOs in the initial stages of their tenure do not have sufficient discretion and are bound to follow the board's mandate to retain their jobs (Shen, 2003; Zona, 2016). Hence, they are more likely to take value-maximizing leverage decisions to decrease the risk of their dismissal.

Consistent with the preceding discourse, it can be concluded that the observed impact of controlling ownership and board independence is likely to differ in the different stages of CEO tenure. In order to test this prediction, the sample values are divided using the quartile value of a CEO's tenure into the categories of short-tenured, medium-tenured, and long-tenured CEOs. The related empirical findings from the empirical investigation are presented in Table 4.5.

Table 4.5 depicts that the observed effect of promoter shareholding and board independence does not vary with the stages of a CEO's tenure. However, Column 3 shows that in companies with long-tenured CEOs, the leverage ratio (*LEV*) tends to be lower when auditor independence is impaired by a high proportion of non-audit fees (*NAF*). A lengthy tenure expands the influence of CEOs over capital structure decisions (Chen et al., 2012). In order to preserve their discretion and

Table 4.5 Corporate governance monitoring mechanisms and the leverage ratio: Role of CEO tenure

Dependent variable: *LEV*	Short-tenured CEOs	Medium-tenured CEOs	Long-tenured CEOs
Variables	(1)	(2)	(3)
L.LEV	0.868***	0.795***	0.771***
	(0.0567)	(0.0680)	(0.0534)
BSIZE	−0.00232	−0.00199	0.00132
	(0.00336)	(0.00388)	(0.00337)
BIND	−0.000165	0.000618	0.000124
	(0.000367)	(0.000838)	(0.000655)
CEODUAL	−0.0113	0.0138	−0.0143
	(0.0182)	(0.0272)	(0.0141)
BGD	−0.000610	0.000253	0.000399
	(0.000467)	(0.000429)	(0.000919)
PROMOTER	−0.000222	−0.000288	4.94e−05
	(0.000400)	(0.000261)	(0.000309)
NPD	−0.00235	−0.00645	−0.00375
	(0.0232)	(0.0105)	(0.0262)
NAF	0.0248	−0.00732	−0.0227**
	(0.0164)	(0.0117)	(0.0114)
FSIZE	0.0139**	0.0158	0.00147
	(0.00570)	(0.0120)	(0.00990)
FAGE	−0.000249	−0.000160	−0.000351*
	(0.000185)	(0.000253)	(0.000206)
GROWTII	0.00213	0.00629	0.0127*
	(0.00487)	(0.00946)	(0.00754)
NDTS	−0.469	−0.218	−1.082**
	(0.684)	(0.679)	(0.433)
PROFIT	−0.255*	−0.290*	−0.668***
	(0.138)	(0.154)	(0.142)
BRISK	−0.0322	0.0565	0.170
	(0.0938)	(0.107)	(0.198)
TANG	0.0545	0.0201	0.0738
	(0.0713)	(0.0617)	(0.0655)
ZSCORE	−0.000181	−0.00136	−0.00474**
	(0.00172)	(0.00389)	(0.00227)
LIQUIDP	−0.00203	−0.0111	0.00823
	(0.00657)	(0.00816)	(0.00728)
DIVIDEND	0.0593	0.394	0.139

(continued)

Table 4.5 (continued)

Dependent variable: *LEV*	Short-tenured CEOs	Medium-tenured CEOs	Long-tenured CEOs
Variables	(1)	(2)	(3)
	(0.0774)	(0.332)	(0.152)
AGENCYC	−0.0369	−0.0647	−0.0296
	(0.0516)	(0.0484)	(0.0466)
Constant	−0.233**	−0.241	0.0438
	(0.0993)	(0.245)	(0.235)
Industry & Year FE	Yes	Yes	Yes
Wald F (p-value)	235.8 (0.000)	283.4 (0.000)	379.1 (0.000)
AR (2) (p-value)	0.687 (0.492)	0.0509 (0.959)	−0.447 (0.655)
Hansen J (p-value)	76.59 (0.492)	62.04 (0.475)	130.3 (0.266)

Notes This table summarizes the results from the empirical estimation of Eq. 4.1 when the sample is segregated based on CEO tenure. Short-tenured CEOs encompass years of CEO tenure in the lowest quartile (CEO tenure < 2.416667 years). Years of CEO tenure in the upper quartile are designated as long-tenured CEOs (CEO tenure > 18.75 years). Firm-year observations in the middle two quartiles are clubbed together medium-tenured CEOs (CEO tenure from 2.416667 to 18.75 years). Windmeijer's (2005) corrected-robust standard errors are shown in parentheses. ***, **, and * indicate significance at 1, 5, and 10% levels, respectively

undiversified wealth, long-tenured CEOs may prefer to avoid debt financing and its accompanying pre-committed payouts (Caliskan & Doukas, 2015; Chao et al., 2017). In these conditions, employment of non-audit services can facilitate the adoption of low capital gearing levels. A higher provision of non-audit services strengthens the financial relationship between the auditor and the client firm (Ashbaugh et al., 2003; Mitra, 2007). The augmented income stream from the client can deter an auditor from raising any accounting concerns and ensuring the complete reliability of financial statements (Dhaliwal et al., 2008). Thus, a large non-audit fee payment creates doubt about the credibility of financials, which can intensify information asymmetry. The governance constituents that rely on audited financials may not be able to clearly appraise managerial actions (Hoelscher & Seavey, 2014). They may find it difficult to determine a corporation's liquidity position from such biased reports and, accordingly, are unable to recommend increased debt levels (Bley et al., 2019). Hence, an opaque information environment can provide latitude to long-tenured CEOs to pursue a leverage policy of their choice. This result aligns with H7 and highlights the adverse effects of excessive non-audit fees in comparison to audit fees.

4.3.2 Role of Firm Size

Relative to their smaller counterparts, large-sized business entities are in a better position to withstand situations of financial distress (Chakraborty, 2018; Matemilola et al., 2019). These firms are usually characterized by widespread and diversified business operations, which moderate the volatility in their earnings (Lee & Kuo, 2014; Ramalho et al., 2018). As a result, larger companies have a lower risk of bankruptcy. In addition, these enterprises have superior borrowing capacity as they possess large amounts of tangible assets that can be pledged as collateral while securing debt financing (Schmid, 2013; Tarus & Ayabei, 2016). Importantly, large-sized corporations can benefit from the disciplinary role of debt as they are generally mature corporations that have substantial accumulated cash available under the wilful control of corporate insiders (Belghitar & Khan, 2013; DeAngelo et al., 2006). Therefore, effective corporate governance mechanisms in large companies can deploy borrowed capital to curtail management's discretion by binding it with contracted interest payouts.

The empirical analysis checks the validity of the proposed expectation by segregating the firm-year observations based on the quartile values of firm size (Prakash et al., 2024). The results from the empirical estimation of Eq. 4.1 conducted for small-sized, medium-sized, and large-sized corporations are shown in Table 4.6. It is inferred from Column 3 that the observed positive impact of board independence (*BIND*) on the leverage ratio (*LEV*) is more pronounced in large-sized firms. Since large companies have higher borrowing capacity and lower bankruptcy risk (Matemilola et al., 2019), their non-affiliated outside directors can urge for the usage of debt as borrowed funds can restrict the availability of surplus cash at the disposal of corporate insiders by requiring it to make periodic installment payments (Jensen, 1986).

4.3.3 Role of Firm Age

Filatotchev et al. (2006) argue that managerial expropriation intensifies when a company reaches the mature stage of its lifecycle. At this phase of their lifecycle, corporations have amassed massive reserves that significantly outweigh their limited growth options (Cole, 2013; La Rocca et al., 2011). Therefore, self-interested corporate insiders can be incentivized to misallocate the excess corporate funds to value-destroying activities. Furthermore, strategy literature also emphasizes that older corporations are vulnerable to the problem of organizational inertia (Petruzzelli et al., 2018; Teofilus et al., 2022). Constrained by their formalized structures and a dated knowledge base, the management of these firms tends to follow long-established corporate practices and avoid any complex and radical changes to improve efficiency (Bouncken et al., 2021; Coad et al., 2016). Since debt financing imposes certain

Table 4.6 Corporate governance monitoring mechanisms and the leverage ratio: Role of firm size

Dependent variable: *LEV*	Small-sized firms	Medium-sized firms	Large-sized firms
Variables	(1)	(2)	(3)
L.LEV	0.676***	0.656***	0.744***
	(0.0851)	(0.0672)	(0.0718)
BSIZE	−0.00325	0.00231	0.000312
	(0.00436)	(0.00371)	(0.00431)
BIND	0.000845	−0.000205	0.00142**
	(0.000803)	(0.000702)	(0.000716)
CEODUAL	−0.0156	0.000963	−0.0188
	(0.0144)	(0.0165)	(0.0208)
BGD	−0.00146	−0.000315	0.000262
	(0.00142)	(0.00125)	(0.000690)
PROMOTER	0.000730	−0.000486	−0.000263
	(0.000740)	(0.000913)	(0.000463)
NPD	0.0331	−0.0106	0.00568
	(0.0220)	(0.0162)	(0.0201)
NAF	−0.0139	−0.000906	0.0160
	(0.0190)	(0.00766)	(0.0197)
FSIZE	−0.00447	0.0161*	0.0122
	(0.0118)	(0.00841)	(0.0165)
FAGE	−0.000421	−0.000250	−0.000518
	(0.000276)	(0.000188)	(0.000336)
GROWTH	0.0113	0.00736	0.00876*
	(0.00756)	(0.0116)	(0.00499)
NDTS	−1.311***	−0.180	−1.859**
	(0.485)	(0.538)	(0.800)
PROFIT	−0.198*	−0.735***	−0.487***
	(0.105)	(0.112)	(0.186)
BRISK	−0.141	0.441*	−0.321
	(0.134)	(0.251)	(0.355)
TANG	0.149**	0.0658	0.0294
	(0.0655)	(0.0813)	(0.0982)
ZSCORE	−0.00658**	−0.00129	−0.00238
	(0.00326)	(0.00431)	(0.00242)
LIQUIDP	0.00713	−0.00794	0.000425
	(0.00866)	(0.00705)	(0.00666)
DIVIDEND	0.207	0.236	0.0308
	(0.145)	(0.324)	(0.191)

(continued)

Table 4.6 (continued)

Dependent variable: *LEV*	Small-sized firms	Medium-sized firms	Large-sized firms
Variables	(1)	(2)	(3)
AGENCYC	−0.0302	−0.117	−0.0731
	(0.0466)	(0.0794)	(0.108)
Constant	0.0319	−0.193	−0.165
	(0.253)	(0.215)	(0.362)
Industry & Year FE	Yes	Yes	Yes
Wald F (p-value)	326.7 (0.000)	290.8 (0.000)	635.6 (0.000)
AR(2) (p-value)	0.594 (0.553)	0.0968 (0.923)	−0.223 (0.824)
Hansen J (p-value)	89.23 (0.473)	64.70 (0.487)	35.99 (0.330)

Notes This table summarizes the findings from the empirical estimation of Eq. 4.1 when the sample is classified using the quartile values of firm size. The values in the bottom quartile are grouped as small-sized firms (firm size < 19.41277). Observations of firm size in the top quartile are categorized as large-sized firms (firm size > 21.26125). The remaining firm-year observations in the middle two quartiles are termed as medium-sized firms (firm size from 19.41277 to 21.26125). Parentheses denote Windmeijer's (2005) corrected-robust standard errors. ***, **, and * indicate significance at 1, 5, and 10% levels, respectively

performance expectations, executives of mature entities can purposely circumvent lender monitoring by maintaining a low leverage ratio (Berger et al., 1997).

In light of the highlighted circumstances, it can be conjectured that stronger corporate governance mechanisms can play a valuable role in older corporations by employing the disciplinary device of debt capital. For examining this assertion, the sample is partitioned using the critical values of firm age. The findings from the empirical estimation of Eq. 4.1 for younger, middle-aged, and mature corporations are depicted in Table 4.7.

Column 3 demonstrates that the observed positive influence of board independence (*BIND*) on the leverage ratio (*LEV*) is prominent in older firms. This inference evinces the stated expectation and alludes that independent directors ameliorate the problem of free cash flow and organizational inertia in aged corporations through constant supervision and advisory. As these directors have reputational concerns, they can provide unbiased viewpoints and valuable expertise on various corporate matters (Rashid, 2015; Solomon, 2007). Considering that mature companies can easily access external financing due to a better record of performance history (La Rocca et al., 2011), outside directors can insist that the management leverage the corporation (Jiraporn et al., 2012). Debt reduces discretionary cash and forces managers to ensure good profitability to comply with the loan covenants (Jensen, 1986). Thus, a highly independent board uses borrowed capital as an additional bonding mechanism in old business enterprises.

Table 4.7 Corporate governance monitoring mechanisms and the leverage ratio: Role of firm age

Dependent variable: *LEV*	Younger firms	Middle-aged firms	Older firms
Variables	(1)	(2)	(3)
L.LEV	0.506***	0.785***	0.708***
	(0.0848)	(0.0415)	(0.0595)
BSIZE	−0.00719	−5.77e−05	0.00184
	(0.00596)	(0.00161)	(0.00432)
BIND	−0.000494	0.000389	0.000861*
	(0.000935)	(0.000448)	(0.000454)
CEODUAL	0.0209	−0.00290	0.00440
	(0.0292)	(0.0122)	(0.0146)
BGD	−0.00126	0.000422	0.000143
	(0.00148)	(0.000720)	(0.000409)
PROMOTER	−0.000986	−0.000615	−0.000197
	(0.000693)	(0.000448)	(0.000460)
NPD	0.0211	−0.00428	−0.00578
	(0.0266)	(0.0172)	(0.0131)
NAF	−0.0170	0.00454	0.0161
	(0.0167)	(0.0118)	(0.0235)
FSIZE	0.0257***	0.00670	0.0104
	(0.00957)	(0.00736)	(0.00626)
FAGE	−0.000185	−0.000634**	0.000302
	(0.000924)	(0.000301)	(0.000327)
GROWTH	0.0144**	0.00389	0.00480
	(0.00653)	(0.00394)	(0.00565)
NDTS	−0.383	−0.768**	−0.544
	(0.626)	(0.385)	(0.818)
PROFIT	−0.682***	−0.434***	−0.579***
	(0.150)	(0.0862)	(0.145)
BRISK	0.114	−0.0729	0.273
	(0.0992)	(0.167)	(0.232)
TANG	0.0481	0.0608	0.00654
	(0.0801)	(0.0572)	(0.0572)
ZSCORE	−0.00771**	−0.00110	−0.00229
	(0.00387)	(0.00137)	(0.00272)
LIQUIDP	−0.0118	−0.00327	−0.00520
	(0.00845)	(0.00413)	(0.00597)
DIVIDEND	0.524*	0.172	0.202
	(0.295)	(0.159)	(0.187)

(continued)

Table 4.7 (continued)

Dependent variable: *LEV*	Younger firms	Middle-aged firms	Older firms
Variables	(1)	(2)	(3)
AGENCYC	−0.107	−0.0288	−0.0699
	(0.0678)	(0.0422)	(0.0925)
Constant	−0.261	−0.0189	−0.168
	(0.252)	(0.178)	(0.155)
Industry & Year FE	Yes	Yes	Yes
Wald F (p-value)	141.1 (0.000)	383.4 (0.000)	241.7 (0.000)
AR (2) (p-value)	0.136 (0.892)	0.388 (0.698)	0.682 (0.495)
Hansen J (p-value)	96.71 (0.489)	115.7 (0.184)	70.77 (0.485)

Notes This table presents the results from the empirical estimation when the sample is disaggregated based on firm age. Firm-year observations within quartile one are assigned as younger firms (firm age < 21.46944 years). Observations above quartile three make up the sample of older firms (firm age > 53 years). The remaining values of firm age ranging from quartile one to quartile three are grouped as middle-aged firms (firm age from 21.46944 to 53 years). Parentheses denote Windmeijer's (2005) corrected-robust standard errors. ***, **, and * represent significance at 1, 5, and 10% levels, respectively

4.3.4 *Role of Firm Growth Opportunities*

The utilization of debt can be beneficial in low-growth companies because it can restrict the management's misuse of funds by binding it with periodic payouts of interest payments (Benkraiem et al., 2018; Flavin et al., 2021). Such firms have usually exhausted most of their investment opportunities set and have cumulated a significant amount of internal funds. Since these retained funds are in excess of the limited growth prospects, low-growth entities are susceptible to the problem of free cash flow (Florackis, 2008; Jensen, 1986). Corporate insiders may dissipate the surplus funds for satisfying their selfish interests (John et al., 2015). Hence, self-interested dominant owners and managers of low-growth business enterprises can avoid the bonding mechanism of debt to maintain their consumption of private benefits. In contrast, robust corporate governance monitoring mechanisms can stimulate increased capital gearing levels to curb the managerial extraction of corporate resources in these corporations.

In line with the previous discussion, the empirical study investigates whether the effect of various corporate governance attributes is stronger in low-growth companies. The same is probed by disaggregating the sampled observations on the basis of growth opportunities, which is indicated by Tobin's Q. The relevant results for low-growth, moderate-growth, and high-growth companies have been summarized in Table 4.8.

It can be observed from Column 1 that the significant negative effect of controlling shareholding (*PROMOTER*) on the leverage ratio (*LEV*) is present only in low-growth firms. Low-growth corporations usually have excessive retained funds,

Table 4.8 Corporate governance monitoring mechanisms and the leverage ratio: Role of firm growth opportunities

Dependent variable: *LEV*	Low-growth firms	Moderate-growth firms	High-growth firms
Variables	(1)	(2)	(3)
L.LEV	0.679***	0.823***	0.604***
	(0.0665)	(0.0430)	(0.104)
BSIZE	−0.00189	0.000165	−8.24e−05
	(0.00367)	(0.00279)	(0.00703)
BIND	−0.000170	0.000370	0.000180
	(0.000550)	(0.000237)	(0.00108)
CEODUAL	−0.0263	0.00322	0.0100
	(0.0171)	(0.0132)	(0.0157)
BGD	0.000396	8.55e−05	0.000672
	(0.000831)	(0.000306)	(0.00107)
PROMOTER	−0.00101**	4.76e−05	−6.19e−06
	(0.000500)	(0.000181)	(0.000725)
NPD	−0.0160	−0.00627	−0.00332
	(0.0146)	(0.0125)	(0.0431)
NAF	−0.00420	−0.00951	0.0188
	(0.0248)	(0.00646)	(0.0292)
FSIZE	0.0198	0.00541	0.00477
	(0.0122)	(0.00344)	(0.0146)
FAGE	−0.000624**	−0.000158	−0.000611**
	(0.000277)	(0.000120)	(0.000260)
GROWTH	0.0138	−0.00152	0.00274
	(0.0129)	(0.00392)	(0.00617)
NDTS	−1.621**	−1.354**	−0.361
	(0.811)	(0.632)	(0.554)
PROFIT	−0.339**	−0.307**	−0.380**
	(0.146)	(0.152)	(0.154)
BRISK	−0.141	0.116	−0.0110
	(0.275)	(0.0835)	(0.0986)
TANG	0.0897	0.0346	0.0166
	(0.0605)	(0.0578)	(0.0555)
ZSCORE	−0.00748	−0.00110	−0.00372
	(0.00623)	(0.00194)	(0.00267)
LIQUIDP	−0.0179***	−0.00412	0.00671
	(0.00638)	(0.00515)	(0.00960)
DIVIDEND	0.0368	0.121	0.163

(continued)

Table 4.8 (continued)

Dependent variable: *LEV*	Low-growth firms	Moderate-growth firms	High-growth firms
Variables	(1)	(2)	(3)
	(0.150)	(0.196)	(0.146)
AGENCYC	−0.0314	−0.0367*	−0.0722
	(0.0649)	(0.0187)	(0.0635)
Constant	−0.139	−0.0499	−0.0320
	(0.251)	(0.0672)	(0.260)
Industry & Year FE	Yes	Yes	Yes
Wald F (p-value)	290 (0.000)	388.2 (0.000)	45.56 (0.000)
AR (2) (p-value)	0.838 (0.402)	0.662 (0.508)	−0.139 (0.890)
Hansen J (p-value)	65.54 (0.458)	76.01 (0.109)	71.50 (0.461)

Notes This table shows the findings from the empirical estimation conducted for firms in different stages of growth. Growth opportunities are measured by Tobin's Q. All the firm-year observations less than the lowest quartile value of Tobin's Q constitute the group of low-growth firms (Tobin's Q < 1.1674). The sample of high-growth firms represents observations whose values exceed the upper quartile of the Q ratio (Tobin's Q > 3.3138). The remaining values in the middle two quartiles are categorized as moderate-growth firms (Tobin's Q from 1.1674 to 3.3138). Windmeijer's (2005) corrected-robust standard errors are depicted in parentheses. ***, **, and * indicate significance at 1, 5, and 10% levels, respectively

which provide an opportunity for promoter owners to misappropriate these corporate resources (Jensen, 1986). As the deployment of debt lessens the funds at their disposal, controlling owners will tend to decrease the capital gearing levels (Jiraporn et al., 2012). A lower leverage ratio can also diminish the lender monitoring and performance expectations associated with borrowed capital (Berger et al., 1997; Jung et al., 1996). Thus, dominant shareholders underleverage the company to minimize the disciplinary effect of debt financing.

4.3.5 Role of Firm Financial Condition

The deployment of debt as a disciplinary device is likely to be affected by a firm's financial condition. As the risk of default intensifies, the corporation's ability to service its debt obligation diminishes (Balasubramanian et al., 2019). In addition, using more capital gearing can further exacerbate bankruptcy risk and make the company's financial position more fragile (Pindado et al., 2006). Moreover, lenders are expected to supply funds only at a higher risk premium to financially weaker business entities (D'Mello et al., 2008; Gupta & Mahakud, 2022). Therefore, a lower leverage ratio is presumed desirable in firms with a high risk of financial distress. Contrastingly, financially sound enterprises can afford a higher debt ratio as they can better fulfill their contractual obligations and easily access external financing (Arslan-Ayaydin Ö et al., 2014).

Corollary to the previously elaborated discourse, it can be reckoned that a corporation's financial condition is predicted to matter when considering the ramifications of corporate governance attributes on the debt levels. Hence, their contingent effects on the leverage ratio are ascertained using the quartile values of the Altman-Z score. A higher Altman-Z score is an indicator of low bankruptcy risk and financially sound operations (Habib et al., 2020). Hence, the firm-year observations are grouped into three categories: corporations in financial distress, entities with moderate financial conditions, and financially sound companies. The empirical findings for the obtained sub-samples are depicted in Table 4.9.

It can be noted from Column 1 that the negative influence of stakeholding by the controlling owner (*PROMOTER*) on the leverage ratio (*LEV*) is more prominent for firms in financial distress conditions. The heightened risk of default in financially distressed companies can precipitate the risk aversion of dominant shareholders. These owners have a significant portion of their wealth concentrated in the business enterprise (Chakraborty, 2018; González et al., 2013). As the employment of debt can further worsen the financial position of a corporation that is at a greater likelihood of bankruptcy, promoter owners are anticipated to discourage its use to protect against the loss of their wealth and control arising from the default situations (Rossi et al., 2018a, 2018b). Similar observations are also reported in respect of non-controlling large owners (*NPD*) as they are shown to impact *LEV* negatively in firms experiencing financial distress. Inflated debt levels can endanger the survival of a financially weaker entity and cause the depletion of the substantial economic wealth of its additional blockholders (Boubaker et al., 2017). Therefore, the other large shareholders of financially distressed companies also attempt to keep the leverage ratio low to preserve the value of their holdings.

4.3.6 Role of Industry Concentration

Highly concentrated markets are marked by the presence of few competing firms (Cheng et al., 2013; Schmidt, 1997). Since these corporations are in control of a significant portion of the market and consequently assume substantial market power, their managers have little or no incentives to improve the efficiency of business operations (Melville et al., 2007; Srivastava et al., 2023). In addition, the presence of a limited number of rivals hampers the ability to benchmark a company's performance, which can further provide opportunities for managers to implement self-interested policies (El Diri et al., 2020; Nalebuff & Stiglitz, 1983). Given the heightened agency conflicts in concentrated industries, the deployment of the bonding mechanism of debt can be beneficial in minimizing managerial entrenchment (Jensen, 1986).

In contrast, the disciplinary forces of competition in low-concentrated industries can substitute for the governance role of debt (Boubaker et al., 2018). Intensively high competition can drive down the profit margin of the enterprise if it continues

Table 4.9 Corporate governance monitoring mechanisms and the leverage ratio: Role of firm financial condition

Dependent variable: *LEV*	Financial distress conditions (Low Altman-Z scores)	Moderate financial conditions (Medium range Altman-Z scores)	Financially sound conditions (High Altman-Z scores)
Variables	(1)	(2)	(3)
L.LEV	0.757***	0.704***	0.485***
	(0.0852)	(0.0450)	(0.0921)
BSIZE	0.00411	0.00179	0.00383
	(0.00422)	(0.00256)	(0.00441)
BIND	0.000523	3.91e−05	0.000232
	(0.00103)	(0.000528)	(0.000764)
CEODUAL	0.0213	7.10e−05	−0.0235
	(0.0333)	(0.0128)	(0.0183)
BGD	0.000772	−0.000291	0.000247
	(0.000908)	(0.000702)	(0.00143)
PROMOTER	−0.000717*	−0.000306	0.000124
	(0.000382)	(0.000529)	(0.000294)
NPD	−0.0323**	−0.00623	0.0161
	(0.0161)	(0.0120)	(0.0238)
NAF	0.0108	−0.00151	−0.00281
	(0.0208)	(0.0139)	(0.0271)
FSIZE	−0.000772	0.0227***	0.00579
	(0.00664)	(0.00664)	(0.00848)
FAGE	−0.000183	−0.000351**	−0.000609**
	(0.000272)	(0.000169)	(0.000284)
GROWTH	0.0308	0.0107*	0.00298
	(0.0186)	(0.00616)	(0.00413)
NDTS	−0.505	−1.270***	−0.140
	(0.923)	(0.336)	(0.482)
PROFIT	−0.610*	−0.479***	−0.301**
	(0.319)	(0.0800)	(0.117)
BRISK	0.129	0.0843	−0.0221
	(0.201)	(0.196)	(0.0971)
TANG	0.0901	0.0748	−0.0967
	(0.0827)	(0.0503)	(0.0680)
ZSCORE	−0.0245***	−0.00255	−0.00208
	(0.00658)	(0.00279)	(0.00157)
LIQUIDP	0.00321	−0.0144***	0.000123
	(0.0108)	(0.00416)	(0.00657)

(continued)

Table 4.9 (continued)

Dependent variable: *LEV*	Financial distress conditions (Low Altman-Z scores)	Moderate financial conditions (Medium range Altman-Z scores)	Financially sound conditions (High Altman-Z scores)
Variables	(1)	(2)	(3)
DIVIDEND	0.835	0.217	0.0282
	(1.991)	(0.133)	(0.0698)
AGENCYC	−0.108	−0.0139	−0.0221
	(0.0808)	(0.0577)	(0.0611)
Constant	0.0614	−0.369**	−0.00996
	(0.145)	(0.148)	(0.195)
Industry & Year FE	Yes	Yes	Yes
Wald F (p-value)	500.7 (0.000)	197.1 (0.000)	12.78 (0.000)
AR (2) (p-value)	0.874 (0.382)	0.361 (0.718)	0.00388 (0.997)
Hansen J (p-value)	42.52 (0.492)	155.8 (0.118)	48.61 (0.448)

Notes This table highlights the results from the empirical estimation when the sample is divided using the Altman Z-scores. Altman Z-score signals a firm's financial condition. A higher score indicates lower default risk (Habib et al., 2020). Hence, Z score values in the bottom quartile are classified as firms in financial distress conditions (Z score < 2.058483). Observations in the top quartile comprise the sample of firms with financially sound conditions (Z score > 7.7275). The middle two quartiles with remaining values are labeled as firms with moderate financial conditions (Z score from 2.058483 to 7.7275). Parentheses denote Windmeijer's (2005) corrected-robust standard errors. ***, **, and * represent significance at 1, 5, and 10% levels, respectively

to incur a relatively steeper expenditure on production costs and overheads (El Diri et al., 2020; Hart, 1983). Thus, the threat of competition compels management to reduce their self-serving activities and focus on enhancing productivity (Srivastava et al., 2024).

Debt financing also has strategic implications when dealing with rivals. On the one hand, borrowed capital can be employed to invest and produce aggressively to fend off new and existing competitors (Brander & Lewis, 1986; Campello, 2003). On the other hand, high indebtedness can impede a company's capacity to respond to rival firms' predatory actions as it can be constrained in implementing tactical investments (Boubaker et al., 2018; Chevalier, 1995).

It can be inferred from the preceding deliberations that the industry structure and accompanying competition affect the utility of debt. Therefore, it can be expected that the effect of corporate governance monitoring mechanisms on the leverage ratio is contingent upon the degree of industry concentration. In order to test this prediction, the sample is segregated using the quartile values of the Herfindahl–Hirschman Index (HHI). The corresponding results from the empirical estimation of Eq. 4.1 for low-concentrated, medium-concentrated, and highly-concentrated industries are presented in Table 4.10.

Table 4.10 Corporate governance monitoring mechanisms and the leverage ratio: Role of industry concentration

Dependent variable: *LEV*	Low-concentrated industries	Medium-concentrated industries	Highly-concentrated industries
Variables	(1)	(2)	(3)
L.LEV	0.762***	0.551***	0.658***
	(0.0506)	(0.0704)	(0.0531)
BSIZE	−0.00703	−0.00423	0.00213
	(0.00457)	(0.00339)	(0.00332)
BIND	0.000350	0.000174	5.42e−05
	(0.000645)	(0.000932)	(0.000573)
CEODUAL	−0.000490	0.0173	−0.0436
	(0.0182)	(0.0158)	(0.0340)
BGD	0.000134	0.00118	−0.000842
	(0.000629)	(0.000813)	(0.000514)
PROMOTER	−0.000583	0.000155	−0.00121**
	(0.000436)	(0.000455)	(0.000531)
NPD	−0.0109	−0.00321	−0.0129
	(0.0146)	(0.0252)	(0.0127)
NAF	0.000529	−0.0181*	0.00915
	(0.0103)	(0.00971)	(0.0160)
FSIZE	0.0128	0.0110	0.00953
	(0.00854)	(0.0122)	(0.00903)
FAGE	−0.000349	−0.000192	4.20e−05
	(0.000272)	(0.000208)	(0.000251)
GROWTH	0.00856	0.00888	0.00102
	(0.00546)	(0.00733)	(0.00756)
NDTS	−1.785***	−0.743	−0.140
	(0.535)	(0.465)	(0.454)
PROFIT	−0.577***	−0.852***	−0.452***
	(0.123)	(0.165)	(0.117)
BRISK	0.104	0.104	0.112
	(0.148)	(0.0925)	(0.208)
TANG	0.120***	0.158**	0.105**
	(0.0433)	(0.0698)	(0.0520)
ZSCORE	−0.00183	−0.00430	−0.00118
	(0.00268)	(0.00299)	(0.00211)
LIQUIDP	−0.0106*	−0.00196	−0.00761
	(0.00553)	(0.00587)	(0.00461)

(continued)

Table 4.10 (continued)

Dependent variable: *LEV*	Low-concentrated industries	Medium-concentrated industries	Highly-concentrated industries
Variables	(1)	(2)	(3)
DIVIDEND	0.394***	0.134	0.0392
	(0.0958)	(0.222)	(0.140)
AGENCYC	−0.0542	−0.282***	−0.0789*
	(0.0487)	(0.0936)	(0.0452)
Constant	−0.0660	−0.00601	−0.0570
	(0.190)	(0.277)	(0.200)
Industry & Year FE	Yes	Yes	Yes
Wald F (p-value)	282 (0.000)	232.8 (0.000)	264.5 (0.000)
AR (2) (p-value)	−0.364 (0.716)	−1.259 (0.208)	1.253 (0.210)
Hansen J (p-value)	103.6 (0.382)	143.5 (0.313)	100.1 (0.478)

Notes This table provides an overview of the findings from the system GMM estimation of Eq. 4.1 when the sample is partitioned based on the degree of industry concentration. HHI is used to proxy for the severity of concentration in a given market. Sample values below quartile one of HHI are termed as low-concentrated industries (HHI < 0.0329862). Firm-year observations that lie above the value of quartile three of HHI are classified as highly-concentrated industries (HHI > 0.0771521). The observations ranging from quartiles one and three constitute the sample of medium-concentrated industries (HHI from 0.0329862 to 0.0771521). Parentheses report Windmeijer's (2005) corrected-robust standard errors. ***, **, and * indicate significance at 1, 5, and 10% levels, respectively

Column 2 depicts that a higher proportion of non-audit fees (*NAF*) negatively affects the leverage ratio (*LEV*) when a corporation is operating in a medium-concentrated industry. Since such a company does not hold considerable market power, it may attempt to strengthen its position in the industry by implementing large-scale investments in new production and distribution facilities (Kim, 2015). Aggressive investments can erect high-entry barriers for new entrant firms (Akdoğu & MacKay, 2008; Park et al., 2017). In addition, over-production can facilitate price reduction, which can severely erode the rivals' profit margins (Fosu, 2013; Guney et al., 2011). However, when the capital gearing levels are high, it can limit the capacity of a firm in medium-concentrated markets to undertake the underlined strategic investments (Boubaker et al., 2018; Chevalier, 1995). Further, highly levered entities risk losing their market shares as their constrained liquidity situation can prevent them from responding to these predatory investments from competitors (Haushalter et al., 2007).

In view of the specified circumstances, the contracted auditors of companies in medium-concentrated industries can advise them to keep the debt levels under control through non-audit services. Auditors can provide valuable company-specific expertise as they have significant private information about the client's business gathered over the course of multiple audits (Cai et al., 2016; Dhaliwal et al., 2016).

Further, they have amassed substantial knowledge about different industrial structures and conditions by auditing several corporations across various sectors (Bae et al., 2017; Elaoud & Jarboui, 2017). Thus, auditors can provide useful input on different corporate matters by providing non-audit services.

Column 3 of Table 4.10 also demonstrates that dominant ownership (*PROMOTER*) negatively influences *LEV* in companies affiliated with highly concentrated markets. Inadequate competition in concentrated industries permits corporate insiders to operate the firm as per their discretion (Cheng et al., 2013; Melville et al., 2007). Hence, promoters can continue with wasteful spending in the absence of competitive pressures. Since debt reduces the free cash flow and enforces certain performance requirements, controlling shareholders in corporations of heavily concentrated markets tend to keep leverage levels low (Jensen, 1986; Jiraporn et al., 2012).

4.4 Summary and Concluding Observations

This chapter explores the linkage between corporate governance monitoring mechanisms and the long-term financing composition. In this regard, borrowed funds are a relatively cheaper source of financing and render the benefit of tax deductibility of interest payouts (Myers & Majluf, 1984). A reasonable proportion of debt in the capital structure can also discipline managerial actions. It curtails surplus funds available at the disposal of corporate insiders by binding the firm to make periodic interest and principal payments (Jensen, 1986). Further, borrowing companies are also consistently monitored by lenders to ensure the repayment of debt (Chauhan et al., 2018; Jung et al., 196). Therefore, debt can be deployed as a bonding mechanism to minimize managerial discretion. Apart from its governance role, the literature also documents that the dominant shareholders and executives can use more loan financing to prevent the dilution of voting rights or engage in tunnelling of raised funds (Boateng & Huang, 2017; Ramalho et al., 2018). On the other hand, the research studies also recognize that since debt increases the likelihood of bankruptcy, risk-averse corporate insiders may avoid gearing up the firm (Baysinger et al., 1991; Chakraborty, 2018).

As agency conflicts are noted to have diverse implications on debt levels, the role of corporate governance in determining the leverage ratio also remains unclear. Hence, an empirical investigation using non-financial NIFTY 500 entities is carried out to uncover the effect of the characteristics of the board of directors, concentrated ownership, and auditor independence on the debt ratio. The analysis is conducted from FY 2010 to FY 2019 and the key observations from the same are presented in Table 4.11.

Table 4.11 Summary of results from empirical investigation of corporate governance monitoring mechanisms on the leverage ratio

Variables	Analyses	Results
Board size	Main effect	• No significant main effect
	Contingent effect	• No significant contingent effect
Board independence	Main effect	• Positive impact, present in the post-reform period
	Contingent effect	*Firm size* • Positive impact in the case of larger firms *Firm age* • Positive impact in the case of older firms *Other contingency factors* • No significant effect
CEO duality	Main effect	• No significant main effect
	Contingent effect	• No significant contingent effect
Board gender diversity	Main effect	• No significant main effect
	Contingent effect	• No significant contingent effect
Controlling shareholder	Main effect	• Negative impact, present in the pre-reform period
	Contingent effect	*Firm growth opportunities* • Negative impact in the case of low-growth firms *Firm financial condition* • Negative impact in the case of financially distressed firms *Industry concentration* • Negative impact in the case of highly-concentrated industries *Other contingency factors* • No significant effect
Non-controlling large shareholders	Main effect	• No significant main effect
	Contingent effect	*Firm financial condition* • Negative impact in the case of financially distressed firms *Other contingency factors* • No significant effect
Auditor independence	Main effect	• No significant main effect

(continued)

Table 4.11 (continued)

Variables	Analyses	Results
	Contingent effect	*CEO tenure* • Negative impact in the late stages of a CEO's tenure *Industry concentration* • Negative impact in the case of medium-concentrated industries *Other contingency factors* • No significant effect

Notes This table provides a brief overview of all the results gathered from the current empirical investigation

References

Abor, J., & Biekpe, N. (2006). Does board characteristics affect the capital structure decisions of Ghanaian SMEs? *Corporate Ownership and Control, 4*(1), 113–118.

Al-Najjar, B. (2011). Empirical modelling of capital structure: Jordanian evidence. *Journal of Emerging Market Finance, 10*(1), 1–19.

Al-Najjar, B., & Taylor, P. (2008). The relationship between capital structure and ownership structure: New evidence from Jordanian panel data. *Managerial Finance, 34*(12), 919–933.

Akdoğu, E., & MacKay, P. (2008). Investment and competition. *Journal of Financial and Quantitative Analysis, 43*(2), 299–330.

Arellano, M., & Bond, S. (1991). Some tests of specification for panel data: Monte Carlo evidence and an application to employment equations. *The Review of Economic Studies, 58*(2), 277–297.

Arslan-Ayaydin, Ö., Florackis, C., & Ozkan, A. (2014). Financial flexibility, corporate investment and performance: Evidence from financial crises. *Review of Quantitative Finance and Accounting, 42*(2), 211–250.

Ashbaugh, H., LaFond, R., & Mayhew, B. W. (2003). Do non-audit services compromise auditor independence? *Further Evidence. the Accounting Review, 78*(3), 611–639.

Bae, G. S., Choi, S. U., Dhaliwal, D. S., & Lamoreaux, P. T. (2017). Auditors and client investment efficiency. *The Accounting Review, 92*(2), 19–40.

Bajaj, Y., Kashiramka, S., & Singh, S. (2021a). Application of capital structure theories: A systematic review. *Journal of Advances in Management Research, 18*(2), 173–199.

Bajaj, Y., Kashiramka, S., & Singh, S. (2021b). Economic policy uncertainty and leverage dynamics: Evidence from an emerging economy. *International Review of Financial Analysis, 77*, Article 101836.

Bajaj, Y., Kashiramka, S., & Singh, S. (2024). Does economic state matter for leverage adjustments? *An India-China Comparison. the World Economy, 47*(2), 492–518.

Balasubramanian, S. A., Radhakrishna, G. S., Sridevi, P., & Natarajan, T. (2019). Modeling corporate financial distress using financial and non-financial variables: The case of Indian listed companies. *International Journal of Law and Management, 61*(3/4), 457–484.

Baysinger, B. D., Kosnik, R. D., & Turk, T. A. (1991). Effects of board and ownership structure on corporate R&D strategy. *Academy of Management Journal, 34*(1), 205–214.

Belghitar, Y., & Khan, J. (2013). Governance mechanisms, investment opportunity set and SMEs cash holdings. *Small Business Economics, 40*(1), 59–72.

Benkraiem, R., Hamrouni, A., Miloudi, A., & Uyar, A. (2018). Access to finance for French firms: Do boardroom attributes matter? *Economics Bulletin, 38*(3), 1267–1278.

Berger, P. G., Ofek, E., & Yermack, D. L. (1997). Managerial entrenchment and capital structure decisions. *The Journal of Finance, 52*(4), 1411–1438.

Bley, J., Saad, M., & Samet, A. (2019). Auditor choice and bank risk taking. *International Review of Financial Analysis, 61*, 37–52.

Blundell, R., & Bond, S. (2000). GMM estimation with persistent panel data: An application to production functions. *Econometric Reviews, 19*(3), 321–340.

Boateng, A., & Huang, W. (2017). Multiple large shareholders, excess leverage and tunneling: Evidence from an emerging market. *Corporate Governance: An International Review, 25*(1), 58–74.

Boateng, A., Cai, H., Borgia, D., Bi, X. G., & Ngwu, F. N. (2017). The influence of internal corporate governance mechanisms on capital structure decisions of Chinese listed firms. *Review of Accounting and Finance, 16*(4), 444–461.

Boubaker, S., Rouatbi, W., & Saffar, W. (2017). The role of multiple large shareholders in the choice of debt source. *Financial Management, 46*(1), 241–274.

Boubaker, S., Saffar, W., & Sassi, S. (2018). Product market competition and debt choice. *Journal of Corporate Finance, 49*, 204–224.

Bouncken, R. B., Ratzmann, M., & Kraus, S. (2021). Anti-aging: How innovation is shaped by firm age and mutual knowledge creation in an alliance. *Journal of Business Research, 137*, 422–429.

Brander, J. A., & Lewis, T. R. (1986). Oligopoly and financial structure: The limited liability effect. *The American Economic Review, 76*(5), 956–970.

Cai, Y., Kim, Y., Park, J. C., & White, H. D. (2016). Common auditors in M&A transactions. *Journal of Accounting and Economics, 61*(1), 77–99.

Caliskan, D., & Doukas, J. A. (2015). CEO risk preferences and dividend policy decisions. *Journal of Corporate Finance, 35*, 18–42.

Campello, M. (2003). Capital structure and product markets interactions: Evidence from business cycles. *Journal of Financial Economics, 68*(3), 353–378.

Chakraborty, I. (2018). Effects of ownership structure on capital structure of Indian listed firms: Role of business groups vis-à-vis stand-alone firms. *Emerging Markets Finance and Trade, 54*(10), 2315–2332.

Chao, C. C., Hu, M., Munir, Q., & Li, T. (2017). The impact of CEO power on corporate capital structure: New evidence from dynamic panel threshold analysis. *International Review of Economics & Finance, 51*, 107–120.

Chauhan, Y., Pathak, R., & Kumar, S. (2018). Do bank-appointed directors affect corporate cash holding? *International Review of Economics & Finance, 53*, 39–56.

Chen, C. X., Lu, H., & Sougiannis, T. (2012). The agency problem, corporate governance, and the asymmetrical behavior of selling, general, and administrative costs. *Contemporary Accounting Research, 29*(1), 252–282.

Cheng, P., Man, P., & Yi, C. H. (2013). The impact of product market competition on earnings quality. *Accounting & Finance, 53*(1), 137–162.

Chevalier, J. A. (1995). Do LBO supermarkets charge more? An empirical analysis of the effects of LBOs on supermarket pricing. *The Journal of Finance, 50*(4), 1095–1112.

Coad, A., Segarra, A., & Teruel, M. (2016). Innovation and firm growth: Does firm age play a role? *Research Policy, 45*(2), 387–400.

Cole, R. A. (2013). What do we know about the capital structure of privately held US firms? Evidence from the surveys of small business finance. *Financial Management, 42*(4), 777–813.

D'Mello, R., Krishnaswami, S., & Larkin, P. J. (2008). Determinants of corporate cash holdings: Evidence from spin-offs. *Journal of Banking & Finance, 32*(7), 1209–1220.

DeAngelo, H., DeAngelo, L., & Stulz, R. M. (2006). Dividend policy and the earned/contributed capital mix: A test of the life-cycle theory. *Journal of Financial Economics, 81*(2), 227–254.

Dhaliwal, D. S., Gleason, C. A., Heitzman, S., & Melendrez, K. D. (2008). Auditor fees and cost of debt. *Journal of Accounting, Auditing & Finance, 23*(1), 1–22.

Dhaliwal, D. S., Lamoreaux, P. T., Litov, L. P., & Neyland, J. B. (2016). Shared auditors in mergers and acquisitions. *Journal of Accounting and Economics, 61*(1), 49–76.

Dimitropoulos, P. (2014). Capital structure and corporate governance of soccer clubs: European evidence. *Management Research Review, 37*(7), 658–678.

El Diri, M., Lambrinoudakis, C., & Alhadab, M. (2020). Corporate governance and earnings management in concentrated markets. *Journal of Business Research, 108*, 291–306.

Elaoud, A., & Jarboui, A. (2017). Auditor specialization, accounting information quality and investment efficiency. *Research in International Business and Finance, 42*, 616–629.

Erkan, A., Fainshmidt, S., & Judge, W. Q. (2016). Variance decomposition of the country, industry, firm, and firm-year effects on dividend policy. *International Business Review, 25*(6), 1309–1320.

Ezeani, E., Salem, R., Kwabi, F., Boutaine, K., & Komal, B. (2022). Board monitoring and capital structure dynamics: Evidence from bank-based economies. *Review of Quantitative Finance and Accounting, 58*, 473–498.

Fama, E. F. (1980). Agency problems and the theory of the firm. *Journal of Political Economy, 88*, 288–307.

Feng, Z., Ghosh, C., & Sirmans, C. F. (2007). On the capital structure of real estate investment trusts (REITs). *The Journal of Real Estate Finance and Economics, 34*(1), 81–105.

Filatotchev, I., Toms, S., & Wright, M. (2006). The firm's strategic dynamics and corporate governance life-cycle. *International Journal of Managerial Finance, 2*(4), 256–279.

Flavin, T., Goyal, A., & O'Connor, T. (2021). Corporate governance, life cycle, and payout precommitment: An emerging market study. *Journal of Financial Research, 44*(1), 179–209.

Florackis, C. (2008). Agency costs and corporate governance mechanisms: Evidence for UK firms. *International Journal of Managerial Finance, 4*(1), 37–59.

Fosu, S. (2013). Capital structure, product market competition and firm performance: Evidence from South Africa. *The Quarterly Review of Economics and Finance, 53*(2), 140–151.

González, M., Guzmán, A., Pombo, C., & Trujillo, M. A. (2013). Family firms and debt: Risk aversion versus risk of losing control. *Journal of Business Research, 66*(11), 2308–2320.

Goyal, V. K., & Park, C. W. (2002). Board leadership structure and CEO turnover. *Journal of Corporate Finance, 8*(1), 49–66.

Goyal, V. K., Nova, A., & Zanetti, L. (2011). Capital market access and financing of private firms. *International Review of Finance, 11*(2), 155–179.

Guney, Y., Li, L., & Fairchild, R. (2011). The relationship between product market competition and capital structure in Chinese listed firms. *International Review of Financial Analysis, 20*(1), 41–51.

Gupta, G., & Mahakud, J. (2022). Impact of financial distress on investment-cash flow sensitivity: Evidence from emerging economy. *International Journal of Managerial Finance, 19*(4), 713–743.

Habib, A., Costa, M. D., Huang, H. J., Bhuiyan, M. B. U., & Sun, L. (2020). Determinants and consequences of financial distress: Review of the empirical literature. *Accounting & Finance, 60*, 1023–1075.

Hair, J. F. J., Anderson, R. E., Tatham, R. L., & Black, W. C. (1998). *Multivariate data analysis*. Macmillan.

Haque, F., Arun, T. G., & Kirkpatrick, C. (2011). Corporate governance and capital structure in developing countries: A case study of Bangladesh. *Applied Economics, 43*(6), 673–681.

Hart, O. D. (1983). The market mechanism as an incentive scheme. *The Bell Journal of Economics, 14*(2), 366–382.

Haushalter, D., Klasa, S., & Maxwell, W. F. (2007). The influence of product market dynamics on a firm's cash holdings and hedging behavior. *Journal of Financial Economics, 84*(3), 797–825.

Hoelscher, J. L., & Seavey, S. E. (2014). Auditor industry specialization and corporate risk-taking. *Managerial Auditing Journal, 29*(7), 596–620.

Jensen, M. C. (1986). Agency costs of free cash flow, corporate finance, and takeovers. *The American Economic Review, 76*(2), 323–329.

Jiraporn, P., Kim, J. C., Kim, Y. S., & Kitsabunnarat, P. (2012). Capital structure and corporate governance quality: Evidence from the Institutional Shareholder Services (ISS). *International Review of Economics & Finance, 22*(1), 208–221.

John, K., Knyazeva, A., & Knyazeva, D. (2015). Governance and payout precommitment. *Journal of Corporate Finance, 33*, 101–117.

Jung, K., Kim, Y. C., & Stulz, R. (1996). Timing, investment opportunities, managerial discretion, and the security issue decision. *Journal of Financial Economics, 42*(2), 159–185.

Kang, J., & Kim, J. S. (2006). Private benefits of control and firm leverage: An analysis of Korean firms. *Review of Quantitative Finance and Accounting, 27*(4), 439–463.

Kieschnick, R., & Moussawi, R. (2018). Firm age, corporate governance, and capital structure choices. *Journal of Corporate Finance, 48*, 597–614.

Kim, J. B., Lee, J. J., & Park, J. C. (2015). Audit quality and the market value of cash holdings: The case of office-level auditor industry specialization. *Auditing: A Journal of Practice & Theory, 34*(2), 27–57.

King, M. R., & Santor, E. (2008). Family values: Ownership structure, performance and capital structure of Canadian firms. *Journal of Banking & Finance, 32*(11), 2423–2432.

Kyriazopoulos, G. (2017). Corporate governance and capital structure in the periods of financial distress. Evidence from Greece. *Investment Management and Financial Innovations, 14*(1.1), 254–262.

La Porta, R., Lopez-de-Silanes, F., Shleifer, A., & Vishny, R. W. (2000). Agency problems and dividend policies around the world. *The Journal of Finance, 55*(1), 1–33.

La Rocca, M., La Rocca, T., & Cariola, A. (2011). Capital structure decisions during a firm's life cycle. *Small Business Economics, 37*(1), 107–130.

Lee, C. F., & Kuo, N. T. (2014). Effects of ultimate ownership structure and corporate tax on capital structures: Evidence from Taiwan. *International Review of Economics & Finance, 29*, 409–425.

Liu, Q., & Tian, G. (2012). Controlling shareholder, expropriations and firm's leverage decision: Evidence from Chinese Non-tradable share reform. *Journal of Corporate Finance, 18*(4), 782–803.

López-Delgado, P., & Diéguez-Soto, J. (2020). Indebtedness in family-managed firms: The moderating role of female directors on the board. *Review of Managerial Science, 14*(4), 727–762.

Lorsch, J. W., & MacIver, E. (1989). *Pawns or potentates: The reality of America's corporate boards*. Harvard Business School Press.

Matemilola, B. T., Bany-Ariffin, A. N., Azman-Saini, W. N. W., & Nassir, A. M. (2019). Impact of institutional quality on the capital structure of firms in developing countries. *Emerging Markets Review, 39*, 175–209.

Melville, N., Gurbaxani, V., & Kraemer, K. (2007). The productivity impact of information technology across competitive regimes: The role of industry concentration and dynamism. *Decision Support Systems, 43*(1), 229–242.

Mendiratta, A., Singh, S., Yadav, S. S., & Mahajan, A. (2023). The impact of corporate social irresponsibility media coverage on firm performance. *Journal of Advances in Management Research, 21*(1), 1–19.

Mishra, C. S., & McConaughy, D. L. (1999). Founding family control and capital structure: The risk of loss of control and the aversion to debt. *Entrepreneurship Theory and Practice, 23*(4), 53–64.

Mitra, S. (2007). Nonaudit service fees and auditor independence: Empirical evidence from the oil and gas industry. *Journal of Accounting, Auditing & Finance, 22*(1), 85–107.

Myers, S. C., & Majluf, N. S. (1984). Corporate financing and investment decisions when firms have information that investors do not have. *Journal of Financial Economics, 13*(2), 187–221.

Nalebuff, B. J., & Stiglitz, J. E. (1983). Prizes and incentives: Towards a general theory of compensation and competition. *The Bell Journal of Economics, 14*(1), 21–43.

Paligorova, T., & Xu, Z. (2012). Complex ownership and capital structure. *Journal of Corporate Finance, 18*(4), 701–716.

Park, K., Yang, I., & Yang, T. (2017). The peer-firm effect on firm's investment decisions. *The North American Journal of Economics and Finance, 40*, 178–199.

Pathak, M., & Chandani, A. (2023). The nexus between capital structure and firm-specific factors: Evidence from Indian companies. *Journal of Economic and Administrative Sciences, 39*(2), 470–487.

Petruzzelli, A. M., Ardito, L., & Savino, T. (2018). Maturity of knowledge inputs and innovation value: The moderating effect of firm age and size. *Journal of Business Research, 86*, 190–201.

Pindado, J., Rodrigues, L., & De La Torre, C. (2006). How does financial distress affect small firms' financial structure? *Small Business Economics, 26*(4), 377–391.

Prakash, N., Singh, S., & Sharma, S. (2024). Technological diffusion, bank performance, and Solow's paradox: Insights from an emerging economy. *Journal of the Knowledge Economy*. Advanced online publication. https://doi.org/10.1007/s13132-024-02347-4

PwC India (2013). *Companies Act, 2013 Key Highlights and analysis*. Retrieved January 4, 2025 from companies-act-2013-key-highlights-and-analysis.pdf (pwc.in).

Ramalho, J. J., Rita, R. M., & Silva, J. V. (2018). The impact of family ownership on capital structure of firms: Exploring the role of zero-leverage, size, location and the global financial crisis. *International Small Business Journal, 36*(5), 574–604.

Rashid, A. (2015). Revisiting agency theory: Evidence of board independence and agency cost from Bangladesh. *Journal of Business Ethics, 130*(1), 181–198.

Rossi, F., Cebula, R. J., & Barth, J. R. (2018a). Female representation in the boardroom and firm debt: Empirical evidence from Italy. *Journal of Economics and Finance, 42*, 315–338.

Rossi, F., Boylan, R., & Cebula, R. J. (2018b). Financial decisions and ownership structure as control mechanisms of agency problems: Evidence from Italy. *Corporate Governance: The International Journal of Business in Society, 18*, 531–563.

Sarkar, J., & Selarka, E. (2021). Women on board and performance of family firms: Evidence from India. *Emerging Markets Review, 46*, Article 100770.

Sethiya, A., & Thenmozhi, M. (2020). Impact of blockholder promoters on debt financing of Indian firms. *International Journal of Corporate Governance, 11*(1), 1–22.

Schmid, T. (2013). Control considerations, creditor monitoring, and the capital structure of family firms. *Journal of Banking & Finance, 37*(2), 257–272.

Schmidt, K. M. (1997). Managerial incentives and product market competition. *The Review of Economic Studies, 64*(2), 191–213.

Shen, W. (2003). The dynamics of the CEO-board relationship: An evolutionary perspective. *Academy of Management Review, 28*(3), 466–476.

Shleifer, A., & Vishny, R. W. (1997). A survey of corporate governance. *The Journal of Finance, 52*(2), 737–783.

Simsek, Z. (2007). CEO tenure and organizational performance: An intervening model. *Strategic Management Journal, 28*(6), 653–662.

Solomon, J. (2007). *Corporate governance and accountability*. John Wiley & Sons.

Srivastava, B., Singh, S., & Jain, S. (2023). Bank competition, risk-taking and financial stability: Insights from an emerging economy. *Competitiveness Review: An International Business Journal, 33*(5), 959–992.

Srivastava, B., Singh, S., & Jain, S. (2024). A frontier-based parametric framework for exploring the competition–efficiency nexus in commercial banking: Insights from an emerging economy. *Managerial Finance, 50*(5), 854–889.

Stulz, R. (1988). Managerial control of voting rights: Financing policies and the market for corporate control. *Journal of Financial Economics, 20*, 25–54.

Suman, S., & Singh, S. (2022). The role of multiple large shareholders in dividend payouts: Evidence from India. *American Business Review, 25*(1), 120–151.

Tarus, D. K., & Ayabei, E. (2016). Board composition and capital structure: Evidence from Kenya. *Management Research Review, 39*(9), 1056–1079.

Tekin, H., & Polat, A. Y. (2021). Do market differences matter on dividend policy? *Borsa Istanbul Review, 21*(2), 197–208.

Teofilus, T., Ardyan, E., Sutrisno, T., Sabar, S., & Sutanto, V. (2022). Managing Organizational Inertia: Indonesian Family Business Perspective. *Frontiers in Psychology, 13*, Article 839266.

Windmeijer, F. (2005). A finite sample correction for the variance of linear efficient two-step GMM estimators. *Journal of Econometrics, 126*(1), 25–51.

Zona, F. (2016). Agency models in different stages of CEO tenure: The effects of stock options and board independence on R&D investment. *Research Policy, 45*(2), 560–575.

Chapter 5
Corporate Governance and Cost of Capital

The previous chapter highlighted the role of corporate governance monitoring mechanisms in determining a firm's long-term financing composition. The empirical framework is augmented in this chapter to understand the impact of corporate governance on the cost of acquiring funds from the financial markets. The cost of capital represents the required rate of return that the debtholders and equity investors demand based on their perceived exposure to firm risk (Boubaker et al., 2018; De Moura et al., 2020). The presence of severe information asymmetry and agency conflicts can adversely affect this perception leading to inflated risk premiums (Luo et al., 2015; Ma et al., 2017). Correspondingly, costly financing can constrain the ability of companies at high expropriation risk to undertake all profitable projects (Attig et al., 2008; Ben-Nasr et al., 2012). In view of the deleterious effects of information opacity and managerial entrenchment, a robust state of corporate governance can reduce these concerns and, subsequently, the requisite rate demanded by external capital providers. Consistent with the discussion, the empirical analysis is conducted for a sample of non-financial NIFTY 500 corporations from FY 2010 to FY 2019 to detect the ramifications of various governance attributes on the cost of financing. Further, the sample is partitioned into pre-reform and post-reform periods to infer if there is any change in the effect of board directors, large ownership holdings, and auditor independence after the institution of the Companies Act, 2013. The contingent effects of corporate governance are also identified by dividing the firm-year observations based on particular CEO-, firm-, and industry-level contextual factors.

The chapter outline is presented in the following manner. Section 5.1 the research problem. The findings from the main empirical investigation are summarized and expounded in Sect. 5.2. Section 5.3 elaborates on the results from the additional analyses that glean the contingent effects of corporate governance monitoring mechanisms. Finally, Sect. 5.4 culminates the research study by reviewing the important observations from the empirical examination.

S. Singh and S. Suman, *Corporate Governance Monitoring Mechanisms and Corporate Performance and Valuation*, India Studies in Business and Economics,
https://doi.org/10.1007/978-981-96-9736-6_5

5.1 Introduction

The cost of capital affects a firm's value as it denotes the rate at which the investors discount the expected future cash flows (Ben-Nasr et al., 2012). The discount rate is expected to rise when external capital providers perceive that the entrenchment of corporate insiders[1] is high (Lugo, 2019; Luo et al., 2015). Controlling shareholders and management may engage in expropriating corporate resources to derive private benefits through empire-building, payment of extravagant compensations, excessive consumption of perquisites, and tunneling (Lin et al., 2011). An increment in the discount rate is also likely to occur when there is a wider information disparity between the management and outside finance suppliers regarding a corporation's true valuation (Boubaker et al., 2018; Ma et al., 2017). Hence, lenders and equity owners consider the agency costs and information environment while determining the required rate of return on funds to be provided.

Strong corporate governance structures can ameliorate managerial opportunism and mitigate information asymmetry by encouraging quality financial reporting (Aldamen & Duncan, 2012; Zhu, 2014). Consequently, they tend to decrease the monitoring costs incurred by outside investors, which results in lower financing costs (Chen et al., 2009; Luo et al., 2015). The underlying effect of each governance mechanism on the cost of capital is expounded in detail as follows (Table 5.1).

5.2 Main Empirical Analysis and Discussion

Sample description

The cost of capital of NIFTY 500 non-financial corporations is considered from FY 2010 to FY 2019 for the empirical examination. Due to the missing data on the cost of capital estimates and other variables, certain observations are dropped from the sample. Hence, the total number of investigated observations amounts to 2969 for 371 firms.

Regression model and variables

Equation 5.1 is employed to analyze the relationship between corporate governance monitoring mechanisms and the cost of financing. It presents a dynamic panel regression model that takes into account the persistence in the cost of capital (Guyot et al., 2014; Wintoki et al., 2012). Equation 5.1 is stated in the following manner:

---

[1] Corporate insiders include the controlling owner and managers.

Table 5.1 Summary of the predicted relationship between corporate governance monitoring mechanisms and the cost of capital

Variables	Relationship
Board size *(BSIZE)*	If a large board is associated with expanded advisory and monitoring capabilities, investors are expected to charge a lower risk premium, leading to a decreased cost of financing (Upadhyay & Sriram, 2011). Alternatively, if they believe that oversized boards are ineffective as they are prone to structural issues innate to large groups, they would demand a higher rate of return on the funds supplied (Wahab et al., 2020) **H1:** Board size has a significant association with the cost of capital
Board independence *(BIND)*	An investor is predicted to supply funds at a lower rate of return as independent directors are linked to lower agency concerns since they possess the ability to bring objective and unbiased scrutiny on managerial actions (Anderson et al., 2004; Thu & Khanh, 2021) **H2:** Board independence has a negative association with the cost of capital
CEO duality *(CEODUAL)*	Dual CEOs can be viewed as entrenched by the debtholders and equity investors as these CEOs simultaneously head the managerial operations and board of directors. Therefore, external capital providers are likely to charge inflated risk premiums in the presence of CEO duality (Chen et al., 2022; Moss, 2016) **H3:** CEO duality has a positive association with the cost of capital
Board gender diversity *(BGD)*	Women directors can also reduce the issue of groupthink and enrich board decision-making by contributing fresh and distinctive viewpoints on various corporate matters (Upadhyay, 2014). The financing providers are expected to weigh these benefits of gender-diverse boards and thence charge a lower cost of capital (Aksoy & Yilmaz, 2023; Tanaka, 2014) **H4:** Board gender diversity has a negative association with the cost of capital
Controlling shareholder *(PROMOTER)*	The substantial controlling rights of a dominant owner can heighten the expropriation concerns of lenders and minority shareholders, thereby leading to a higher cost of capital (Gao et al., 2020; Lin et al., 2018). On the other hand, the significant shareholding of the promoters[2] may be considered as their commitment that they will not expropriate the interests of debtholders and small equity owners (Selarka, 2005) **H5:** Controlling shareholder has a significant association with the cost of capital
Non-controlling large shareholders *(NPD)*	The presence of non-controlling large owners can lower the expropriation risk for minority shareholders and debtholders as these blockholders can deploy their significant voting rights to monitor and question managerial actions to ensure that only value-maximizing decisions are implemented (Attig et al., 2008) **H6:** Non-controlling large shareholders have a negative association with the cost of capital

(continued)

[2] In the milieu of Indian corporations, promoters are presumed to be controlling shareholders. (Selarka, 2005).

Table 5.1 (continued)

Variables	Relationship
Auditor independence *(NAF)*	Large payments for non-audit services may raise questions about the auditor's objectivity, as they might face a conflict of interest when reporting material errors in the financial statements they prepared, fearing the potential loss of substantial income (DeFond et al., 2002). In light of increased information risk, the required rate of return on funds supplied would be relatively higher (Alsadoun et al., 2018; Friedrich et al., 2024) **H7:** A higher proportion of non-audit fees has a significant association with the cost of capital

Notes This table describes the hypotheses for examining the relationship between corporate governance and cost of capital

$$\begin{aligned} COC_{it} = {} & \beta_0 + \beta_1 COC_{t-1} + \beta_2 BSIZE_{it} + \beta_3 BIND_{it} \\ & + \beta_4 CEODUAL_{it} + \beta_5 BGD_{it} + \beta_6 PROMOTER_{it} \\ & + \beta_7 NPD_{it} + \beta_8 NAF_{it} + \sum_{j=9}^{N} \beta_j CONTROLS_{it} \\ & + Industry\ effects_i + Year\ effects_t + \varepsilon_{it} \end{aligned} \tag{5.1}$$

where, *COC* is the dependent variable, which is proxied by the weighted average cost of capital estimates obtained from Bloomberg®. The explanatory variables include characteristics of the board of directors as indicated by its size (*BSIZE*), diversity (*BGD*), and independence as affected by the percentage of outside directors (*BIND*) and the practice of CEO duality (*CEODUAL*). The influence of large owners is also considered by distinguishing between the controlling owner (*PROMOTER*) and non-controlling blockholders (*NPD*). Lastly, the effect of higher non-audit fee payments (*NAF*) on the required rate of return on the invested funds is also examined. The measurement of specified corporate governance variables is stated in Chapter 1.

CONTROLS comprise firm-level financial variables that are likely to influence the cost of financing. Larger and aged firms are likely to be liable to a lower information risk premium as their sizeable operations assist in building a reputation in capital markets (Alsadoun et al., 2018; Dahiya & Singh, 2021). Hence, the variable proxying firm size *(FSIZE)* and firm age *(FAGE)* is incorporated into the empirical model. Furthermore, the effect of growth opportunities *(GROWTH)* on the cost of financing is also considered. Since growth firms hold the potential to generate substantial increases in revenues and net income over a longer period, their suppliers of capital are expected to demand a lower rate of return (Lin et al., 2011; Rahaman & Al Zaman, 2013).

The influence of profitability *(PROFIT)* is also addressed as profitable business ventures are perceived to carry a lower bankruptcy risk by the external capital providers, due to which they may be willing to supply funds at a lower rate (Aksoy & Yilmaz, 2023). On the other hand, companies with volatile earnings can be considered risky since they may be constrained in their ability to honor their debt obligations and undertake required investments (Guizani, 2017). As volatile earnings can magnify business risk premium *(BRISK)*, their effect is taken into account in the empirical examination. In addition, severe variability in equity returns can also intensify the risk perception and concerns about a firm's future performance (Anderson et al., 2004; Cook & Luo, 2023). Therefore, the impact of stock return volatility *(RETVOL)* on the cost of capital is also appraised.

The effect of the leverage ratio *(LEV)* on the cost of financing is also investigated. A higher degree of financial leverage can increase the weighted average cost of capital as it raises the risk of default and encumbers a corporation with substantial repayment obligations (Aksoy & Yilmaz, 2023; Zhu, 2014). Furthermore, the role of asset tangibility *(TANG)* in influencing the cost of financing is also analyzed. An increase in tangible assets enhances the amount of fixed costs incurred by the corporation (Sohn et al., 2013). In the circumstances of relatively low and uncertain revenues, the existence of a larger amount of fixed costs can cause a sharp markdown in a firm's profits (Guthrie, 2011; Huffman, 1983). As the uncertainty concerning profits increases when there are additions to the stock of tangible assets, outside financing suppliers may demand a higher rate of return to compensate for the increased risk (Tuzel, 2010). The implication of financial distress *(ZSCORE)* is also addressed as external capital providers are expected to allocate funds at a reasonable cost to economically sound corporations due to decreased default risk (Graham et al., 2008). Agency costs *(AGENCYC)* are also taken into consideration since risk premiums are likely to be high when expenditures under the management's discretionary control are exorbitant (Belkhir et al., 2021).

The empirical model also includes industry effects to address the impact of industry characteristics on the cost of capital (Ben-Nasr et al., 2012). Further, year effects are also considered in the model to deal with variations in the cost of financing arising from changes in macroeconomic conditions (De Moura et al., 2020). Table 5.2 summarizes all the variables utilized in the empirical study.

Research methodology

As a dynamic panel data model is employed, the problems of autocorrelation and endogeneity occur (Guyot et al., 2014; Shailer & Wang, 2015). Endogeneity issues can also arise because of corporate governance and other financial control variables. In this regard, there could be causation concerns as there can be a likelihood that independent directors may avoid companies with a higher cost of capital as they may presume it to be risky. In addition, an unobserved effect, such as company culture, may simultaneously affect the governance mechanisms and the cost of capital. In such a scenario, endogeneity also arises as the explanatory variables are correlated to the error term. Lastly, despite following the extant literature, there can be measurement errors in the variables, which will also produce endogeneity (Arellano & Bond, 1991).

Table 5.2 Summary of control variables used in examining the impact of corporate governance monitoring mechanisms on the cost of capital

Variables	Measurement	Data Source
Firm size *(FSIZE)*	Natural logarithm of total assets (Aksoy & Yilmaz, 2023; Ben-Nasr et al., 2012)	Datastream®
Firm age (*FAGE*)	Number of years since the firm's inception (Upadhyay, 2014)	Datastream®
Growth opportunities *(GROWTH)*	Tobin's Q (Lin et al., 2018; Rahaman & Al Zaman, 2013)	Bloomberg®
Profitability *(PROFIT)*	Ratio of net income to total assets (Aksoy & Yilmaz, 2023; Zhu, 2014)	Datastream®
Business risk *(BRISK)*	Standard deviation of the profitability (*PROFIT*) over the last five years (Boubakri & Ghouma, 2010; Chan & Hsu, 2013)	Datastream®
Stock return volatility (*RETVOL*)	Standard deviation of monthly stock returns over the previous sixty months (Anderson et al., 2004; Zhu, 2014)	Datastream®
Leverage ratio *(LEV)*	Total debt to total assets ratio (Ma et al., 2017; Upadhyay & Sriram, 2014)	Datastream®
Asset tangibility *(TANG)*	Net plant, property, and equipment divided by total assets (Upadhyay, 2014)	Datastream®
Financial distress *(ZSCORE)*	Altman-Z score (Lin et al., 2018)	Datastream®
Agency costs *(AGENCYC)*	Ratio of a firm's SGA expenses to its annual sales (Belkhir et al., 2021; Shailer & Wang, 2015)	Datastream®

Notes This table provides the definitions of the control variables utilized in the empirical investigation to uncover the ramifications of corporate governance mechanisms on the cost of capital

The two-step system GMM estimation of Eq. 5.1 is appropriate to address the highlighted endogeneity and autocorrelation concerns (Bajaj et al., 2020; Suman & Singh, 2022). Subsequent to empirical investigation, diagnostic tests of Hansen J and AR (2) are also conducted to evaluate the validity of system GMM for the stated dynamic panel regression model. Before undertaking the analysis, winsorization of all the financial variables is done at 1% to mitigate the impact of outliers.

Descriptive statistics

Table 5.3 displays the summary statistics of all the variables that are under the scope of the present empirical examination. It demonstrates that an average firm in the sample pays about a weighted average cost (*COC*) of 9.15% on the total capital employed. The inferences concerning corporate governance attributes are comparable to those reported in Chapter 2.

Multivariate regression analysis

Table 5.4 summarizes the results from the two-step system GMM estimation of Eq. 5.1, which examines the relationship between corporate governance monitoring mechanisms and the weighted average cost of capital. They provide support for the deployment of the dynamic panel regression model as the coefficients on lagged values of the cost of capital are positive and statistically significant. Further, the diagnostic tests across all the specifications also corroborate the suitability of the system GMM estimator. The insignificant Hansen J test suggests that the instruments employed by the estimator exhibit exogeneity. In addition, the AR (2) test is also not

Table 5.3 Summary statistics of the cost of capital, corporate governance monitoring mechanisms, and other firm-level variables

Variables	Mean	Standard deviation	Minimum	Maximum
COC	0.0915	0.0199	0.0417	0.1596
BSIZE	9.6777	2.5899	3	22
BIND	51.8575	10.9905	0	100
CEODUAL	0.3011	0.4588	0	1
BGD	9.7032	8.1077	0	42.857
PROMOTER	55.3291	16.7741	8.2	90
NPD	0.1192	0.3241	0	1
NAF	0.3696	0.4451	0	2.6496
FSIZE	20.5379	1.4581	16.9363	24.306
FAGE	39.6251	23.5865	3	155
GROWTH	2.6545	2.3706	0.6725	13.779
PROFIT	0.0804	0.069	−0.1345	0.2623
BRISK	0.0324	0.0337	0.0027	0.2893
RETVOL	0.1464	0.0457	0.0673	0.2798
LEV	0.2269	0.1872	0	0.7268
TANG	0.3261	0.2024	0.0059	0.8044
ZSCORE	5.8524	6.0527	0.1494	35.7928
AGENCYC	0.2435	0.1769	0.0084	0.9615

Notes This table provides an overview of the descriptive statistics of variables utilized in the empirical examination

significant, thereby alluding to the absence of second-order autocorrelation. Lastly, the Wald F statistic validates the joint significance of variables.

Column 1 demonstrates that a higher percentage of ownership by the controlling shareholder (*PROMOTER*) reduces the weighted average cost of capital (*COC*). This finding affirms H5 and indicates that external capital providers consider concentrated holdings a reasonable incentive for the promoters to undertake only value-maximizing actions. A promoter has a relatively large and undiversified wealth invested in the firm (Boubakri & Ghouma, 2010; Caixe et al., 2019). The value of their economic wealth depends upon the profitability and valuation of the corporation (Anderson & Reeb, 2003). Correspondingly, they are more likely to bear the adverse consequences of their expropriation activities as reflected by the drastic decline in the worth of their stakeholding (Chau & Gray, 2010). Hence, substantial equity ownership can be perceived as a significant deterrent for the dominant shareholders to engage in self-serving activities (Selarka, 2005). In view of the restraining behavior of large blockholdings, finance suppliers can be willing to provide capital at a lower rate when controlling ownership is significantly high. Lastly, it is also noted that the monitoring mechanisms of the board of directors, non-controlling large shareholders, and the degree of auditor independence do not affect the cost of capital in the overall sample.

In respect of the control variables, it is observed that highly levered firms (*LEV*) are associated with a lower cost of capital (*COC*). Loan financing provides tax deductions on interest payments, which decreases its effective cost to the corporation (Dhaliwal et al., 2006; Modigliani & Miller, 1963). Furthermore, existing and long-standing lenders can issue fresh borrowings at a reduced rate as they are now more informed about the entity's financial position and can better supervise its management (Bonini et al., 2016; Hernández-Cánovas & Martínez-Solano, 2010). Hence, the employment of more debt in the capital structure can bring down the weighted average cost of capital. In addition, it also noted that an increase in tangible assets (*TANG*) raises *COC*. When a company owns a higher proportion of tangible assets, it incurs a large amount of fixed costs (Sohn et al., 2013). In the event of declining and unpredictable revenues, heavy expenditure on fixed costs can deteriorate a corporation's profit margin and even cause huge losses (Guthrie, 2011; Huffman, 1983). Since uncertainty regarding earnings magnifies when a firm owns most of its assets in physical form, the outside capital providers can charge a higher risk premium on the invested funds (Tuzel, 2010).

The empirical study is also supplemented to understand how the perceived effectiveness of various monitoring mechanisms differs after the launch of the improved governance regime through the enactment of the Companies Act, 2013. In order to investigate the same, the firm-year observations are partitioned into pre-reform and post-reform periods. The pre-reform period for the investigated sample commences at the beginning of FY 2010 and extends until the end of FY 2014.[3] Years subsequent

[3] As elaborated in Chapter 2, the Companies Act, 2013 was instituted on August 30, 2013. Considering that the new Act was enacted in the middle of FY 2014, the study follows Sarkar and Selarka (2021) and takes the pre-reform period until the end of FY 2014.

Table 5.4 Corporate governance monitoring mechanisms and the cost of capital: Main regression analysis

Dependent variable: *COC*	Overall sample (2010–2019)	Pre-reform period (2010–2014)	Post-reform period (2015–2019)
Variables	(1)	(2)	(3)
L.COC	0.633***	0.254**	0.835**
	(0.128)	(0.105)	(0.336)
BSIZE	−0.000144	−0.000445	0.000652
	(0.000751)	(0.000801)	(0.00200)
BIND	−0.000190	8.63e−05	−0.000821**
	(0.000134)	(0.000110)	(0.000411)
CEODUAL	−0.000101	0.00242	−0.00311
	(0.00408)	(0.00406)	(0.00530)
BGD	0.000102	0.000105	−0.00110
	(0.000135)	(0.000142)	(0.000783)
PROMOTER	−0.000319**	−0.000115	−0.000213**
	(0.000151)	(0.000170)	(0.0000845)
NPD	−0.00508	−0.00414	−0.000318
	(0.00340)	(0.00252)	(0.00850)
NAF	−0.00207	−0.00101	0.00206
	(0.00584)	(0.00157)	(0.0102)
FSIZE	−0.00157	−0.00172	0.00166
	(0.00211)	(0.00205)	(0.00216)
FAGE	−1.71e−05	−1.64e−05	−5.60e−05
	(3.30e−05)	(6.22e−05)	(8.59e−05)
GROWTH	−0.000228	−0.00340*	0.00463
	(0.00111)	(0.00195)	(0.00366)
PROFIT	−0.0156	−0.0212	−0.0656
	(0.0323)	(0.0453)	(0.111)
BRISK	0.0407	0.0188	0.223*
	(0.0374)	(0.0447)	(0.125)
RETVOL	0.0186	0.0919***	0.0416
	(0.0282)	(0.0339)	(0.0987)
LEV	−0.0372*	−0.0752***	−0.0568
	(0.0216)	(0.0231)	(0.0641)
TANG	0.0218*	0.0291	0.0104
	(0.0112)	(0.0243)	(0.0142)
ZSCORE	7.60e−05	0.00109	−0.00183
	(0.000445)	(0.000832)	(0.00123)

(continued)

Table 5.4 (continued)

Dependent variable: *COC*	Overall sample (2010–2019)	Pre-reform period (2010–2014)	Post-reform period (2015–2019)
Variables	(1)	(2)	(3)
AGENCYC	0.00572	0.0412*	0.0337
	(0.00908)	(0.0250)	(0.0645)
Constant	0.0832*	0.0901	0.0270
	(0.0472)	(0.0562)	(0.0575)
Industry & Year FE	Yes	Yes	Yes
Wald F (p−value)	2079.58 (0.000)	887.35 (0.000)	1485.19 (0.000)
AR (2) (p−value)	−1.578 (0.115)	0.553 (0.580)	−1.504 (0.133)
Hansen J (p-value)	37.96 (0.425)	54.43 (0.114)	16.14 (0.443)

Notes This table reports the findings of the two-step system GMM estimation of Eq. 5.1. Columns 1 show the results when the empirical investigation is undertaken for the overall sample from FY 2010-FY 2019. Column 2 depicts findings for the period before the launch of the Companies Act, 2013 (Pre-reform period). Column 3 represents the results for years when the Companies Act, 2013 is in effect (Post-reform period). Windmeijer's corrected-robust standard errors are indicated in parentheses. ***, **, and * denote significance at 1, 5, and 10% levels, respectively

to FY 2014 represent the post-reform period when the new corporate governance regulations are in place. The system GMM estimation of Eq. 5.1 is carried out separately for the pre-reform and post-reform periods and the related results are reported in Columns 2 and 3, respectively.

Column 3 demonstrates that the negative impact of controlling ownership (*PROMOTER*) on the cost of financing (*COC*) is prominent in the post-reform period. The increased scrutiny and stricter punitive actions under the new robust corporate governance framework make the costs of engaging in self-serving activities more consequential for the dominant shareholders (Busru & Singh, 2016; Das & Dey, 2016). As these costs magnify with the increase in promoters' stakeholdings, they are dissuaded from expropriating corporate resources (Chau & Gray, 2010; Selarka, 2005). Hence, in the strengthened governance environment, external capital providers can supply funds at a lower rate of return to firms with a higher controlling stake.

Interestingly, it is also noted from Column 3 that a highly independent board (*BIND*) decreases the cost of capital (*COC*) in the post-reform period. Debtholders and minority shareholders expect independent directors to enhance a corporation's governance since these board members bring an impartial and objective judgment on corporate insiders' actions (Anderson et al., 2004; Thu & Khanh, 2021). With the independence criteria becoming stringent under the new corporate governance provisions (Grant Thornton, 2013), non-affiliated outside directors can be presumed to supervise the management more strictly. Since agency concerns are reduced with greater board independence, outside investors can charge a lower cost of capital from the corporation. Altogether, this finding supports H2.

5.3 Additional Analyses

5.3.1 *Role of CEO Tenure*

The empirical investigation is also augmented to glean the contingent effects of corporate governance monitoring mechanisms on the cost of accessing outside financing. The first contingent variable that is considered is the tenure that the present CEO has completed in the current position.

A CEO yields significant clout over the board of directors and the top management team in the later stages of their tenure (Iatridis, 2012; Smith et al., 2017). Owing to their prior successes, the long-tenured CEOs tend to enjoy massive confidence from the board members in their abilities (Lorsch & MacIver, 1989; Shen, 2003). As a consequence, the sitting directors may blindly approve of their proposed plans without adequate questioning and checks (Walters et al., 2007). The lax supervision may also be an outcome of their close liaisons with the directors built over the course of their lengthy tenure (Alayo et al., 2023; Smith et al., 2017). Thus, long-tenured CEOs are in a position to undertake unilateral decisions, which they can use to further their personal interests at the expense of corporate goals (Sheikh, 2019). Furthermore, they also tend to propagate previously profitable practices that may no longer be optimal in contemporary circumstances (Hambrick & Fukutomi, 1991; Walters et al., 2007). In contrast, CEOs in the initial years of their tenure are under pressure to attain superior performance to retain their jobs (Shen, 2003; Walters et al., 2007). These short-tenured CEOs are also subjected to the board's mandate and continuous scrutiny, which constrain their discretion (Hambrick & Fukutomi, 1991). Hence, CEO entrenchment is expected to be lower when they have been recently appointed.

In essence, the scope for managerial opportunism is a function of the years that the incumbent CEOs have completed in their present position. Therefore, it can be anticipated that the influence of corporate governance monitoring mechanisms on the cost of capital is contingent upon the length of a CEO's tenure. The proposed prediction is tested by segregating the sample based on the quartile values of a CEO's term. The corresponding results from the empirical estimation of Eq. 5.1 for the subgroups of short-tenured, medium-tenured, and long-tenured CEOs are depicted in Table 5.5.

Table 5.5 demonstrates that corporate governance devices do not have a significant effect on the cost of financing (*COC*) in the case of short-tenured and medium-tenured CEOs. It is also noted from Column 3 that the observed negative effect of promoter ownership (*PROMOTER*) on the weighted average cost of capital (*COC*) is more prominent when the corporations have long-tenured CEOs at the helm (Iatridis, 2012; Smith et al., 2017). The power of CEOs over corporate decisions is magnified as they advance in their tenure. In addition, as the length of their tenure increases, CEOs develop close relationships with the members of the promoter group and associate more with its values and beliefs (Alayo et al., 2023; Huybrechts et al., 2012). Moreover, in the Indian corporate milieu, CEOs with considerably longer tenures are

Table 5.5 Corporate governance monitoring mechanisms and the cost of capital: Role of CEO tenure

Dependent variable: *COC*	Short-tenured CEOs	Medium-tenured CEOs	Long-tenured CEOs
Variables	(1)	(2)	(3)
L.COC	0.483***	0.729**	0.790***
	(0.166)	(0.337)	(0.230)
BSIZE	−0.000796	−0.000428	−1.06e−06
	(0.000990)	(0.00318)	(0.000906)
BIND	6.94e−06	−0.000384	−1.81e−05
	(0.000122)	(0.000268)	(0.000192)
CEODUAL	−0.000118	−0.00221	9.83e−05
	(0.00622)	(0.0148)	(0.00372)
BGD	0.000131	0.000130	−4.89e−05
	(0.000234)	(0.000584)	(0.000434)
PROMOTER	3.53e−05	−0.000195	−0.000111**
	(9.95e−05)	(0.000271)	(0.0000525)
NPD	−0.00232	−0.000377	−0.00660
	(0.00247)	(0.0103)	(0.00683)
NAF	−0.00182	0.00123	−0.00402
	(0.00363)	(0.00156)	(0.00735)
FSIZE	0.00150	2.95e−05	−0.000197
	(0.00114)	(0.00200)	(0.00130)
FAGE	−3.24e−06	−1.32e−05	−1.66e−05
	(3.00e−05)	(5.58e−05)	(3.21e−05)
GROWTH	−0.00122	−0.00440	−0.000317
	(0.00106)	(0.00303)	(0.000485)
PROFIT	−0.0325	−0.0267	−0.00840
	(0.0354)	(0.0633)	(0.0215)
BRISK	0.00765	0.0640	0.00563
	(0.0318)	(0.132)	(0.0354)
RETVOL	0.139**	0.00982	0.0347
	(0.0649)	(0.144)	(0.0471)
LEV	−0.0742***	−0.0292	−0.0210
	(0.0236)	(0.0507)	(0.0196)
TANG	0.0100	0.00432	0.00615
	(0.0103)	(0.0287)	(0.00473)
ZSCORE	0.000314	0.00140	0.000160
	(0.000467)	(0.00133)	(0.000160)

(continued)

Table 5.5 (continued)

Dependent variable: *COC*	Short-tenured CEOs	Medium-tenured CEOs	Long-tenured CEOs
Variables	(1)	(2)	(3)
AGENCYC	−0.00594	−0.00516	0.0101
	(0.0157)	(0.0273)	(0.0178)
Constant	0.00265	0.0511	0.0232
	(0.0238)	(0.0856)	(0.0333)
Industry & Year FE	Yes	Yes	Yes
Wald F (p-value)	2061 (0.000)	1703 (0.000)	3130 (0.000)
AR (2) (p-value)	−1.621 (0.105)	−1.098 (0.272)	−1.579 (0.114)
Hansen J (p-value)	29.39 (0.497)	9.934 (0.446)	27.41 (0.286)

Notes This table depicts the findings from the empirical estimation of Eq. 5.1 when the sample is divided using the quartile values of CEO tenure. Short-tenured CEOs include years of CEO tenure in the bottom quartile (CEO tenure < 2.579167 years). Years of CEO tenure in the top quartile are termed as long-tenured CEOs (CEO tenure > 19.63194 years). Sample values in the middle two quartiles are grouped together as medium-tenured CEOs (CEO tenure from 2.579167 to 19.63194 years). Windmeijer's corrected-robust standard errors are reported in parentheses. ***, **, and * denote significance at 1, 5, and 10% levels, respectively

usually related to the promoter group (Mampatta, 2017). Consequently, long-tenured CEOs can use their significant influence to espouse policies that protect and further the promoter's interests. In such a scenario, concerns regarding expropriation by the controlling owners and management tend to be salient among outside investors. The large blockholdings of the dominant shareholders can then allay these fears of outside finance suppliers. Promoters can suffer a drastic deterioration in their economic wealth ex-post if they abuse corporate resources to extract private benefits (Chau & Gray, 2010; Ma et al., 2017). Therefore, their undiversified shareholdings can prevent them from partaking in self-serving activities (Selarka, 2005). Hence, in the context of increasing entrenchment of CEOs, high controlling ownership can instill confidence in debtholders and small shareholders, due to which they may require a lower rate on the invested funds.

5.3.2 *Role of Firm Size*

Smaller corporations are more informationally opaque in comparison to large enterprises (Graham et al., 2008; Lin et al., 2011). They are less reputed since they have a relatively lower analyst following and media coverage (Gupta et al., 2018; Lin et al., 2011). Due to a higher degree of information asymmetry, the concerns for agency issues also increase. However, effective governance mechanisms can minimize the incidence of agency conflicts and allay investors' fears, thereby leading to a reduced cost of capital.

In essence, it is anticipated that the impact of corporate governance monitoring mechanisms on the cost of financing will be stronger in the case of small companies. The firm-year observations are divided using the quartiles of firm size to examine the specified prediction (Prakash et al., 2024). The findings from the empirical estimation of Eq. 5.1 undertaken for small-sized, medium-sized, and large-sized entities are provided in Table 5.6.

Column 1 evinces the underlined prediction as it is inferred that the negative effect of controlling ownership (*PROMOTER*) on the weighted average cost of capital (*COC*) is present only in small-sized firms. In the opaque information environment of smaller companies, the promoters' substantial shareholdings can signal their commitment that they will not expropriate outside investors (Selarka, 2005). The cost of exploiting corporate resources rises with the increase in their stakeholdings (Chau & Gray, 2010; Selarka, 2005). Correspondingly, an investor can consider large equity ownership by dominant shareholders to deter them from misusing funds for their benefit. Therefore, when small corporations have high promoter holdings, debtholders and minority shareholders can provide funds at a lower rate. In addition, Columns 2 and 3 indicate that corporate governance mechanisms do not significantly influence the cost of accessing funds for medium-sized and large-sized companies.

5.3.3 Role of Firm Age

Younger firms usually have a weaker reputation and have a relatively shorter credit and operating history (Gupta et al., 2018; Shailer & Wang, 2015). In addition, these companies typically have higher growth prospects (Kuo, 2017). However, there is uncertainty regarding these investment opportunities since external financing providers cannot precisely determine their true worth. As a result, the problem of information asymmetry is more pronounced in the case of young business enterprises. On the one hand, older organizations enjoy greater repute in the capital markets as they have a well-established credit and performance record (Bonini et al., 2016; Selarka, 2005). While information opacity is lowered in the case of mature corporations, they are likely to be disposed to the tendencies of organizational inertia (Teofilus et al., 2022). Bound by their previously accumulated knowledge, the management of such entities generally adheres to their long-standing capital allocation practices (Petruzzelli et al., 2018; Shailer & Wang, 2015). Consequently, older companies can fail to innovate and undertake strategic changes in response to changes in their business environment (Coad et al., 2016).

Table 5.6 Corporate governance monitoring mechanisms and the cost of capital: Role of firm size

Dependent variable: *COC*	Small-sized firms	Medium-sized firms	Large-sized firms
Variables	(1)	(2)	(3)
L.COC	0.320*	0.641***	0.404***
	(0.168)	(0.165)	(0.126)
BSIZE	−0.00104	−0.000312	−0.000683
	(0.00189)	(0.00115)	(0.000606)
BIND	−9.40e−05	−0.000112	6.17e−05
	(0.000191)	(0.000269)	(8.69e−05)
CEODUAL	0.00390	−0.00156	0.00426
	(0.00395)	(0.00519)	(0.00358)
BGD	0.000122	−0.000211	9.63e−05
	(0.000159)	(0.000236)	(0.000141)
PROMOTER	−0.000162*	−5.25e−05	−6.52e−05
	(0.000086)	(5.44e−05)	(6.35e−05)
NPD	−0.00274	−0.00197	−0.00266
	(0.00348)	(0.00288)	(0.00275)
NAF	−0.000529	−0.00128	−0.00488
	(0.00438)	(0.00435)	(0.00327)
FSIZE	0.000381	0.000530	−0.000316
	(0.00362)	(0.00230)	(0.00197)
FAGE	−4.29e−05	−7.43e−07	−1.51e−06
	(5.73e−05)	(2.30e−05)	(5.18e−05)
GROWTH	−0.000613	−0.000881	0.000602
	(0.00175)	(0.00197)	(0.00185)
PROFIT	−0.0124	−0.00132	−0.0879***
	(0.0497)	(0.0377)	(0.0313)
BRISK	−0.0461	0.0691	0.0601
	(0.0651)	(0.0856)	(0.0545)
RETVOL	0.0325	0.0373	0.0100
	(0.0339)	(0.0368)	(0.0498)
LEV	−0.0525*	−0.0259	−0.0575***
	(0.0300)	(0.0165)	(0.0128)
TANG	0.00955	0.0106	0.00839
	(0.0175)	(0.0120)	(0.0111)
ZSCORE	0.000558	0.000430	0.000679
	(0.000630)	(0.000820)	(0.000483)
AGENCYC	−0.0157	0.00316	−0.00794
	(0.0223)	(0.0149)	(0.0211)

(continued)

Table 5.6 (continued)

Dependent variable: *COC*	Small-sized firms	Medium-sized firms	Large-sized firms
Variables	(1)	(2)	(3)
Constant	0.0920	0.0144	0.0688*
	(0.0745)	(0.0606)	(0.0396)
Industry & Year FE	Yes	Yes	Yes
Wald F (p−value)	3165 (0.000)	2336 (0.000)	1833 (0.000)
AR (2) (p−value)	−1.004 (0.316)	−1.604 (0.109)	−1.404 (0.160)
Hansen J (p-value)	25.49 (0.435)	31.19 (0.457)	75.69 (0.330)

Notes This table summarizes the results from the empirical estimation of Eq. 5.1 for corporations with varying ranges of firm size. The values of firm size in the lower quartile are classified as small-sized firms (firm size < 19.50064). Observations in the upper quartile comprise large-sized firms (firm size > 21.35681). The remaining firm-year observations in the middle two quartiles are assigned as medium-sized firms (firm size from 19.50064 to 21.35681). Parentheses demonstrate. Windmeijer's corrected-robust standard errors. ***, **, and * show significance at 1, 5, and 10% levels, respectively

In line with the preceding discussion, it can be gathered that the degree of information asymmetry and the nature of agency conflicts differ according to a corporation's lifecycle. Hence, the impact of corporate governance monitoring mechanisms on the weighted average cost of capital is expected to depend on a firm's age. In order to investigate the same, the sample is partitioned based on the quartile values of firm age in years. The related results from the empirical estimation of Eq. 5.1 for younger, middle-aged, and older companies are presented in Table 5.7.

Column 1 shows that a decrease in auditor independence (*NAF*), as indicated by an increasing proportion of non-audit fees, raises the cost of financing (*COC*) in younger firms. The provision of non-audit services can further exacerbate information asymmetry in early-stage corporations. As the auditor renders non-auditor services, its financial bond with the client firm strengthens (Meuwissen & Quick, 2019; Mitra, 2007). Hence, they can be doubted in their capabilities to point out and report any misstatements in the financials truthfully as they will lose a significant amount of earnings if they do so (DeFond et al., 2002). The perceived impairment of the auditor's objectivity creates questions about the credibility of the financial statements leading to magnified information risk in younger enterprises (Karjalainen, 2011). Resultantly, lenders and minority shareholders charge a higher cost of capital from such companies when they pay large non-audit fees to the contracted auditors. This finding aligns with the assertions of H7.

Column 2 of Table 5.7 reports that the effect of corporate governance attributes on *COC* is not prominent in the case of middle-aged firms. It is also observed from Column 3 that CEO duality (*CEODUAL*) decreases *COC* in older firms. A joint CEO-Chairman post provides an individual with a unified and strong authority which

Table 5.7 Corporate governance monitoring mechanisms and the cost of capital: Role of firm age

Dependent variable: *COC*	Younger firms	Middle-aged firms	Older firms
Variables	(1)	(2)	(3)
L.COC	0.405*	0.795***	0.537***
	(0.209)	(0.199)	(0.144)
BSIZE	−0.000520	−0.00121	−0.000254
	(0.00108)	(0.00126)	(0.000566)
BIND	−7.59e−06	−5.86e−05	5.86e−05
	(0.000316)	(0.000348)	(8.23e−05)
CEODUAL	3.45e−05	0.00290	−0.00383*
	(0.00328)	(0.00758)	(0.00199)
BGD	0.000114	−1.79e−06	−3.87e−05
	(0.000245)	(0.000206)	(8.29e−05)
PROMOTER	−3.03e−05	−4.06e−06	−2.55e−05
	(0.000334)	(0.000151)	(6.08e−05)
NPD	−0.00216	−0.00793	0.00267
	(0.00612)	(0.00522)	(0.00315)
NAF	0.0114*	−0.00505	−0.00219
	(0.00638)	(0.00876)	(0.00279)
FSIZE	−0.000982	−0.000314	−0.00137
	(0.00273)	(0.00148)	(0.000834)
FAGE	−0.000241	6.64e−05	1.45e−05
	(0.000185)	(0.000104)	(5.26e−05)
GROWTH	−0.000659	−0.00125	−0.000329
	(0.00224)	(0.00270)	(0.000984)
PROFIT	−0.0330	−0.0505	−0.0235
	(0.0661)	(0.0587)	(0.0359)
BRISK	0.00813	0.00660	0.0118
	(0.0386)	(0.0915)	(0.0354)
RETVOL	0.0760	0.0292	0.0663*
	(0.0524)	(0.0473)	(0.0365)
LEV	−0.0240	−0.0320	−0.0642***
	(0.0391)	(0.0291)	(0.0209)
TANG	0.00179	0.0449*	0.00784
	(0.0152)	(0.0263)	(0.00950)
ZSCORE	0.000534	−9.55e−05	−0.000551
	(0.000878)	(0.000555)	(0.000547)
AGENCYC	−0.0195	0.00609	−0.0115
	(0.0208)	(0.0213)	(0.0111)

(continued)

Table 5.7 (continued)

Dependent variable: *COC*	Younger firms	Middle-aged firms	Older firms
Variables	(1)	(2)	(3)
Constant	0.0647	0.0202	0.0703**
	(0.0731)	(0.0426)	(0.0328)
Industry & Year FE	Yes	Yes	Yes
Wald F (p-value)	1005 (0.000)	990.4 (0.000)	2081 (0.000)
AR (2) (p-value)	−1.499 (0.134)	−1.547 (0.122)	−0.700 (0.484)
Hansen J (p-value)	26.12 (0.457)	9.856 (0.453)	61.49 (0.494)

Notes This table shows the findings from the two-step system GMM estimation of Eq. 5.1 when the sample is disaggregated based on firm age in years. Firm-year observations within the first quartile are assigned as younger firms (firm age < 22 years). Observations above quartile three constitute the sample of older firms (firm age > 54.1222 years). The remaining values of firm age ranging from quartile one to quartile three are categorized as middle-aged firms (firm age from 22 to 54.1222 years). Parentheses indicate Windmeijer's corrected-robust standard errors. ***, **, and * represent significance at 1, 5, and 10% levels, respectively

facilitates them to make speedier decisions in response to dynamic business conditions (Finkelstein & D'aveni, 1994; Peng et al., 2010). As the Chair of the board, they can quickly convince and take the board's approvals for various corporate matters (Yang & Zhao, 2014). Further, they also possess firm- and industry-specific knowledge that can also aid in implementing required strategic changes (Hirshleifer et al., 2012; Tian et al., 2001). Therefore, external capital providers can regard CEO duality to be effective in reducing organizational inertia in aged corporations. Correspondingly, they will be willing to provide funds at a lower rate when a joint CEO-Chair is at the top in mature entities. Altogether, this result rejects arguments underlying H3.

5.3.4 *Role of Firm Growth Opportunities*

A high-growth company can generate attractive returns for investors as it has the potential to produce a substantial increment in its sales and net earnings over a long-term period (Lin et al., 2011; Rahaman & Al Zaman, 2013). However, the actual value of growth opportunities is difficult to be ascertained by the external capital providers. The information asymmetry regarding growth prospects can also give rise to expropriation concerns. In light of the severe information asymmetry of growing corporations, the presence of robust corporate governance mechanisms in these entities can assure investors that their interests will be protected by ensuring that the acquired funds are invested in only value-maximizing growth opportunities (Chen, 2008; Chen et al., 2009). Therefore, it can be expected that the impact of corporate governance on the cost of financing will be more salient in growth companies.

The empirical investigation checks for the significance of the purported assertion by creating sub-samples based on the quartile values of Tobin's Q, which indicates a corporation's growth prospects. The results from the empirical estimation of Eq. 5.1, which is conducted for low-growth, moderate-growth, and high-growth companies, are depicted in Table 5.8.

It can be inferred from Columns 1 and 2 that no corporate governance variable significantly impacts the cost of financing (*COC*) for low-growth and moderate-growth entities. Furthermore, Column 3 proffers a striking observation as it can be noted that the presence of CEO duality (*CEODUAL*) brings down the weighted average cost of capital (*COC*) in high-growth firms. In order to take full advantage of their investment opportunity set ahead of their competitors, growing enterprises often require swift decision-making and timely implementation of investment projects (Yang & Zhao, 2014). In this regard, a combined CEO-Chairman position can be associated with faster decisions by the outside finance providers as it imparts an organization with a united leadership (Tzabbar & Margolis, 2017). By taking charge of the board too, the CEO ensures a better flow of information between the management and board, which facilitates taking rapid actions as per the dynamic business conditions (Cabrera-Suárez & Martín-Santana, 2015; Hsu et al., 2021). Considering the benefits of a singular direction for growth companies, outside investors can be willing to supply funds at a lower cost when a dual CEO leads these firms.

5.3.5 Role of Firm Financial Condition

Financial distress situations can cast doubt on a corporation's ability to honor its debt obligations (Graham et al., 2008). Such circumstances also give rise to uncertainty concerning a firm's survival (Gupta & Mahakud, 2022). As a result, financially weaker companies are likely to be restricted from accessing external financing at a reasonable rate from the financial markets. However, the presence of strong governance structures in a financially distressed organization can lower its constraints in acquiring outside financing at reduced risk premiums. In worsening financial conditions, good governance practices can be presumed to be critical in propelling the management to improve the company's performance and control excessive risk exposure (Malik et al., 2021; Sharfman & Fernando, 2008). Hence, effective corporate governance mechanisms can help financially distressed entities secure external capital at a low cost.

The stated expectation is examined by disaggregating the overall sample based on the quartiles of the Altman-Z score. The Altman-Z score predicts a corporation's financial condition, whereby its lower value connotes a higher risk of default. Correspondingly, observations in the bottom quartile constitute the group of firms in financial distress conditions. The relevant results obtained from the empirical estimation of Eq. 5.1 for distressed firms, companies with moderate financial conditions, and financially sound entities are shown in Table 5.9.

Table 5.8 Corporate governance monitoring mechanisms and the cost of capital: Role of firm growth opportunities

Dependent variable: *COC*	Low-growth firms	Moderate-growth firms	High-growth firms
Variables	(1)	(2)	(3)
L.COC	0.591***	0.537***	0.277**
	(0.184)	(0.154)	(0.111)
BSIZE	0.000225	−0.000623	7.18e−05
	(0.000652)	(0.00111)	(0.000577)
BIND	2.54e−05	−0.000422	0.000104
	(0.000144)	(0.000351)	(0.000124)
CEODUAL	−0.00497	−0.00275	−0.00564**
	(0.00457)	(0.00403)	(0.00220)
BGD	0.000129	1.02e−05	−0.000100
	(0.000229)	(0.000162)	(8.45e−05)
PROMOTER	−4.68e−05	−8.61e−05	2.19e−05
	(5.28e−05)	(5.43e−05)	(0.000107)
NPD	−0.00107	−0.00236	0.00881
	(0.00274)	(0.00239)	(0.00607)
NAF	−0.000270	0.00351	0.00186
	(0.00279)	(0.00464)	(0.00260)
FSIZE	−0.000399	−0.000304	0.000622
	(0.00193)	(0.00173)	(0.000864)
FAGE	−2.26e−05	−2.46e−05	8.80e−07
	(2.97e−05)	(2.75e−05)	(3.08e−05)
GROWTH	0.000604	−0.000662	6.99e−05
	(0.00241)	(0.00126)	(0.000591)
PROFIT	−0.0405	−0.0148	−0.0199
	(0.0520)	(0.0293)	(0.0251)
BRISK	0.00446	0.0112	0.0417
	(0.0413)	(0.0325)	(0.0314)
RETVOL	0.0542	0.0236	0.103***
	(0.0336)	(0.0422)	(0.0296)
LEV	−0.0502***	−0.0307*	−0.0670***
	(0.0188)	(0.0156)	(0.0177)
TANG	0.0119	0.0132	−0.000422
	(0.0100)	(0.0141)	(0.00929)
ZSCORE	−0.000109	1.74e−05	8.68e−05
	(0.000339)	(0.000422)	(0.000325)
AGENCYC	−0.00605	0.00364	−0.00260

(continued)

Table 5.8 (continued)

Dependent variable: *COC*	Low-growth firms	Moderate-growth firms	High-growth firms
Variables	(1)	(2)	(3)
	(0.0116)	(0.0155)	(0.00886)
Constant	0.0377	0.0684	0.0151
	(0.0550)	(0.0435)	(0.0282)
Industry & Year FE	Yes	Yes	Yes
Wald F (p-value)	1910 (0.000)	1619 (0.000)	1547 (0.000)
AR (2) (p-value)	−0.935 (0.350)	−1.575 (0.115)	−1.345 (0.179)
Hansen J (p-value)	37.04 (0.375)	30.54 (0.338)	75.95 (0.415)

Notes This table shows the findings from the empirical estimation, which is undertaken for firms in different stages of growth. Growth opportunities are proxied by Tobin's Q. All the firm-year observations below the bottom quartile value of Tobin's Q make up the group of low-growth firms (Tobin's Q < 1.1491). The sample of high-growth firms encompasses observations whose values lie in the upper quartile of the Q ratio (Tobin's Q > 3.1837). The remaining observations in the middle two quartiles are classified as moderate-growth firms (Tobin's Q from 1.1491 to 3.1837). Windmeijer's corrected-robust standard errors are indicated in parentheses. ***, **, and * denote significance at 1, 5, and 10% levels, respectively

It can be observed from Column 1 that board independence (*BIND*) lessens the weighted average cost of capital (*COC*) for firms in financial distress conditions. Since independent directors are unaffiliated with the business enterprise and have reputational concerns, they tend to exercise strict and objective supervision over corporate matters (Anderson et al., 2004; Thu & Khanh, 2021). Considering the financial distress conditions, a highly independent board is better positioned to urge the executive directors to alter the current strategy and implement measures to improve business performance and control operational risk (Dowell et al., 2011; Malik et al., 2021). Independent directors can also bring valuable knowledge and experiences to advise the management on structural changes that can be undertaken to arrest a further decline in financial conditions (Filatotchev & Toms, 2003). They also provide legitimacy to the firm in times of crisis and can use their connections to assist it in procuring external capital and other critical corporate resources (Daily & Dalton, 1994; Mangena et al., 2020). Due to the perceived benefits of independent directors, their higher representation can facilitate a financially weaker corporation in acquiring funds from the capital market at reduced risk premiums.

Column 1 also demonstrates that a higher percentage of equity ownership by the controlling shareholder (*PROMOTER*) also reduces the cost of financing (*COC*) for financially distressed companies. In the event of bankruptcy, promoters risk losing their huge wealth invested in the firm (Chau & Gray, 2010; Ma et al., 2017). As a result, their substantial shareholding can cause them to initiate organizational changes in financial distress situations to ensure the business's survival (Donker et al., 2009; Johnson et al., 1993). They can also advocate decisions that lower cash flow uncertainty to strengthen the corporation's precarious financial position (Gottardo & Moisello, 2017). Consequently, external capital providers can be willing to give

Table 5.9 Corporate governance monitoring mechanisms and the cost of capital: Role of firm financial condition

Dependent variable: *COC*	Financial distress conditions (Low Altman-Z scores)	Moderate financial conditions (Medium range Altman-Z scores)	Financially sound conditions (High Altman-Z scores)
Variables	(1)	(2)	(3)
L.COC	0.318**	0.676***	0.491***
	(0.144)	(0.160)	(0.108)
BSIZE	−0.000918	−0.000169	5.57e−05
	(0.000975)	(0.000415)	(0.000302)
BIND	−0.000470**	6.09e−06	−2.02e−05
	(0.000236)	(8.78e−05)	(0.000165)
CEODUAL	0.00556	−0.000271	−0.00157
	(0.00816)	(0.00290)	(0.00326)
BGD	0.000595	−2.52e−05	−0.000100
	(0.000439)	(0.000175)	(0.000187)
PROMOTER	−0.000236***	−3.25e−06	5.15e−06
	(0.0000867)	(0.000109)	(5.40e−05)
NPD	−0.00537	−0.00148	0.000486
	(0.00683)	(0.00171)	(0.00716)
NAF	−0.00197	0.000827	0.000309
	(0.00563)	(0.00142)	(0.00194)
FSIZE	−0.00211	−0.000207	0.000822
	(0.00244)	(0.000480)	(0.00111)
FAGE	2.63e−05	−3.34e−05	3.00e−05
	(6.47e−05)	(2.67e−05)	(3.64e−05)
GROWTH	−0.0178**	−0.000128	−9.79e−05
	(0.00722)	(0.00153)	(0.000972)
PROFIT	−0.0364	−0.0239	−0.00851
	(0.0580)	(0.0257)	(0.0364)
BRISK	0.0568	−0.0223	0.00830
	(0.132)	(0.0136)	(0.0282)
RETVOL	0.0551	0.0364	0.0950**
	(0.0986)	(0.0326)	(0.0460)
LEV	−0.0271	−0.0317*	−0.0512*
	(0.0300)	(0.0173)	(0.0274)
TANG	0.0270*	0.00787	0.00475
	(0.0153)	(0.00797)	(0.00445)
ZSCORE	0.00762**	−8.04e−07	0.000241
	(0.00296)	(0.000650)	(0.000441)

(continued)

Table 5.9 (continued)

Dependent variable: *COC*	Financial distress conditions (Low Altman-Z scores)	Moderate financial conditions (Medium range Altman-Z scores)	Financially sound conditions (High Altman-Z scores)
Variables	(1)	(2)	(3)
AGENCYC	0.00691	−0.00714	0.00293
	(0.0300)	(0.0121)	(0.0137)
Constant	0.114	0.0274	−0.00167
	(0.0729)	(0.0222)	(0.0523)
Industry & Year FE	Yes	Yes	Yes
Wald F (p-value)	443.3 (0.000)	2872 (0.000)	93.82 (0.000)
AR (2) (p-value)	−0.657 (0.511)	−1.616 (0.106)	−1.466 (0.143)
Hansen J (p-value)	32.10 (0.462)	77.86 (0.171)	50.95 (0.358)

Notes This table depicts the findings from the empirical estimation of Eq. 5.1 when the sample is divided using the Altman Z-scores. A higher Z score suggests lower bankruptcy risk (Graham et al., 2008). Therefore, sample values in the lower quartile are grouped as firms in financial distress conditions (Z score < 2.028901). Observations in the upper quartile are designated as firms with financially sound conditions (Z score > 7.477723). The middle two quartiles with remaining values are categorized as firms with moderate financial conditions (Z score from 2.028901 to 7.477723). Parentheses report Windmeijer's corrected-robust standard errors. ***, **, and * denote significance at 1, 5, and 10% levels, respectively

funds at a lower cost to financially weaker entities when they have a high controlling ownership stake. Lastly, Columns 2 and 3 also demonstrate that corporate governance devices have an insignificant effect on the cost of external financing for firms with relatively stronger financial conditions.

5.3.6 Role of Industry Concentration

The presence of a few dominating firms in highly concentrated industries grants these entities significant market power, which permits their management to implement policies of their choice (Cheng et al., 2013; Schmidt, 1997). As the forces of competition do not threaten such corporations, their executives can run the business operations inefficiently and pass on any increment in the costs to the customers without any substantial loss in the market share (Bertrand & Mullainathan, 2003; Hicks, 1935). In addition, the problem of information asymmetry is also notable in concentrated markets because the limited number of competitors constrains the scope of taking a comprehensive peer performance evaluation (Holmstrom, 1982; Nalebuff & Stiglitz, 1983). Consequently, corporate insiders can make use of this information disparity to engage in self-dealing activities. In contrast, managerial discretion is curtailed by the competitive pressures accompanying industries with a lower degree of concentration (Srivastava et al., 2024). Given the intense competition, managers and controlling owners are forced to cut down on extravagant expenditures to control the costs and enlarge the profit margin for the purpose of maintaining the firm's competitive position (Schmidt, 1997; Singla & Singh, 2019). The identification of unprofitable operations also becomes easier in competitive industries as performance can be compared with numerous competitors (Nalebuff & Stiglitz, 1983; Shleifer, 1985). Thus, managerial entrenchment is minimized in low-concentrated industries.

Consistent with the previous discourse, it can be inferred that the severity of agency conflicts varies with the degree of industry concentration. Commensurately, the effect of corporate governance monitoring mechanisms on the cost of financing can be contingent on the industry structure. In order to investigate this possibility, the sample is sorted into different groups based on the quartile values of the Herfindahl–Hirschman Index (HHI). The concerned empirical findings from the system GMM estimation of Eq. 5.1 for the categories of firms affiliated to low-concentrated, medium-concentrated, and highly concentrated markets are depicted in Table 5.10.

It can be observed from Columns 1 and 2 that corporate governance mechanisms do not significantly affect the cost of financing (*COC*) for companies operating in low-concentrated and medium-concentrated markets. Further, Column 3 also shows that the presence of non-controlling large shareholders (*NPD*) negatively influences the weighted average cost of capital (*COC*) of firms affiliated with highly concentrated industries. The significant market power and information asymmetry in concentrated markets extend latitude to the corporate insiders to operate the business as per their will (Cheng et al., 2013; Schmidt, 1997). In light of heightened expropriation concerns, the monitoring role of additional blockholders can gain prominence. They can use their considerable voting rights to dispute sub-optimal policies of the management and coax it to make only value-maximizing decisions (Attig et al., 2008). Hence, minority shareholders and lenders can associate the existence of non-promoter large owners with the increased discipline of managers. Correspondingly, they can charge a lower cost of capital from corporations in a concentrated market when they have multiple large shareholders. Hence, the reported result is in consonance with H6.

5.4 Summary and Concluding Observations

The current chapter analyzes the effect of corporate governance monitoring mechanisms on the cost of financing. As the problem of agency conflicts and information asymmetry becomes severe, the outside capital providers are likely to demand a higher rate of return to compensate for the increased perceived risk level (Lugo, 2019; Ma et al., 2017). However, the presence of robust corporate governance structures in a company can limit managerial entrenchment and promote more information transparency (Aldamen & Duncan, 2012; Zhu, 2014). The reduced expropriation concerns arising from the stronger corporate governance environment can cause a

Table 5.10 Corporate governance monitoring mechanisms and the cost of capital: Role of industry concentration

Dependent variable: *COC*	Low-concentrated industries	Medium-concentrated industries	Highly-concentrated industries
Variables	(1)	(2)	(3)
L.COC	0.496*	0.671***	0.492***
	(0.261)	(0.243)	(0.185)
BSIZE	−0.000368	−7.82e−05	−0.000363
	(0.000793)	(0.000836)	(0.00125)
BIND	−6.29e−07	−0.000178	5.66e−05
	(6.87e−05)	(0.000274)	(0.000166)
CEODUAL	0.000393	−0.000216	−9.66e−05
	(0.00163)	(0.00473)	(0.00955)
BGD	0.000323	−6.91e−05	0.000187
	(0.000234)	(0.000288)	(0.000423)
PROMOTER	−1.17e−05	−0.000104	−1.72e−05
	(7.15e−05)	(6.27e−05)	(6.64e−05)
NPD	−0.00143	−0.00310	−0.00450*
	(0.00710)	(0.00572)	(0.00245)
NAF	−0.00819	0.00110	0.000541
	(0.00551)	(0.00125)	(0.00170)
FSIZE	0.00109	−5.59e−05	−0.00147
	(0.00248)	(0.000835)	(0.00298)
FAGE	−1.64e−05	−9.52e−06	−3.59e−05
	(5.38e−05)	(2.81e−05)	(4.56e−05)
GROWTH	−0.00118	−0.000657	3.98e−05
	(0.00199)	(0.000690)	(0.00292)
PROFIT	0.00892	0.0690	−0.0856*
	(0.0804)	(0.0724)	(0.0479)
BRISK	0.0606	0.0548	0.0688
	(0.0990)	(0.0589)	(0.0641)
RETVOL	0.0384	0.0507*	−0.00160
	(0.0676)	(0.0305)	(0.0683)
LEV	−0.0512*	−0.0251	−0.0484**
	(0.0277)	(0.0431)	(0.0198)
TANG	0.00150	0.0140	0.00354
	(0.00594)	(0.0186)	(0.0283)
ZSCORE	−0.000335	−0.000196	0.000313
	(0.00104)	(0.000452)	(0.000633)

(continued)

Table 5.10 (continued)

Dependent variable: *COC*	Low-concentrated industries	Medium-concentrated industries	Highly-concentrated industries
Variables	(1)	(2)	(3)
AGENCYC	0.0185	0.00943	−0.0160
	(0.0278)	(0.0189)	(0.0167)
Constant	0.0307	0.0251	0.0874
	(0.0609)	(0.0444)	(0.0885)
Industry & Year FE	Yes	Yes	Yes
Wald F (p-value)	1456 (0.000)	3630 (0.000)	917.1 (0.000)
AR (2) (p-value)	−1.546 (0.122)	−1.578 (0.115)	−1.502 (0.133)
Hansen J (p-value)	17.63 (0.346)	11.30 (0.419)	23.16 (0.393)

Notes This table summarizes the results from the empirical estimation of Eq. 5.1 when the sample is segregated based on the degree of industry concentration. HHI indicates the severity of concentration in a given market. Sample values less than quartile one of HHI are classified as low-concentrated industries (HHI < 0.0329862). Firm-year observations exceeding the value of quartile three of HHI are assigned as highly-concentrated industries (HHI > 0.0773149). The observations ranging from quartiles one to three are grouped as medium-concentrated industries (HHI from 0.0329862 to 0.0773149). Parentheses summarize Windmeijer's corrected-robust standard errors. ***, **, and * represent significance at 1, 5, and 10% levels, respectively

reduction in the required rate of return by outside investors. Therefore, the role of the board of directors, large owners, and auditor independence in determining a firm's cost of capital is investigated.

The empirical examination is done for a period of ten years ranging from FY 2010 to FY 2019, for non-financial enterprises listed on the NIFTY 500 index. The pivotal results from analysis undertaken are reported in Table 5.11.

Table 5.11 Summary of results from empirical investigation of corporate governance monitoring mechanisms on the cost of capital

Variables	Analyses	Results
Board size	Main effect	• No significant main effect
	Contingent effect	• No significant contingent effect
Board independence	Main effect	• Negative impact in the post-reform period
	Contingent effect	*Firm financial condition* • Negative impact in the case of financially distressed firms *Other contingency factors* • No significant effect
CEO duality	Main effect	• No significant main effect
	Contingent effect	*Firm age* • Negative impact in the case of older firms *Firm growth opportunities* • Negative impact in the case of high-growth firms *Other contingency factors* • No significant contingent effect
Board gender diversity	Main effect	• No significant main effect
	Contingent effect	• No significant contingent effect
Controlling shareholder	Main effect	• Negative impact, present in the post-reform period
	Contingent effect	*CEO tenure* • Negative impact in the late stages of a CEO's tenure *Firm size* • Negative impact in the case of smaller firms *Firm financial condition* • Negative impact in the case of financially distressed firms *Other contingency factors* • No significant effect
Non-controlling large shareholders	Main effect	• No significant main effect
	Contingent effect	*Industry concentration* • Negative impact in the case of highly-concentrated industries *Other contingency factors* • No significant effect
Auditor independence	Main effect	• No significant main effect

(continued)

Table 5.11 (continued)

Variables	Analyses	Results
	Contingent effect	*Firm age* • Positive impact in the case of younger firms *Other contingency factors* • No significant effect

Notes This table presents a concise summary of all the findings obtained from the current empirical investigation

References

Aksoy, M., & Yilmaz, M. K. (2023). Does board diversity affect the cost of debt financing? Empirical evidence from Turkey. *Gender in Management: An International Journal, 38*(4), 504–524.

Alayo, M., Maseda, A., Iturralde, T., & Calabrò, A. (2023). We are family! The role of family members' identification in the internationalization of family firms. *European Management Journal, 41*(5), 792–801.

Aldamen, H., & Duncan, K. (2012). Does adopting good corporate governance impact the cost of intermediated and non-intermediated debt? *Accounting & Finance, 52*, 49–76.

Alsadoun, N., Naiker, V., Navissi, F., & Sharma, D. S. (2018). Auditor-provided tax nonaudit services and the implied cost of equity capital. *Auditing: A Journal of Practice & Theory, 37*(3), 1–24.

Anderson, R. C., & Reeb, D. M. (2003). Founding-family ownership and firm performance: Evidence from the S&P 500. *The Journal of Finance, 58*(3), 1301–1328.

Anderson, R. C., Mansi, S. A., & Reeb, D. M. (2004). Board characteristics, accounting report integrity, and the cost of debt. *Journal of Accounting and Economics, 37*(3), 315–342.

Arellano, M., & Bond, S. (1991). Some tests of specification for panel data: Monte Carlo evidence and an application to employment equations. *The Review of Economic Studies, 58*(2), 277–297.

Attig, N., Guedhami, O., & Mishra, D. (2008). Multiple large shareholders, control contests, and implied cost of equity. *Journal of Corporate Finance, 14*(5), 721–737.

Bajaj, Y., Kashiramka, S., & Singh, S. (2020). Capital structure dynamics: China and India (Chindia) perspective. *European Business Review, 32*(5), 845–868.

Belkhir, M., Naceur, S. B., Chami, R., & Samet, A. (2021). Bank capital and the cost of equity. *Journal of Financial Stability, 53*, Article 100843.

Ben-Nasr, H., Boubakri, N., & Cosset, J. C. (2012). The political determinants of the cost of equity: Evidence from newly privatized firms. *Journal of Accounting Research, 50*(3), 605–646.

Bertrand, M., & Mullainathan, S. (2003). Enjoying the quiet life? Corporate governance and managerial preferences. *Journal of Political Economy, 111*(5), 1043–1075.

Bonini, S., Dell'Acqua, A., Fungo, M., & Kysucky, V. (2016). Credit market concentration, relationship lending and the cost of debt. *International Review of Financial Analysis, 45*, 172–179.

Boubaker, S., Boubakri, N., Grira, J., & Guizani, A. (2018). Sovereign wealth funds and equity pricing: Evidence from implied cost of equity of publicly traded targets. *Journal of Corporate Finance, 53*, 202–224.

Boubakri, N., & Ghouma, H. (2010). Control/ownership structure, creditor rights protection, and the cost of debt financing: International evidence. *Journal of Banking & Finance, 34*(10), 2481–2499.

Busru, S., & Singh, S. (2016). Indian redefined corporate governance: In the context of companies act 2013. *Research Journal of Finance and Accounting, 7*(5), 48–52.

Cabrera-Suárez, M. K., & Martín-Santana, J. D. (2015). Board composition and performance in Spanish non-listed family firms: The influence of type of directors and CEO duality. *BRQ Business Research Quarterly, 18*(4), 213–229.

Caixe, D. F., Kalatzis, A. E. G., & de Castro, L. R. K. (2019). Controlling shareholders and investment-risk sensitivity in an emerging economy. *Emerging Markets Review, 39*, 133–153.

Chan, A. L., & Hsu, A. W. H. (2013). Corporate pyramids, conservatism and cost of debt: Evidence from Taiwan. *The International Journal of Accounting, 48*(3), 390–413.

Chau, G., & Gray, S. J. (2010). Family ownership, board independence and voluntary disclosure: Evidence from Hong Kong. *Journal of International Accounting, Auditing and Taxation, 19*(2), 93–109.

Chen, C., Cui, H., & Zhang, Y. (2022). CEO duality and bank loan contracting: Evidence from China. *Emerging Markets Finance and Trade, 58*(12), 3526–3540.

Cheng, P., Man, P., & Yi, C. H. (2013). The impact of product market competition on earnings quality. *Accounting & Finance, 53*(1), 137–162.

Cheng, S. (2008). Board size and the variability of corporate performance. *Journal of Financial Economics, 87*(1), 157–176.

Chen, Y. R., & Chuang, W. T. (2009). Alignment or entrenchment? Corporate governance and cash holdings in growing firms. *Journal of Business Research, 62*(11), 1200–1206.

Coad, A., Segarra, A., & Teruel, M. (2016). Innovation and firm growth: Does firm age play a role? *Research Policy, 45*(2), 387–400.

Cook, D. O., & Luo, S. S. (2023). Fund flow-induced volatility and the cost of debt. *Journal of Banking & Finance, 146*, Article 106702.

Dahiya, M., & Singh, S. (2021). The linkage between CSR and cost of equity: An Indian perspective. *Sustainability Accounting, Management and Policy Journal, 12*(3), 499–521.

Daily, C. M., & Dalton, D. R. (1994). Bankruptcy and corporate governance: The impact of board composition and structure. *Academy of Management Journal, 37*(6), 1603–1617.

Das, A., & Dey, S. (2016). Role of corporate governance on firm performance: A study on large Indian corporations after implementation of Companies' Act 2013. *Asian Journal of Business Ethics, 5*, 149–164.

De Moura, A. A. F., Altuwaijri, A., & Gupta, J. (2020). Did mandatory IFRS adoption affect the cost of capital in Latin American countries? *Journal of International Accounting, 38*, Article 100301.

DeFond, M. L., Raghunandan, K., & Subramanyam, K. R. (2002). Do non–audit service fees impair auditor independence? Evidence from going concern audit opinions. *Journal of Accounting Research, 40*(4), 1247–1274.

Dhaliwal, D., Heitzman, S., & Zhen Li, O. (2006). Taxes, leverage, and the cost of equity capital. *Journal of Accounting Research, 44*(4), 691–723.

Donker, H., Santen, B., & Zahir, S. (2009). Ownership structure and the likelihood of financial distress in the Netherlands. *Applied Financial Economics, 19*(21), 1687–1696.

Dowell, G. W., Shackell, M. B., & Stuart, N. V. (2011). Boards, CEOs, and surviving a financial crisis: Evidence from the internet shakeout. *Strategic Management Journal, 32*(10), 1025–1045.

Filatotchev, I., & Toms, S. (2003). Corporate governance, strategy and survival in a declining industry: A study of UK cotton textile companies. *Journal of Management Studies, 40*(4), 895–920.

Finkelstein, S., & D'aveni, R. A. (1994). CEO duality as a double-edged sword: How boards of directors balance entrenchment avoidance and unity of command. *Academy of Management Journal, 37*(5), 1079–1108.

Friedrich, C., Quick, R., & Schmidt, F. (2024). Auditor-provided non-audit services and perceived audit quality: Evidence from the cost of equity and debt capital. *International Journal of Auditing, 28*(2), 388–407.

Gao, H., He, J., Li, Y., & Qu, Y. (2020). Family control and cost of debt: Evidence from China. *Pacific-Basin Finance Journal, 60*, Article 101286.

Gottardo, P., & Moisello, A. M. (2017). Family firms, risk-taking and financial distress. *Problems and Perspectives in Management, 15*(2–1), 168–177.
Graham, J. R., Li, S., & Qiu, J. (2008). Corporate misreporting and bank loan contracting. *Journal of Financial Economics, 89*(1), 44–61.
Grant Thornton (2013). *Implications of Companies Act, 2013*. Retrieved January 4, 2025 from http://gtw3.grantthornton.in/assets/Companies_Act-Governance.pdf
Guizani, M. (2017). The financial determinants of corporate cash holdings in an oil rich country: Evidence from Kingdom of Saudi Arabia. *Borsa Istanbul Review, 17*(3), 133–143.
Gupta, G., & Mahakud, J. (2022). Impact of financial distress on investment-cash flow sensitivity: Evidence from emerging economy. *International Journal of Managerial Finance, 19*(4), 713–743.
Gupta, K., Krishnamurti, C., & Tourani-Rad, A. (2018). Financial development, corporate governance and cost of equity capital. *Journal of Contemporary Accounting & Economics, 14*(1), 65–82.
Guthrie, G. (2011). A note on operating leverage and expected rates of return. *Finance Research Letters, 8*(2), 88–100.
Guyot, A., Lagoarde-Segot, T., & Neaime, S. (2014). Foreign shocks and international cost of equity destabilization. Evidence from the MENA region. *Emerging Markets Review, 18*, 101–122.
Hambrick, D. C., & Fukutomi, G. D. (1991). The seasons of a CEO's tenure. *Academy of Management Review, 16*(4), 719–742.
Hernández-Cánovas, G., & Martínez-Solano, P. (2010). Relationship lending and SME financing in the continental European bank-based system. *Small Business Economics, 34*(4), 465–482.
Hicks, J. R. (1935). Annual survey of economic theory: The theory of monopoly. *Econometrica: Journal of the Econometric Society*, 1–20.
Hirshleifer, D., Low, A., & Teoh, S. H. (2012). Are overconfident CEOs better innovators? *The Journal of Finance, 67*(4), 1457–1498.
Holmstrom, B. (1982). Moral hazard in teams. *The Bell Journal of Economics*, 324–340.
Hsu, S., Lin, S. W., Chen, W. P., & Huang, J. W. (2021). CEO duality, information costs, and firm performance. *The North American Journal of Economics and Finance, 55*, Article 101011.
Huffman, L. (1983). Operating leverage, financial leverage, and equity risk. *Journal of Banking & Finance, 7*(2), 197–212.
Huybrechts, J., Voordeckers, W., & Lybaert, N. (2012). Entrepreneurial risk taking of private family firms: The influence of a nonfamily CEO and the moderating effect of CEO tenure. *Family Business Review, 26*(2), 161–179.
Iatridis, G. E. (2012). Audit quality in common-law and code-law emerging markets: Evidence on earnings conservatism, agency costs and cost of equity. *Emerging Markets Review, 13*(2), 101–117.
Johnson, R. A., Hoskisson, R. E., & Hitt, M. A. (1993). Board of director involvement in restructuring: The effects of board versus managerial controls and characteristics. *Strategic Management Journal, 14*(S1), 33–50.
Karjalainen, J. (2011). Audit quality and cost of debt capital for private firms: Evidence from Finland. *International Journal of Auditing, 15*(1), 88–108.
Kuo, L. W. (2017). Reputation as a governance mechanism? Evidence from payout policy of insider-controlled firms in Taiwan. *Journal of Business Finance & Accounting, 44*(9–10), 1443–1476.
Lin, C., Ma, Y., Malatesta, P., & Xuan, Y. (2011). Ownership structure and the cost of corporate borrowing. *Journal of Financial Economics, 100*(1), 1–23.
Lin, C. Y., Tsai, W. C., & Hasan, I. (2018). Private benefits of control and bank loan contracts. *Journal of Corporate Finance, 49*, 324–343.
Lorsch, J. W., & MacIver, E. (1989). *Pawns or potentates: The reality of America's corporate boards*. Harvard Business School Press.
Lugo, S. (2019). Insider ownership and the cost of debt capital: Evidence from bank loans. *International Review of Financial Analysis, 63*, 357–368.

Luo, Q., Li, H., & Zhang, B. (2015). Financing constraints and the cost of equity: Evidence on the moral hazard of the controlling shareholder. *International Review of Economics & Finance, 36*, 99–106.

Ma, L., Ma, S., & Tian, G. (2017). Corporate opacity and cost of debt for family firms. *European Accounting Review, 26*(1), 27–59.

Malik, M. F., Nowland, J., & Buckby, S. (2021). Voluntary adoption of board risk committees and financial constraints risk. *International Review of Financial Analysis, 73*, Article 101611.

Mampatta, S.P. (2017). *How long does an Indian CEO last in the corner office?* Retrieved January 4, 2025 from https://www.livemint.com/Companies/Kek9zqK4tT4MVhtFYK957I/How-long-does-an-Indian-CEO-stay-in-the-corner-office.html

Mangena, M., Priego, A. M., & Manzaneque, M. (2020). Bank power, block ownership, boards and financial distress likelihood: An investigation of Spanish listed firms. *Journal of Corporate Finance, 64*, Article 101636.

Meuwissen, R., & Quick, R. (2019). The effects of non-audit services on auditor independence: An experimental investigation of supervisory board members' perceptions. *Journal of International Accounting, Auditing and Taxation, 36*, Article 100264.

Mitra, S. (2007). Non-audit service fees and auditor independence: Empirical evidence from the oil and gas industry. *Journal of Accounting, Auditing & Finance, 22*(1), 85–107.

Modigliani, F., & Miller, M. H. (1963). Corporate income taxes and the cost of capital: A correction. *The American Economic Review, 53*(3), 433–443.

Moss, S. S. (2016). The impact of corporate governance and earnings management practices on cost of equity capital: Evidence from thai listed companies. *ACRN Oxford Journal of Finance and Risk Perspectives, 5*(1), 160–182.

Nalebuff, B. J., & Stiglitz, J. E. (1983). Prizes and incentives: Towards a general theory of compensation and competition. *The Bell Journal of Economics, 14*(1), 21–43.

Peng, M. W., Li, Y., Xie, E., & Su, Z. (2010). CEO duality, organizational slack, and firm performance in China. *Asia Pacific Journal of Management, 27*(4), 611–624.

Petruzzelli, A. M., Ardito, L., & Savino, T. (2018). Maturity of knowledge inputs and innovation value: The moderating effect of firm age and size. *Journal of Business Research, 86*, 190–201.

Prakash, N., Singh, S., & Sharma, S. (2024). Technological diffusion, bank performance, and Solow's paradox: Insights from an emerging economy. *Journal of the Knowledge Economy*. Advanced online publication. https://doi.org/10.1007/s13132-024-02347-4

Rahaman, M. M., & Al Zaman, A. (2013). Management quality and the cost of debt: Does management matter to lenders? *Journal of Banking & Finance, 37*(3), 854–874.

Sarkar, J., & Selarka, E. (2021). Women on board and performance of family firms: Evidence from India. *Emerging Markets Review, 46*, Article 100770.

Schmidt, K. M. (1997). Managerial incentives and product market competition. *The Review of Economic Studies, 64*(2), 191–213.

Selarka, E. (2005). Ownership concentration and firm value: A study from the Indian corporate sector. *Emerging Markets Finance and Trade, 41*(6), 83–108.

Shailer, G., & Wang, K. (2015). Government ownership and the cost of debt for Chinese listed corporations. *Emerging Markets Review, 22*, 1–17.

Sharfman, M. P., & Fernando, C. S. (2008). Environmental risk management and the cost of capital. *Strategic Management Journal, 29*(6), 569–592.

Sheikh, S. (2019). CEO power and corporate risk: The impact of market competition and corporate governance. *Corporate Governance: An International Review, 27*(5), 358–377.

Shen, W. (2003). The dynamics of the CEO-board relationship: An evolutionary perspective. *Academy of Management Review, 28*(3), 466–476.

Shleifer, A. (1985). A theory of yardstick competition. *The RAND Journal of Economics*, 319–327.

Singla, M., & Singh, S. (2019). Board monitoring, product market competition and firm performance. *International Journal of Organizational Analysis, 27*(4), 1036–1052.

Smith, D. D., Pennathur, A. K., & Marciniak, M. R. (2017). Why do CEOs agree to the discipline of dividends? *International Review of Financial Analysis, 52*, 38–48.

Sohn, J., Tang, C. H. H., & Jang, S. S. (2013). Does the asset-light and fee-oriented strategy create value? *International Journal of Hospitality Management, 32*, 270–277.

Srivastava, B., Singh, S., & Jain, S. (2024). A frontier-based parametric framework for exploring the competition–efficiency nexus in commercial banking: Insights from an emerging economy. *Managerial Finance, 50*(5), 854–889.

Suman, S., & Singh, S. (2022). The role of multiple large shareholders in dividend payouts: Evidence from India. *American Business Review, 25*(1), 120–151.

Tanaka, T. (2014). Gender diversity in the boards and the pricing of publicly traded corporate debt: Evidence from Japan. *Applied Financial Economics, 24*(4), 247–258.

Teofilus, T., Ardyan, E., Sutrisno, T., Sabar, S., & Sutanto, V. (2022). Managing organizational inertia: Indonesian family business perspective. *Frontiers in Psychology, 13*, Article 839266.

Thu, P. A., & Khanh, T. H. T. (2021). Corporate social responsibility, board independence, state ownership and cost of debt in Vietnamese firms. *Journal of Legal, Ethical and Regulatory Issues, 24*(S5), 1–12.

Tian, J. J., & Chung-Ming, L. A. U. (2001). Board composition, leadership structure and performance in Chinese shareholding companies. *Asia Pacific Journal of Management, 18*(2), 245.

Tuzel, S. (2010). Corporate real estate holdings and the cross-section of stock returns. *The Review of Financial Studies, 23*(6), 2268–2302.

Tzabbar, D., & Margolis, J. (2017). Beyond the startup stage: The founding team's human capital, new venture's stage of life, founder–CEO duality, and breakthrough innovation. *Organization Science, 28*(5), 857–872.

Upadhyay, A. (2014). Social concentration on boards, corporate information environment and cost of capital. *Journal of Business Finance & Accounting, 41*(7–8), 974–1001.

Upadhyay, A., & Sriram, R. (2011). Board size, corporate information environment and cost of capital. *Journal of Business Finance & Accounting, 38*(9–10), 1238–1261.

Wahab, E. A. A., Agustia, D., Azmi, N. A., Harymawan, I., Ramli, R., & Zakaria, N. B. (2020). Political connections, corporate governance, and the cost of equity in Malaysia. *International Journal of Innovation, Creativity and Change, 10*(10), 710–731.

Walters, B. A., Kroll, M. J., & Wright, P. (2007). CEO tenure, boards of directors, and acquisition performance. *Journal of Business Research, 60*(4), 331–338.

Wintoki, M. B., Linck, J. S., & Netter, J. M. (2012). Endogeneity and the dynamics of internal corporate governance. *Journal of Financial Economics, 105*(3), 581–606.

Yang, T., & Zhao, S. (2014). CEO duality and firm performance: Evidence from an exogenous shock to the competitive environment. *Journal of Banking & Finance, 49*, 534–552.

Zhu, F. (2014). Corporate governance and the cost of capital: An international study. *International Review of Finance, 14*(3), 393–429.

Chapter 6
Corporate Governance and Dividend Payouts

The preceding chapter analyzed the impact of corporate governance attributes on the cost of financing. The present chapter adds to the former empirical investigation by examining the implications of corporate governance monitoring mechanisms on a form of payout made to equity shareholders, i.e., cash dividends. Dividends represent a portion of corporate income distributed to the equity owners (Amidu & Abor, 2006). As dividend distribution involves an outflow of cash, it can also help in regulating the problem of free cash flow. These payouts reduce the surplus cash that the corporate insiders[1] could have otherwise misused to extract private gains (Jensen, 1986; Rozeff, 1982). In addition, dividend payments increase a company's reliance on capital markets for raising funds, thereby leading to enhanced scrutiny of various capital market participants on managerial actions (Easterbrook, 1984; Ye et al., 2019). Thus, cash dividends can serve as an effective bonding mechanism that can either substitute or complement various corporate governance devices firms employ. On the one hand, dividends can be an outcome of superior corporate governance practices (La Porta et al., 2000). On the other hand, dividend payments can substitute for poor governance as weakly-governed corporations can utilize them to establish a capital market reputation (La Porta et al., 2000; Sawicki, 2009).

In order to clarify the relationship between corporate governance monitoring mechanisms and dividend payouts, the empirical analysis is conducted from FY 2010 to FY 2019 using a sample of non-financial NIFTY 500 entities. A separate empirical examination is also undertaken by segregating the sample into pre-reform and post-reform periods to understand how the effectiveness of the board of directors attributes, large ownership characteristics, and auditor independence varies post the enactment of the new Companies Act in 2013. Furthermore, the research study is augmented to identify contingent effects and boundary conditions of corporate governance by

[1] Corporate insiders include the controlling owner and managers.

S. Singh and S. Suman, *Corporate Governance Monitoring Mechanisms and Corporate Performance and Valuation*, India Studies in Business and Economics,
https://doi.org/10.1007/978-981-96-9736-6_6

performing sub-sample analyses by considering specific CEO-, firm-, and industry-level contextual factors. Lastly, the impact of governance variables on the extent of dividend smoothing is also investigated.

The structure of the chapter is elaborated as follows. Section 6.1 introduces the current research study. The results from the main empirical analysis are elaborated in Sect. 6.2. The exposition of contingent effects is undertaken through additional analyses that are presented in Sect. 6.3. Section 6.4 throws light on the ramifications of corporate governance on dividend stability. Lastly, Sect. 6.5 ends the study by providing concluding remarks.

6.1 Introduction

The linkage between corporate governance mechanisms and dividend payouts can be expounded by understanding the role of dividends in managing agency conflicts. According to Rozeff (1982), dividends lower the excess cash flow available at management's discretion. If the residual profits are not paid out to the shareholders, they may be tunneled by the corporate insiders for enhancing perquisites or investing in unprofitable projects (Mittal & Singh, 2025). At the same time, the payment of cash dividends compels a firm to raise funds from the capital markets, thereby subjecting it to greater regulatory watch and restrictions (Easterbrook, 1984; Ye et al., 2019). Thus, dividend payout serves as an additional bonding mechanism, which, more often than not, is a permanent commitment that is costly to dishonor (Anwar et al., 2017; Kuo, 2017). This observation is supported by the results of Brav et al. (2005), which indicate that investors react negatively to dividend cuts.

Considering the disciplinary role of dividends, La Porta et al. (2000) purport two major hypotheses that underline the association between corporate governance mechanisms and dividend payouts. The outcome hypothesis asserts that dividends are a result of superior corporate governance mechanisms (La Porta et al., 2000). Since the payment of dividends reduces surplus cash available at the disposal of corporate insiders, it ameliorates the free cash flow problem (Jensen, 1986). Hence, under the outcome hypothesis, well-governed firms will reduce excess cash by paying more dividends.

In contrast, the substitution hypothesis states that weakly-governed firms pay more dividends to compensate for poor governance (La Porta et al., 2000). Essentially, in this case, corporate insiders are using dividend payouts as a commitment that they will not exploit the minority shareholders (Gomes, 2000). The voluntary adoption of this bonding mechanism enables entrenched firms to establish a capital market reputation by fostering credibility amongst external investors. They engage in reputation-building to fund the firm's future growth opportunities on reasonable terms (Kuo, 2017; Sawicki, 2009). Additionally, the controlling owners may be guided to diversify the firm's idiosyncratic risk by selling shares at a higher price that would otherwise have been discounted for expropriation (Gomes, 2000).

Considering the previous discourse, it can be gathered that the outcome and substitution hypothesis make opposite predictions with regard to the linkage between corporate governance monitoring mechanisms and dividend payout intensity. Since there is no clarity regarding the nature of the relationship, only a significant effect of multiple corporate governance attributes on the dividend levels is purported. A concise explanation of each of these mechanisms is presented in Table 6.1 to understand how they may affect a firm's dividend policy.

6.2 Main Empirical Analysis and Discussion

Sample description

The sample deployed is the non-financial firms that are listed on the NIFTY 500 index. The dividend behavior of the sampled entities is analyzed from FY 2010 to FY 2019. After excluding missing observations, the total firm-year observations amount to 3466. In summary, 399 corporations are subjected to empirical examination.

Regression model and variables

As the underlined objective of the chapter is to analyze the impact of corporate governance mechanisms on dividend payout levels and dividend stability, the partial adjustment model of Lintner (1956) is adopted to undertake the same. The adapted Lintner model is given by Eq. 6.1, which is elaborated as follows:

$$\begin{aligned} DIVIDEND_{it} &= \beta_0 + \beta_1 DIVIDEND_{t-1} + \beta_2 BSIZE_{it} + \beta_3 BIND_{it} \\ &\quad + \beta_4 CEODUAL_{it} + \beta_5 BGD_{it} + \beta_6 PROMOTER_{it} \\ &\quad + \beta_7 NPD_{it} + \beta_8 NAF_{it} + \sum_{j=9}^{N} \beta_j CONTROLS_{it} \\ &\quad + Industryeffects_i + Yeareffects_t + \varepsilon_{it} \end{aligned} \tag{6.1}$$

where, *DIVIDEND* is the dividends to total assets ratio, which is the study's dependent variable and the corresponding data is extracted from Datastream®. The independent variables comprise the monitoring characteristics of the board of directors, the equity ownership percentage of large shareholders, and auditor independence. These governance attributes are elaborated in detail in Chapter 1. The coefficient (β_1) on the past year's dividend amount alludes to the extent of smoothed and stable dividends.

CONTROLS include several control variables that are likely to determine the desired level of dividend payouts. First, we take into account the impact of firm size (*FSIZE*) as larger firms are usually mature and can easily access financial markets, owing to which they are expected to make larger payouts (Anwer et al., 2020). Second, we consider the impact of a firm's lifecycle stage *(FAGE)* as older firms have larger accumulated earnings, resulting in higher payouts (DeAngelo et al., 2006;

Table 6.1 Summary of the predicted relationship between corporate governance monitoring mechanisms and the level of dividends

Variables	Relationship
Board size *(BSIZE)*	When large boards bring enhanced monitoring abilities, they can encourage (discourage) dividend payments under the outcome (substitution) hypothesis (Kanojia & Bhatia, 2022). Contrastingly, a large board can entrench a CEO by allowing directors to free-ride. In such a scenario, over-sized boards can reduce (increase) dividends under the outcome (substitution) approach (Chintrakarn et al., 2020) **H1:** Board size has a significant association with the level of dividends
Board independence *(BIND)*	Consistent with their monitoring and advisory role, independent directors can urge the management to distribute higher dividend payments when the outcome hypothesis is applicable (Kanojia & Bhatia, 2022). Conversely, when the assumptions of the substitution hypothesis are valid, independent boards will negatively affect the payout amount (Nazar, 2021) **H2:** Board independence has a significant association with the level of dividends
CEO duality *(CEODUAL)*	A combined CEO-Chair position is associated with magnified power. As the board chair, CEOs can misuse their position to influence the board to accept corporate policies that are consistent with their interests (Smith et al., 2017). Therefore, under the assumptions of the outcome hypothesis, a joint CEO-Chair will curtail dividend payments (Abu Afifa et al., 2024). In contrast, the substitution hypothesis stipulates that such entrenched CEOs will distribute more dividends to reduce expropriation concerns (Bhatia & Gulati, 2022) **H3:** CEO duality has a significant association with the level of dividends
Board gender diversity *(BGD)*	The varied viewpoints brought by women directors can strengthen board independence (Ye et al., 2019). As a result, gender-diverse boards can question the cash retention policy of gender-diverse boards more, thereby resulting in higher payouts under the assumptions of the outcome hypothesis (Shaheen et al., 2023). On the other hand, a negative linkage between board gender diversity and dividends is anticipated when the substitution hypothesis is considered (Nadia & Hanafi, 2023) **H4:** Board gender diversity has a significant association with the level of dividends
Controlling shareholder *(PROMOTER)*	In order to pursue their self-serving activities, controlling shareholders can use their significant voting to push for the retention of excess cash by making lower dividend payments (Pinto & Rastogi, 2022). On the other hand, these owners can also be forced to distribute higher dividends to assuage expropriation concerns of outside minority investors and establish a capital market reputation for acquiring funds at a reasonable cost (Kuo, 2017) **H5:** Controlling shareholder has a significant association with the level of dividends

(continued)

Table 6.1 (continued)

Variables	Relationship
Non-controlling large shareholders *(NPD)*	As external blockholders in Indian corporations (Arora & Srivastava, 2021), non-controlling large owners can use their significant voting rights to question and dispute any apparent value-destroying decisions being implemented by corporate insiders (Pindado et al., 2012; Gonzalez et al., 2017, 2019). In essence, the presence of additional blockholders in the ownership structure can result in higher dividend levels (Pindado et al., 2012). In comparison, their disciplinary role can substitute for cash dividend payments in managing agency conflicts (Gonzalez et al., 2017) **H6:** Non-controlling large shareholders have a significant association with the level of dividends
Auditor independence *(NAF)*	The quality and reliability of the financial statement can be weakened when the proportion of non-audit fees is high as auditors may become reticent in disclosing any financial misrepresentations for fear of loss of a substantial income source (Dhaliwal et al., 2008). As a result, the users of audited reports cannot rely on these compromised financials to scrutinize managerial actions (Hendijani Zadeh, 2022). Therefore, a higher non-audit fees to audit fees ratio can reduce cash dividends under the outcome model. However, under the substitution approach, the company contracting non-audit services from their auditor will make larger payouts to lower expropriation concerns for building a reputation in the financial markets **H7:** A higher proportion of non-audit fees has a significant association with the level of dividends

Notes This table describes the hypotheses for examining the relationship between corporate governance and the level of dividends

Kuo, 2017). Third, growth opportunities *(GROWTH)* are considered in the empirical model as a control. Growing firms are likely to retain their earnings to minimize using expensive external funds to finance their expansionary activities (Aoki, 2014; Rozeff, 1982). However, there is also the possibility that high-growth companies, particularly those operating in weaker institutional regimes, pay dividends to build investor trust (Kuo, 2017).

Fourth, as companies with larger cash holdings (*CASH*) are more likely to make higher cash dividend payouts (Amidu & Abor, 2006; Aoki, 2014), we control for their effects in the empirical specification. Fifth, the impact of profitability *(PROFIT)* is examined since profitable companies are better positioned to distribute higher dividends (Amidu & Abor, 2006; Shaheen et al., 2023). The influence of business risk *(BRISK)* is also addressed as corporations with severe earnings volatility are constrained in making more dividend payouts due to uncertainty about their future profits (Saeed & Sameer, 2017). In addition, the effect of leverage *(LEV)* is also considered since debt restricts the flexibility of corporations to pay out dividends owing to their contractual obligation to make periodic interest and principal payments (Aoki, 2014).

Share repurchases *(SRTA)* are also included as a control variable. They represent an alternate form of payouts that can also help in minimizing the agency problem of free cash flow (Jiraporn & Lee, 2018). Therefore, they can substitute for cash dividend payments in distributing surplus cash to equity investors (Grullon & Michaely, 2002; Lee & Suh, 2011). However, Jagannathan et al. (2000) note that, unlike cash dividends, share repurchases provide flexibility and are generally used to dispense temporary increases in cash flows. In comparison, cash dividend payments tend to be rigid and bind a firm with a seemingly irreversible commitment (Anwar et al., 2017; Kuo, 2017). Consequently, they are normally paid out of sustainable and permanent increases in cash flows (Brook et al., 1998; Guay & Harford, 2000). Thus, share repurchases and dividends can also concurrently occur since they are disbursed out of different components of cash flows (Jiang et al., 2013). Additionally, managerial agency cost *(AGENCYC)* is incorporated into the empirical model. When managerial agency costs are high, it can be anticipated that management can make lower payouts to retain funds for spending on expensive perquisites and providing handsome bonuses (Duygun et al., 2018; Pahi & Yadav, 2022). Contrastingly, organizations with higher agency costs can also pay higher dividends to decrease expropriation concerns of outside minority investors (Flavin et al., 2021).

Lastly, the empirical investigation also takes into account industry and year effects. A concise description of all the control variables utilized in the study is provided in Table 6.2.

Research methodology

Lintner's (1956) partial adjustment model adopted for the current empirical study gives rise to the issue of dynamic endogeneity and serial correlation (Koussis & Makrominas, 2019). Endogeneity concerns can also occur because of corporate governance and control variables. The omission of an unobservable variable, such as managerial ability, which influences both dividend payouts and governance attributes, can result in a correlation between the independent variables and the error term. Therefore, system GMM is utilized for estimating Eq. 6.1 (Dahiya et al., 2023; Suman & Singh, 2022). Furthermore, a two-step estimator with Windmeijer's (2005) corrected robust standard errors is used to mitigate heteroskedasticity concerns. Prior to the commencement of the empirical analysis, the financial variables are winsorized at 1% to reduce the effect of extreme observations (Mendiratta et al., 2023).

Descriptive statistics

Table 6.3 demonstrates the summary statistics of all variables that are subjected to the empirical investigation. The dividend to total assets ratio (*DIVIDEND*) ranges from 0 to 0.2439 and has an average value of 0.0246. In contrast, the proportion of share repurchases (*SRTA*) is a meagre 0.0023, which suggests that they are a relatively lesser preferred form of payout to the equity shareholders for the sampled entities. The observations about corporate governance mechanisms and other explanatory variables are similar to those noted in Chapter 2.

Table 6.2 Summary of control variables used in examining the impact of corporate governance monitoring mechanisms on the level of dividends

Variables	Measurement	Data Source
Firm size *(FSIZE)*	Natural logarithm of total assets (Abu Afifa et al., 2024; Arora & Srivastava, 2021)	Datastream®
Firm age *(FAGE)*	Number of years since the firm's inception (Aoki, 2014; Kuo, 2017)	Datastream®
Growth opportunities *(GROWTH)*	Tobin's Q (Aoki, 2014; Nadia et al., 2023)	Bloomberg®
Cash holdings *(CASH)*	Cash and cash equivalents scaled by total assets (Ye et al., 2019; Zhu & Hou, 2022)	Bloomberg®, Datastream®
Profitability *(PROFIT)*	Ratio of net income to total assets (Duygun et al., 2018; Gyapong et al., 2021)	Datastream®
Business risk *(BRISK)*	Standard deviation of the profitability (*PROFIT*) over the last five years (Kuo, 2017; Zhu & Hou, 2022)	Datastream®
Leverage ratio *(LEV)*	Total debt to total assets ratio (Gonzalez et al., 2017; Ye et al., 2019)	Datastream®
Share repurchases *(SRTA)*	Amount of share repurchases to total assets ratio (Jiraporn & Lee, 2018; Pindado et al., 2012)	Datastream®
Agency costs *(AGENCYC)*	Ratio of a firm's SGA expenses to its annual sales (Duygun et al., 2018; Pahi & Yadav, 2022)	Datastream®

Notes This table gives an overview of the control variables that are used to examine the influence of corporate governance monitoring mechanisms on dividend payout levels

Multivariate regression analysis

Table 6.4 depicts the results from the empirical estimation of Eq. 6.1, which represents a modified partial adjustment model of Lintner (1956). Across all the empirical models, the partial adjustment in dividend payouts is evinced as it is noted that their current levels are significantly and positively affected by their previous year's amount. Further, the diagnostic tests yield that the use of the system GMM estimator is also appropriate. The Hansen J test is not significant and indicates that the system GMM-generated instruments are exogenous. The insignificant AR (2) test signals the absence of second-order autocorrelation. Lastly, the joint significance of variables is also supported by the significant Wald F statistic.

Table 6.3 Summary statistics of the dividends, corporate governance monitoring mechanisms, and other firm-level variables

Variables	Mean	Standard deviation	Minimum	Maximum
DIVIDEND	0.0246	0.0396	0	0.2439
BSIZE	9.5332	2.6236	3	22
BIND	51.5673	11.2074	0	100
CEODUAL	0.2975	0.4572	0	1
BGD	9.5712	8.1674	0	42.857
PROMOTER	56.7048	16.981	8.2	90
NPD	0.1174	0.322	0	1
NAF	0.3785	0.4605	0	2.6496
FSIZE	20.4334	1.4764	16.856	24.306
FAGE	38.737	23.4764	1	155
GROWTH	2.7242	2.4221	0.6562	13.779
CASH	0.078	0.1092	0.0008	0.6016
PROFIT	0.0816	0.0708	−0.1345	0.2623
BRISK	0.0346	0.0374	0.0027	0.2893
LEV	0.2214	0.1895	0	0.7268
SRTA	0.0023	0.0165	0	0.2924
AGENCYC	0.2419	0.1793	0.0075	0.9615

Notes This table shows the summary statistics of all the variables employed in the empirical analysis

Column 1 reports that board gender diversity (*BGD*) has a negative and statistically significant effect on dividend payout intensity (*DIVIDEND*). This observation provides evidence in favor of H4 and appears to be consistent with the assumptions of the substitution model. The improved board governance upon the addition of women directors can minimize managerial entrenchment and reduce the need to distribute excess cash through dividends for managing agency conflicts (Sanan, 2019; Ye et al., 2019). Female directors augment the independence of the board by bringing unique perspectives that tend to be different from the management (Gyapong et al., 2021; Pucheta-Martínez & Bel-Oms, 2016). In addition, their distinctive experiences can assist in examining a corporate matter from fresh and broad angles, which can lead to carefully deliberated and informed decisions (Campbell, 1996; Carter et al., 2003). Thus, gender-diverse boards lower the groupthink problem and ensure that corporate insiders' proposed allocation of corporate cash is not accepted blindly (Carter et al., 2010). Commensurately, the utility of dividend payments as a bonding mechanism is diminished when there is an increasing representation of women directors on the board.

In contrast, the observed findings can also be expounded under the premises of the outcome hypothesis. In this regard, La Porta et al. (2000) state that superior corporate governance mechanisms will result in higher payouts, particularly when the firm has low growth prospects. However, when the company possesses attractive

Table 6.4 Corporate governance monitoring mechanisms and dividends: Main regression analysis

Dependent variable: *DIVIDEND*	Overall sample (2010–2019)	Pre-reform period (2010–2014)	Post-reform period (2015–2019)
Variables	(1)	(2)	(3)
L.DIVIDEND	0.474***	0.555***	0.241***
	(0.104)	(0.159)	(0.0914)
BSIZE	0.000100	0.000202	0.000149
	(0.000276)	(0.000211)	(0.000445)
BIND	−3.32e−05	−1.41e−05	−0.000188
	(4.75e−05)	(4.98e−05)	(0.000122)
CEODUAL	−0.00130	−0.00317	−0.00182
	(0.00230)	(0.00302)	(0.00527)
BGD	−0.000122*	−0.000159**	0.000125
	(0.0000668)	(0.0000786)	(0.000148)
PROMOTER	−7.25e−07	−5.38e−06	4.59e−05
	(2.84e−05)	(3.95e−05)	(0.000220)
NPD	−0.000359	−0.000312	0.00291
	(0.00156)	(0.00178)	(0.00459)
NAF	−0.000274	−0.000253	−0.0105
	(0.00147)	(0.00194)	(0.00867)
FSIZE	0.00117**	8.46e−06	0.00201*
	(0.000546)	(0.000585)	(0.00110)
FAGE	3.54e−05	5.36e−05	9.41e−05
	(3.13e−05)	(3.75e−05)	(5.87e−05)
GROWTH	0.00242**	0.00183	0.000913
	(0.00104)	(0.00200)	(0.00138)
CASH	0.0222	0.0388*	0.00999
	(0.0208)	(0.0234)	(0.0160)
PROFIT	0.104***	0.110***	0.131***
	(0.0180)	(0.0274)	(0.0350)
BRISK	−0.0122	−0.0324	−0.00679
	(0.0237)	(0.0323)	(0.0296)
LEV	−0.00228	0.0100	−0.0255**
	(0.00691)	(0.0125)	(0.0118)
SRTA	−0.0572	−0.0398	−0.0369
	(0.0347)	(0.0597)	(0.0446)
AGENCYC	0.00768	0.0111	0.0229
	(0.00803)	(0.00934)	(0.0163)
Constant	−0.0270**	−0.0118	−0.0306

(continued)

Table 6.4 (continued)

Dependent variable: *DIVIDEND*	Overall sample (2010–2019)	Pre-reform period (2010–2014)	Post-reform period (2015–2019)
Variables	(1)	(2)	(3)
	(0.0123)	(0.0122)	(0.0321)
Industry & Year FE	Yes	Yes	Yes
Wald F (p-value)	77.84 (0.000)	60.94 (0.000)	19.80 (0.000)
AR(2) (p-value)	0.994 (0.320)	−0.0427 (0.966)	0.466 (0.641)
Hansen J (p-value)	143.5 (0.497)	62.47 (0.354)	66.99 (0.477)

Notes This table depicts the findings of the two-step system GMM estimation of Eq. 6.1. Column 1 demonstrates the results when the empirical examination is conducted for the entire sample from FY 2010-FY 2019. Column 2 presents findings for the period before the institution of the Companies Act, 2013 (Pre-reform period). Column 3 shows the results for years when the Companies Act, 2013 is in the application (Post-reform period). Windmeijer's (2005) corrected-robust standard errors are indicated in parentheses. ***, **, and * denote significance at 1, 5, and 10% levels, respectively

growth opportunities, robust corporate governance mechanisms can curtail dividend payments by assuring minority shareholders that the retained funds will only be re-invested in optimal projects (Chen, 2008; Chen et al., 2009). As gender-diverse boards are associated with enhanced independence (Sanan, 2019; Ye et al., 2019), small shareholders can accept lower dividends from growing corporations when they have a high percentage of women directors. Moreover, female directors themselves can exercise conservatism and encourage the build-up of precautionary cash reserves against unexpected exigencies to avoid under-funding future investment opportunities (García-Meca et al., 2022; Saeed & Sameer, 2017). Consequently, these directors will lead to lower payouts when the business enterprises have significant future growth options.

The conflicting explanations regarding the negative effect of board gender diversity on dividends can be clarified by considering a firm's environmental conditions. The distinction between various organizational contexts based on contingency factors, such as growth opportunities, can help better understand the observed inverse relationship. The corresponding empirical examination has been presented in Sect. 6.4. In relation to the main effects of other governance devices, Column 1 does not find any adequate statistical support in favor of them.

As far as the control variables are concerned, it is noted from Column 1 that large corporations (*FSIZE*) pay higher dividends (*DIVIDEND*). Since such firms are well-established in the capital markets, they can easily acquire funds at a reasonable cost (Ben-Nasr, 2015; Shamsabadi et al., 2016). Therefore, the need to maintain a huge cash buffer is reduced in big companies, which allows them to afford to make larger dividend payments. In addition, it is also inferred that high-growth firms (*GROWTH*) distribute more dividends (*DIVIDEND*). Business enterprises can employ cash dividends to signal the investors about their growth prospects (Abreu & Gulamhussen, 2013; Pham et al., 2021). Additionally, higher payouts can be utilized by growing corporations to establish a capital market reputation for accessing external financing at a lower cost (La Porta et al., 2000). Lastly, Column 1 also demonstrates that profitable ventures (*PROFIT*) are associated with higher dividends (*DIVIDEND*) as profitable ventures are able to distribute more dividends. This finding also aligns with Lintner's (1956) partial adjustment model, which states that target payout levels are a function of a corporation's net earnings.

The main empirical examination is also extended to take into account the enactment of the Companies Act, 2013 during the sampled period by segregating the firm-year observations into pre-reform and post-reform periods. The pre-reform period includes years from FY 2010 to FY 2014.[2] The post-reform period encompasses years after FY 2014. The specified analysis can help in ascertaining if there is any variation in the effectiveness of monitoring mechanisms post the institution of strengthened corporate governance regulations. The relevant results have been reported in Columns 3 and 4 of Table 6.4. They indicate that the negative influence of board gender diversity (*BGD*) on dividend payouts (*DIVIDEND*) is stronger only in the pre-reform period. Its effect weakens and turns insignificant after the introduction of mandated board gender quotas by the new Companies Act. Further, it is noted that none of the corporate governance devices significantly impact the level of cash dividends in the post-reform period.

6.3 Additional Analyses

6.3.1 Role of CEO Tenure

The empirical study is supplemented with additional analyses to determine if the effectiveness of corporate governance monitoring mechanisms depends upon different organizational contexts. The first contextual variable that is taken into account is the length of a CEO's tenure. CEOs who have occupied their current position for a considerable time tend to accumulate substantial power over the course of their tenure (Iatridis, 2012). Since the long-tenured CEOs have managed to ensure successful and profitable operations over the years, the board of directors possesses an immense belief in their abilities (Lorsch & MacIver, 1989; Shen, 2003). Furthermore, their extended tenure also permits them to develop close-knit relationships with many board members (Chen et al., 2012; Goyal & Park, 2002). As a result, the board can be under the influence of long-tenured CEOs and is likely to be willing to support any policy proposed by them. In contrast, the actions of recently-appointed CEOs are continuously being evaluated and scrutinized by the board (Shen & Canella, 2002). Their discretion is also curtailed because they must work according to the board's mandate to retain their jobs (Zona, 2016).

Consistent with the previous discussion, it can be understood that managerial entrenchment is more salient when the CEOs have completed a long term in office.

[2] Since the new Companies Act was introduced in the middle of the financial year on August 30, 2013, the pre-reform period is extended until the end of FY 2014 (Sarkar & Selarka, 2021).

As dividends reduce surplus cash at the disposal of CEOs, it can be anticipated that the impact of corporate governance on payout levels will be stronger when a firm has a long-tenured CEO at the helm. In order to investigate this prediction, firm-year observations are divided using the quartile values of the CEO's tenure. The results for corporations with short-tenured, medium-tenured, and long-tenured CEOs are depicted in Table 6.5.

Columns 1 and 2 show that corporate governance monitoring mechanisms do not significantly affect dividend payouts (*DIVIDEND*) in the case of short-tenured and medium-tenured CEOs. Interestingly, it can be noted from Column 3 that board gender diversity (*BGD*) positively affects the amount of cash dividends (*DIVIDEND*) when the CEOs have occupied their present post for a longer time. As discussed earlier, the command of CEOs over board decision-making magnifies with their tenure (Iatridis, 2012; Shen, 2003). They can misuse this significant power that has been acquired over time to push for the retention of excess cash against its distribution to derive private benefits. In light of the increasing entrenchment of CEOs, enhanced gender diversity on the board can augment its independence. By contributing viewpoints that are distinctive from those of management, women directors are able to reduce the problem of groupthink and, thereby, diminish the long-tenured CEO's influence over the board (Pucheta-Martínez & Bel-Oms, 2016; Ye et al., 2019). Furthermore, the deliberation over different perspectives provides scope that such CEOs will be questioned about the rationale behind their proposed dividend policy (Carter et al., 2010). As a result, a higher percentage of female directors on the board can limit the discretion of powerful CEOs over the use and disbursal of surplus cash by urging higher dividend payouts.

Column 3 also shows that board size (*BSIZE*) has a positive effect on *DIVIDEND* when CEOs are in the late stages of their tenure. Although long-tenured CEOs exercise considerable influence over the board, it can become difficult to gather support from all when there are many sitting directors (Haynes et al., 2019). In addition, an increase in the board's size also strengthens its monitoring capabilities (Klein, 2002; Monks & Minnow, 1995). When multiple members are on the board, the likelihood that at least one of them will probe long-term CEOs about their surplus cash distribution strategy increases (Upadhyay & Sriram, 2011). Furthermore, oversized boards also provide an enriched set of knowledge and expertise which can aid in implementing value-maximizing dividend decisions (Anderson et al., 2004). Thus, large-size boards will encourage a higher level of cash dividend payments to constrain the expropriation of corporate resources by long-tenured CEOs. This result is consistent with the theoretical arguments underlying H1.

Altogether, these findings seem to provide evidence in favor of the outcome hypothesis. The improved governance associated with gender-diverse and large boards results in higher payouts when CEO entrenchment becomes severe. This inference with regard to board gender diversity in the case of long-tenured CEOs contrast with its reported negative effect in the main regression analysis. As emphasized earlier, the outcome model does state that highly-governed companies with

Table 6.5 Corporate governance monitoring mechanisms and dividends: Role of CEO tenure

Dependent variable: *DIVIDEND*	Short-tenured CEOs	Medium-tenured CEOs	Long-tenured CEOs
Variables	(1)	(2)	(3)
L.DIVIDEND	0.393***	0.705***	0.345***
	(0.136)	(0.136)	(0.109)
BSIZE	−0.000721	0.000150	0.000793*
	(0.000742)	(0.000228)	(0.000462)
BIND	0.000100	−7.40e−05	−3.27e−05
	(0.000157)	(4.78e−05)	(0.000140)
CEODUAL	0.00801	−0.000662	−0.000968
	(0.0133)	(0.00416)	(0.00611)
BGD	−0.000255	−0.000113	0.00100*
	(0.000223)	(7.09e−05)	(0.000577)
PROMOTER	4.66e−05	−1.60e−05	−9.50e−05
	(0.000143)	(4.15e−05)	(0.000131)
NPD	0.00396	0.000379	−0.00111
	(0.00426)	(0.00167)	(0.00446)
NAF	−0.00644	−0.000503	−0.00194
	(0.00529)	(0.00167)	(0.00533)
FSIZE	0.00153	0.000702	0.00179
	(0.00174)	(0.000577)	(0.00135)
FAGE	2.34e−05	7.84e−06	6.84e−05
	(7.37e−05)	(3.07e−05)	(6.59e−05)
GROWTH	0.00120	0.000615	0.00149
	(0.00251)	(0.000596)	(0.00111)
CASH	0.0207	0.00883	0.0437
	(0.0532)	(0.0234)	(0.0475)
PROFIT	0.167***	0.0680**	0.208***
	(0.0593)	(0.0291)	(0.0591)
BRISK	−0.0640	−0.0264	0.0523
	(0.0743)	(0.0241)	(0.0497)
LEV	−0.0144	−0.00232	−7.15e−05
	(0.0240)	(0.00636)	(0.0226)
SRTA	−0.0516	−0.0717	−0.238***
	(0.0599)	(0.0813)	(0.0913)
AGENCYC	0.0130	0.00828	0.0340
	(0.0418)	(0.0104)	(0.0207)
Constant	−0.0280	−0.0154	−0.0540*

(continued)

Table 6.5 (continued)

Dependent variable: *DIVIDEND*	Short-tenured CEOs	Medium-tenured CEOs	Long-tenured CEOs
Variables	(1)	(2)	(3)
	(0.0356)	(0.0129)	(0.0303)
Industry & Year FE	Yes	Yes	Yes
Wald F (p-value)	21.27 (0.000)	107.86 (0.000)	28.22 (0.000)
AR (2) (p-value)	0.823 (0.410)	1.388 (0.165)	0.457 (0.648)
Hansen J (p-value)	52.64 (0.335)	102.3 (0.473)	132.1 (0.480)

Notes This table presents the findings from the empirical of Eq. 6.1 when the sample is partitioned using the quartile values of CEO tenure. Short-tenured CEOs correspond to years of CEO tenure in the lower quartile (CEO tenure < 2.416667 years). Years of CEO tenure in the upper quartile are grouped as long-tenured CEOs (CEO tenure > 18.88333 years). Sample values in the middle two quartiles are taken together as medium-tenured CEOs (CEO tenure from 2.416667 to 18.88333 years). Windmeijer's (2005) corrected-robust standard errors are reported in parentheses. ***, **, and * indicate significance at 1, 5, and 10% levels, respectively

significant growth opportunities can pay low dividends (La Porta et al., 2000). Therefore, the subsequent additional analyses are based on specific firm characteristics that can also provide an indication of an entity's growth stage.

6.3.2 *Role of Firm Size*

A smaller corporation tends to have abundant profitable investment opportunities to expand and grow (Kuo, 2017). However, relative to a large firm, its access to external financing is limited and costly as it usually has a lower reputation in the financial markets (Baker & Kilincarslan, 2019; Ooi, 2001). As a result, the conservation of earnings is desirable in small entities to minimize their reliance on external capital for financing their future growth opportunities. In comparison, large-sized companies are usually in the maturity stage with abysmal growth opportunities because of which they have surplus cash available at the discretion of corporate insiders (Anwer et al., 2020; Jensen, 1986).

Considering that there are differences in growth prospects and availability of excess cash between companies with varying scales of operations, it can be expected that the impact of corporate governance on dividend distribution will be contingent upon a corporation's size. The empirical study tests this prediction by disaggregating the sample based on the quartile values of the firm size (Prakash et al., 2024). The results for small-sized, medium-sized, and large-sized companies of differing sizes are shown in Table 6.6.

It can be observed from Column 1 that the negative effect of board gender diversity (*BGD*) on dividend payout intensity (*DIVIDEND*), as observed in the primary regression analysis, is prominent in smaller firms. As small-sized corporations have

Table 6.6 Corporate governance monitoring mechanisms and dividends: Role of firm size

Dependent variable: *DIVIDEND*	Small-sized firms	Medium-sized firms	Large-sized firms
Variables	(1)	(2)	(3)
L.DIVIDEND	0.438***	0.455***	0.289*
	(0.109)	(0.0999)	(0.173)
BSIZE	−0.00142	0.000263	4.33e−05
	(0.00108)	(0.000319)	(0.000857)
BIND	−2.53e−05	−7.67e−05	3.14e−05
	(0.000280)	(5.58e−05)	(0.000100)
CEODUAL	−0.00816	−0.00441	0.00173
	(0.0106)	(0.00280)	(0.00682)
BGD	−0.000505**	−1.49e−05	0.000128
	(0.000219)	(9.62e−05)	(0.000314)
PROMOTER	−0.000151	−1.49e−05	4.84e−05
	(0.000383)	(4.54e−05)	(8.26e−05)
NPD	−0.000194	−0.00200	0.00135
	(0.00556)	(0.00216)	(0.00233)
NAF	−0.00451	−0.00166	−0.00217
	(0.00826)	(0.00220)	(0.00394)
FSIZE	0.00160	0.000134	−2.49e−05
	(0.00531)	(0.00126)	(0.00125)
FAGE	6.45e−05	2.73e−05	3.43e−05
	(0.000150)	(3.19e−05)	(8.85e−05)
GROWTH	0.00149	0.00238*	0.00356
	(0.00117)	(0.00121)	(0.00271)
CASH	0.0350	0.00888	0.00591
	(0.0476)	(0.0159)	(0.0485)
PROFIT	0.245***	0.0685**	0.0945*
	(0.0729)	(0.0284)	(0.0511)
BRISK	−0.0990	−0.0446	0.0489
	(0.0809)	(0.0296)	(0.0430)
LEV	0.00975	−0.0117	−0.0230
	(0.0203)	(0.00898)	(0.0148)
SRTA	−0.0656	−0.0208	0.131
	(0.110)	(0.0307)	(0.203)
AGENCYC	0.0256	0.00589	0.0202
	(0.0230)	(0.00892)	(0.0506)
Constant	−0.0212	0.00521	−0.00348
	(0.0967)	(0.0280)	(0.0305)

(continued)

Table 6.6 (continued)

Dependent variable: *DIVIDEND*	Small-sized firms	Medium-sized firms	Large-sized firms
Variables	(1)	(2)	(3)
Industry & Year FE	Yes	Yes	Yes
Wald F (p-value)	971.5 (0.000)	83.79 (0.000)	47.89 (0.000)
AR (2) (p-value)	0.387 (0.698)	0.190 (0.849)	1.647 (0.100)
Hansen J (p-value)	72.23 (0.404)	194.5 (0.376)	57.78 (0.446)

Notes This table summarizes the findings from the empirical estimation of Eq. 6.1 for companies with differing ranges of firm size. The values of firm size in the bottom quartile are sorted into small-sized firms (firm size < 19.41277). Observations in the upper quartile constitute the group of large-sized firms (firm size > 21.27541). The remaining sample values in the middle two quartiles are designated as medium-sized firms (firm size from 19.41277 to 21.27541). Parentheses show Windmeijer's (2005) corrected-robust standard errors. ***, **, and * report significance at 1, 5, and 10% levels, respectively

more scope for growth (Kuo, 2017), women directors can exercise conservatism in dividend policy to mitigate the employment of costly external capital (García-Meca et al., 2022; Saeed & Sameer, 2017). They can encourage the retention of surplus cash against its distribution in smaller entities to provide a cheaper source of funds for financing all their investment requirements. Further, a higher percentage of female directors makes boards more effective and independent, which can assure small shareholders that their interests will be protected (Sanan, 2019; Ye et al., 2019). Consequently, outside minority equity investors will be willing to forgo dividends in favor of re-investment of profits when the boards of smaller companies exhibit high gender diversity (Chen, 2008; Chen et al., 2009). This finding also aligns with La Porta's exposition of the outcome hypothesis, which delineates that highly-governed corporations can pay out lower dividends when they possess good growth opportunities (La Porta et al., 2000). In addition, Columns 2 and 3 suggest that none of the corporate governance variables have a salient impact on dividend payout intensity.

6.3.3 *Role of Firm Age*

According to the lifecycle theory, a younger firm is usually a growing enterprise that generates inadequate profits for financing its expanding operations. Further, young companies are quite unestablished as they have a limited operating history, due to which they can raise only costly external financing (Brockman & Unlu, 2011; Fama & French, 2001). In contrast, mature entities have declining growth opportunities set but substantial internal funds that the corporate insiders can expropriate for pursuing their personal goals (Kuo, 2017).

Corollary to the preceding discourse, it is inferred that the growth prospects and severity of the free cash flow problem are determined by a firm's age. Consequently, the impact of corporate governance monitoring mechanisms on dividend levels is also anticipated to be contingent upon a corporation's lifecycle stage. In order to examine this assertion, the sampled observations are partitioned using quartile values of a company's age. The corresponding findings from the empirical estimation of Eq. 6.1, which is undertaken for younger, middle-aged, and older corporations, are given in Table 6.7.

In relation to younger firms, Column 1 demonstrates that dividend payouts (*DIVIDEND*) are curtailed when a higher payment toward non-audit fees is made (*NAF*). This result evinces H7 and suggests that non-audit services can be of value for corporations that are in their initial years of operations. Auditors are in a position to provide client-specific expertise that can help the company improve its performance (Carcello et al., 2002; Lai & Krishnan, 2009). They usually gather a significant amount of information about the client's operations over multiple audits (Cai et al., 2016; Dhaliwal et al., 2006). Furthermore, the auditor also possesses vast knowledge about different industries from auditing companies across various sectors (Elaoud & Jarboui, 2017). Therefore, auditors can leverage the accumulated knowledge repository to advise younger businesses on their cash management and distribution policies by providing non-audit services. The contracted auditor will consider high investment opportunities and the industrial condition of young companies and accordingly guide them to conserve cash by lowering payouts.

Columns 2 and 3 indicate that corporate governance mechanisms are not significantly associated with dividend levels in middle-aged and older corporations.

6.3.4 Role of Firm Growth Opportunities

A growth firm has a colossal requirement for financial resources to undertake all its investment opportunities (Aoki, 2014; Rozeff, 1982). However, the external capital providers have less knowledge about the true worth of these future growth options, due to which they may be willing to supply funds at a higher rate only (Myers & Majluf, 1984). Therefore, retention of earnings is desirable for growing corporations to finance their expansionary operations. Consistent with empirical results obtained in previous sub-sections concerning small-sized and younger corporations, it can be presumed that the linkage between corporate governance mechanisms and dividend payouts is inverse in the case of a high-growth company. Conversely, the favorable impact of corporate governance mechanisms on dividend payments should be pronounced in low-growth business ventures to mitigate the misuse of excess free cash flow by corporate insiders(La Porta et al., 2000; Shamsabadi et al., 2016).

The empirical investigation uncovers the role of corporate governance devices in companies with differing levels of growth opportunities by splitting the firm-year observations into sub-groups using the quartile values of Tobin's Q. Tobin's Q is employed as a measure to indicate a corporation's growth prospects. The relevant findings from the empirical estimation of Eq. 6.1 for low-growth, moderate-growth, and high-growth firms are summarized in Table 6.8.

Table 6.7 Corporate governance monitoring mechanisms and dividends: Role of firm age

Dependent variable: *DIVIDEND*	Younger firms	Middle-aged firms	Older firms
Variables	(1)	(2)	(3)
L.DIVIDEND	0.650***	0.284***	0.687***
	(0.106)	(0.107)	(0.0723)
BSIZE	1.09e−05	0.000115	−0.000133
	(0.000687)	(0.000342)	(0.000303)
BIND	0.000100	−4.81e−05	−2.41e−05
	(7.91e−05)	(0.000127)	(6.88e−05)
CEODUAL	−0.00574	−0.000578	0.00279
	(0.00546)	(0.00204)	(0.00320)
BGD	−7.95e−05	−6.77e−05	0.000145
	(0.000178)	(0.000123)	(0.000261)
PROMOTER	−0.000112	2.56e−05	−2.95e−06
	(9.76e−05)	(0.000183)	(8.75e−05)
NPD	−0.000468	−0.00165	0.00101
	(0.00406)	(0.00276)	(0.00204)
NAF	−0.0126**	−0.00428	0.00165
	(0.00542)	(0.00299)	(0.00336)
FSIZE	0.00141	0.00206*	0.000438
	(0.00201)	(0.00108)	(0.000837)
FAGE	9.53e−05	3.32e−05	3.59e−05
	(0.000255)	(9.00e−05)	(7.83e−05)
GROWTH	0.00306*	0.00221	0.00150
	(0.00174)	(0.00139)	(0.00126)
CASH	0.0418	0.0145	0.0197
	(0.0377)	(0.0284)	(0.0332)
PROFIT	0.134**	0.140***	0.106**
	(0.0640)	(0.0486)	(0.0510)
BRISK	−0.000722	−0.0753*	−0.00471
	(0.0328)	(0.0442)	(0.0326)
LEV	0.0173	−0.00681	0.00239
	(0.0144)	(0.0119)	(0.0113)
SRTA	−0.160	−0.0175	−0.0784
	(0.108)	(0.0462)	(0.0860)
AGENCYC	2.26e−05	0.0255	0.0162
	(0.0200)	(0.0161)	(0.0172)
Constant	−0.0257	−0.0389	−0.0219
	(0.0414)	(0.0295)	(0.0229)

(continued)

Table 6.7 (continued)

Dependent variable: *DIVIDEND*	Younger firms	Middle-aged firms	Older firms
Variables	(1)	(2)	(3)
Industry & Year FE	Yes	Yes	Yes
Wald F (p-value)	42.41 (0.000)	41.40 (0.000)	178.1 (0.000)
AR (2) (p-value)	0.484 (0.628)	0.731 (0.465)	0.417 (0.677)
Hansen J (p-value)	100.6 (0.466)	134.3 (0.270)	69.79 (0.485)

Notes This table depicts the results from the empirical estimation of Eq. 6.1 when the sample is segregated using the quartile values of firm age. Firm-year observations that are less than the value of the first quartile are grouped as younger firms (firm age < 21.79167 years). Observations exceeding the value quartile three are sorted into the sample of older firms (firm age > 53 years). The remaining sample values that range from quartile one to quartile three are classified as middle-aged firms (firm age from 21.79167 to 53 years). Parentheses demonstrate Windmeijer's (2005) corrected-robust standard errors. ***, **, and * denote significance at 1, 5, and 10% levels, respectively

Column 1 depicts that board size (*BSIZE*) has a positive impact on dividend payout intensity (*DIVIDEND*) in low-growth firms. Low-growth corporations often produce large amounts of free cash flows, which is in excess of their investment requirements (La Porta et al., 2000; Shamsabadi et al., 2016). In light of the heightened free cash flow issue in low-growth entities, oversized boards can discharge enhanced scrutiny on corporate insiders' actions. An increase in the number of sitting directors raises the probability that any one of them will dispute managers about their cash management and distribution policies (Klein, 2002; Upadhyay & Sriram, 2011). Furthermore, larger boards engage in extended deliberation, which allows their members to probe the executives and gather more information about their decisions (Upadhyay & Sriram, 2011). In addition, such boards also provide an enhanced supply of expertise, which can aid in making informed dividend decisions (Anderson et al., 2004). Therefore, large boards can direct the distribution of excess cash through the payment of dividends in low-growth corporations.

It can also be noted from Column 1 that CEO duality (*CEODUAL*) positively influences *DIVIDEND* in low-growth firms. This result contravenes theoretical arguments underlining H3 and points toward the stewardship role of CEOs. According to the stewardship theory, managers are committed to pursuing organizational goals and are intrinsically motivated by opportunities for growth and authority (Donaldson & Davis, 1991; Muth & Donaldson, 1998). Consequently, granting clear and higher power to the CEO by assigning them the Chairman's role can incentivize them to work hard and implement value-maximizing decisions (Davis et al., 1997). Additionally, a dual CEO is in possession of firm- and industry-specific knowledge, which can assist in formulating better corporate policies (Finkelstein & D'aveni, 1994; Tian & Lau., 2001). Consequently, as good stewards of corporate resources, a joint CEO-Chair can disburse excess cash by making higher payouts.

Interestingly, Column 3 of Table 6.8 also evinces the steward role of CEOs as it is inferred that CEO duality (*CEODUAL*) is associated with lower dividend payments (*DIVIDEND*) in high-growth firms. In order to finance future growth options at a

Table 6.8 Corporate governance monitoring mechanisms and dividends: Role of firm growth opportunities

Dependent variable: *DIVIDEND*	Low-growth firms	Moderate-growth firms	High-growth firms
Variables	(1)	(2)	(3)
L.DIVIDEND	0.355*	0.585***	0.400***
	(0.188)	(0.113)	(0.0935)
BSIZE	0.000476**	0.000157	−0.00147
	(0.000232)	(0.000262)	(0.00104)
BIND	−3.32e−05	4.06e−05	−0.000280
	(4.07e−05)	(3.68e−05)	(0.000281)
CEODUAL	0.00488*	−0.00311	−0.0176*
	(0.00254)	(0.00286)	(0.0100)
BGD	1.66e−05	3.17e−06	−0.000479**
	(6.55e−05)	(6.08e−05)	(0.000234)
PROMOTER	1.26e−05	1.37e−05	−9.79e−05
	(3.21e−05)	(7.57e−05)	(0.000152)
NPD	−0.00104	0.000163	0.00471
	(0.00100)	(0.00201)	(0.00904)
NAF	−0.00225	0.00153	−0.00941
	(0.00250)	(0.00501)	(0.00592)
FSIZE	−0.000418	−0.000286	0.00599**
	(0.000546)	(0.000502)	(0.00233)
FAGE	1.20e−05	0.0000393*	0.000210*
	(2.18e−05)	(0.0000201)	(0.000119)
GROWTH	−0.00198	0.00177*	0.00235**
	(0.00126)	(0.000979)	(0.000979)
CASH	0.0263	0.0281	0.00924
	(0.0252)	(0.0172)	(0.0294)
PROFIT	0.101**	0.0448**	0.317***
	(0.0508)	(0.0204)	(0.0698)
BRISK	0.0562	−0.0124	−0.00237
	(0.0431)	(0.0318)	(0.0356)
LEV	0.00190	−0.00166	0.0330
	(0.00534)	(0.00643)	(0.0210)
SRTA	−0.0168	−0.0373	−0.138
	(0.130)	(0.0625)	(0.0846)
AGENCYC	0.00358	0.00436	0.0658**
	(0.0113)	(0.00754)	(0.0313)

(continued)

Table 6.8 (continued)

Dependent variable: *DIVIDEND*	Low-growth firms	Moderate-growth firms	High-growth firms
Variables	(1)	(2)	(3)
Constant	0.00302	0.00305	−0.0951**
	(0.0133)	(0.0145)	(0.0433)
Industry & Year FE	Yes	Yes	Yes
Wald F (p-value)	28.99 (0.000)	75 (0.000)	35.74 (0.000)
AR (2) (p-value)	−0.312 (0.755)	1.113 (0.266)	0.190 (0.849)
Hansen J (p-value)	70.79 (0.234)	144.8 (0.194)	162.2 (0.289)

Notes This table shows the results from the empirical estimation of Eq. 6.1, which is undertaken for corporations in different stages of growth. Growth opportunities are measured by Tobin's Q. Hence, sample values in the lower quartile of Tobin's Q are assigned to the group of low-growth firms (Tobin's Q < 1.1659). Firm-year observations whose values are in the upper quartile of the Q ratio (Tobin's Q > 3.30618) constitute high-growth firms. The remaining observations in the middle two quartiles are classified as moderate-growth firms (Tobin's Q from 1.1659 to 3.30618). Windmeijer's (2005) corrected-robust standard errors are depicted in parentheses. ***, **, and * represent significance at 1, 5, and 10% levels, respectively

reasonable cost, a joint CEO-Chair can maintain a higher amount of internal funds by decreasing the payouts.

Column 3 also shows that the previously observed negative effect of board gender diversity (*BGD*) on *DIVIDEND* is more prominent in high-growth firms. As growing corporations require funds for expansion, women directors can adopt a conservative approach to dividend policy (García-Meca et al., 2022; Saeed & Sameer, 2017). They can encourage the build-up of cash against their distribution to finance all profitable investment projects of growth corporations. Further, outside minority investors can also be willing to pass up current dividends as a higher representation of female directors augment board monitoring, which reassures them that their interests will be protected (Gyapong et al., 2021; Ye et al., 2019). This finding is consistent with the outcome model of La Porta et al. (2000), under which the shareholders of a strongly governed growing corporation will be satisfied to receive lower current dividends since the re-investment into the firm's investment opportunities will yield higher future payouts.

6.3.5 Role of Firm Financial Condition

Financially distressed corporations have relatively low liquidity and profitability levels, which can also affect their ability to fulfill contractual obligations (Balasubramanian et al., 2019; Zhu & Hou, 2022). The weaker financial conditions and increased default risk can also cause external financing providers to charge a higher risk premium on the supplied capital (D'Mello et al., 2008; Gupta & Mahakud, 2022).

As a result, financial distress situations can put a limit on the expropriation of cash by corporate insiders (Walker & Wu, 2022). In contrast, financially healthy companies have a comfortable provision of both internal and external financing markets (Arslan-Ayaydin Ö et al., 2014; Marchica & Mura, 2010). Correspondingly, the free cash flow problem is likely to be exaggerated in financially healthy entities (Gyimah et al., 2021).

In summary, the extent of the prevalence of agency conflicts is likely to differ according to a corporation's financial condition. Therefore, the impact of corporate governance monitoring mechanisms on dividend payout intensity is also anticipated to depend upon the business's financial position. The empirical investigation evaluates the validity of this contention by categorizing the sample values based on the quartiles of the Altman-Z score. A higher Altman- Z score suggests that the business entity is at lower bankruptcy risk (Hu et al., 2019). The results from the empirical estimation of Eq. 6.1 for companies in financial distress, firms with moderate financial conditions, and financially sound entities are reported in Table 6.9.

It can be observed from Column 1 that the presence of non-controlling large shareholders (*NPD*) has a negative effect on the amount of cash dividends (*DIVIDEND*) in firms experiencing financial distress circumstances. In light of lower profitability and costly access to outside financing, the payment of dividends causes decreased corporate liquidity, which can curtail investment in optimal projects (Pathan et al., 2016). Consequently, additional blockholders can utilize their significant voting rights to persuade the management of financially weaker companies to build precautionary cash reserves by minimizing payouts (Gonzalez et al., 2017; Jiang et al., 2019). Furthermore, their concentrated holdings also incentivize them to monitor the allocation of cash by the corporate insiders continuously, thereby lowering investors' expropriation concerns (Pindado et al., 2012). Therefore, multiple large shareholders (MLS) are associated with lower payouts in financially distressed firms. This finding conforms with the governance role of non-controlling blockholders highlighted while formulating H6. Columns 2 and 3 of Table 6.9 also demonstrate that no corporate governance mechanism significantly influences the dividend payment of entities with better financial conditions.

6.3.6 Role of Industry Concentration

Highly concentrated markets lack the disciplinary role of competition, which allows the corporate insiders of companies operating in such industries to run the business as per their discretion (Cheng et al., 2013; Schmidt, 1997). On the other hand, the increasing competition in low-concentrated markets forces the management to abandon self-serving activities and improve the corporation's profitability (Gyimah et al., 2021; Pahi & Yadav, 2022). The failure to control high costs can make the firm incompetent by diminishing its profit margin (Pahi & Yadav, 2022; Schmidt, 1997). Thus, managerial entrenchment is regulated by competitive pressures in low-concentrated markets.

Table 6.9 Corporate governance monitoring mechanisms and dividends: Role of firm financial condition

Dependent variable: *DIVIDEND*	Financial distress conditions (Low Altman-Z scores)	Moderate financial conditions (Medium range Altman-Z scores)	Financially sound conditions (High Altman-Z scores)
Variables	(1)	(2)	(3)
L.DIVIDEND	0.587***	0.430***	0.469***
	(0.118)	(0.101)	(0.0836)
BSIZE	0.000134	0.000222	−0.00126
	(0.000102)	(0.000315)	(0.000812)
BIND	−1.05e−05	0.000103	−0.000321
	(2.25e−05)	(0.000114)	(0.000221)
CEODUAL	0.00176	−0.00235	0.000261
	(0.00159)	(0.00288)	(0.00694)
BGD	3.23e−05	5.37e−05	−0.000230
	(3.23e−05)	(0.000136)	(0.000239)
PROMOTER	−1.05e−05	9.60e−06	−0.000152
	(1.71e−05)	(0.000117)	(0.000111)
NPD	−0.000901*	0.00209	−0.00299
	(0.000515)	(0.00380)	(0.00592)
NAF	−0.000895	0.00406	−0.00468
	(0.00126)	(0.00358)	(0.00637)
FSIZE	0.000240	−0.000203	0.00657***
	(0.000336)	(0.000601)	(0.00171)
FAGE	−2.40e−06	3.53e−05	0.000137
	(9.34e−06)	(3.49e−05)	(9.96e−05)
GROWTH	0.000900	0.00214*	0.00219*
	(0.000863)	(0.00110)	(0.00117)
CASH	0.00200	0.0180	0.0183
	(0.0187)	(0.0202)	(0.0223)
PROFIT	0.0264**	0.0791***	0.307***
	(0.0115)	(0.0267)	(0.0714)
BRISK	0.00966	0.0151	−0.0542
	(0.0165)	(0.0269)	(0.0378)
LEV	−0.00488	−0.00307	0.0272
	(0.00485)	(0.00705)	(0.0229)
SRTA	0.333***	−0.0174	−0.129***
	(0.0986)	(0.0393)	(0.0476)
AGENCYC	0.000345	0.00850	0.0610**
	(0.00507)	(0.00633)	(0.0247)

(continued)

Table 6.9 (continued)

Dependent variable: *DIVIDEND*	Financial distress conditions (Low Altman-Z scores)	Moderate financial conditions (Medium range Altman-Z scores)	Financially sound conditions (High Altman-Z scores)
Variables	(1)	(2)	(3)
Constant	−0.00470	−0.00280	−0.0927*
	(0.00714)	(0.0180)	(0.0492)
Industry & Year FE	Yes	Yes	Yes
Wald F (p-value)	54.19 (0.000)	58.01 (0.000)	42.54 (0.000)
AR (2) (p-value)	−0.709 (0.479)	0.649 (0.516)	1.011 (0.312)
Hansen J (p-value)	71.77 (0.419)	108.5 (0.337)	144.6 (0.232)

Notes This table depicts the findings from the empirical estimation of Eq. 6.1 when the sample is disaggregated based on the quartile values of Altman Z-scores. A higher Z score indicates lower default risk (Hu et al., 2019). Correspondingly, sample values in the bottom quartile are grouped as firms in financial distress conditions (Z score < 2.056614). Observations in the top quartile are designated as firms with financially sound conditions (Z score > 7.727528). The middle two quartiles with remaining values are categorized as firms with moderate financial conditions (Z score from 2.056614 to 7.727528). Parentheses denote Windmeijer's (2005) corrected-robust standard errors. ***, **, and * show significance at 1, 5, and 10% levels, respectively

In line with the prior discourse, it can be expected that the impact of corporate governance attributes on cash dividends will be more prominent in the case of highly concentrated industries. The empirical examination tests this prediction by partitioning the firm-year observations using the quartile values of the Herfindahl–Hirschman Index (HHI), which indicates the severity of a concentration in a given market (Pahi & Yadav, 2022). The corresponding findings for companies affiliated with low-concentrated, medium-concentrated, and highly-concentrated markets are provided in Table 6.10.

It is observed from Columns 1 and 2 that corporate governance variables do not have a statistically significant impact on the payout levels (*DIVIDEND*) of firms operating in low-concentrated and medium-concentrated markets. However, Column 3 shows that board size (*BSIZE*) has a positive effect on the dividend levels (*DIVIDEND*) of companies that are a member of a highly concentrated industry. Oversized boards enhance monitoring capabilities and augment the supply of expertise available to the managers, which can guide them in making better decisions (Anderson et al., 2004; Klein, 2002). In light of increasing managerial entrenchment in concentrated markets that can result in the misuse of cash, large boards can push for a higher dividend distribution. It is also noted from Column 3 that controlling ownership percentage (*PROMOTER*) is also positively associated with *DIVIDEND*. As the risk of expropriation heightens in highly concentrated industries, promoters[3] can encourage dividend payments to assuage investors' concerns (Kuo, 2017). They may

[3] Promoters are considered as controlling shareholders in the Indian institutional context.

Table 6.10 Corporate governance monitoring mechanisms and dividends: Role of industry concentration

Dependent Vvariable: *DIVIDEND*	Low-concentrated industries	Medium-concentrated industries	Highly-concentrated industries
Variables	(1)	(2)	(3)
L.DIVIDEND	0.193*	0.397***	0.390***
	(0.102)	(0.127)	(0.0728)
BSIZE	−0.000253	0.000408	0.000700*
	(0.000439)	(0.000335)	(0.000413)
BIND	−0.000107	−8.07e−05	−8.59e−05
	(0.000148)	(7.50e−05)	(8.20e−05)
CEODUAL	−0.000266	−0.00554	−0.0102
	(0.00234)	(0.00917)	(0.00745)
BGD	−0.000214	−0.000145	9.54e−05
	(0.000237)	(0.000109)	(0.000128)
PROMOTER	5.24e−05	−8.72e−05	0.000145**
	(9.34e−05)	(7.52e−05)	(0.0000611)
NPD	0.00315	−0.000493	−0.000106
	(0.00465)	(0.00267)	(0.00252)
NAF	0.00827	−0.00284	−0.00118
	(0.00652)	(0.00367)	(0.00216)
FSIZE	0.00104	0.000826	0.00148
	(0.00101)	(0.000996)	(0.000994)
FAGE	0.000157**	3.24e−05	−5.22e−06
	(7.50e−05)	(5.83e−05)	(4.68e−05)
GROWTH	0.00153	0.00289**	0.00152
	(0.00182)	(0.00139)	(0.00164)
CASH	0.0157	0.0178	0.0458
	(0.0324)	(0.0311)	(0.0332)
PROFIT	0.177***	0.111***	0.106***
	(0.0564)	(0.0367)	(0.0349)
BRISK	−0.00775	−0.0421	−0.0772*
	(0.0484)	(0.0381)	(0.0457)
LEV	−0.00646	−0.00658	−0.0193*
	(0.0135)	(0.0149)	(0.0105)
SRTA	−0.0711**	−0.0366	−0.136**
	(0.0353)	(0.0716)	(0.0543)
AGENCYC	0.0149	0.00470	0.000102
	(0.0289)	(0.0273)	(0.0138)

(continued)

Table 6.10 (continued)

Dependent Vvariable: *DIVIDEND*	Low-concentrated industries	Medium-concentrated industries	Highly-concentrated industries
Variables	(1)	(2)	(3)
Constant	−0.0273	−0.0107	−0.0390
	(0.0215)	(0.0256)	(0.0252)
Industry & Year FE	Yes	Yes	Yes
Wald F (p-value)	18.13 (0.000)	36.71 (0.000)	45.42 (0.000)
AR (2) (p-value)	−0.129 (0.897)	0.318 (0.751)	1.259 (0.208)
Hansen J (p-value)	112.3 (0.229)	118.2 (0.236)	122.9 (0.384)

Notes This table summarizes the results from the empirical estimation of Eq. 6.1 when the sample is segregated based on the values of HHI. HHI indicates the degree of concentration in a specific industry. Firm-year observations below quartile one of HHI are sorted into low-concentrated industries (HHI < 0.0329862). Sample values above the quartile three of HHI make up the group of highly-concentrated industries (HHI > 0.0771521). The observations ranging from quartiles one to three are assigned to medium-concentrated industries (HHI from 0.0329862 to 0.0771521). Parentheses report Windmeijer's (2005) corrected-robust standard errors. ***, **, and * indicate significance at 1, 5, and 10% levels, respectively

use dividends as a bonding device to establish a capital market reputation and to minimize agency risk discount to the corporation's share value (Gomes, 2000; La Porta et al., 2000). In addition, a reduced discount rate will also prevent a diminution in the worth of their concentrated holdings (Kuo, 2017). This observation concerning the controlling owner aligns with the assumptions of the substitution hypothesis stated in H5.

6.4 Corporate Governance Monitoring Mechanisms and Dividend Stability

Lintner (1956) observes that corporations adopt a target payout ratio and partially adjust their dividend payments toward the target level each year. They avoid making drastic increments in dividend payouts unless they can be sustained by permanent increases in earnings. They are also reluctant to cut dividends when earnings diminish. Thus, firms prefer paying a steady stream of predictable dividends. Besides payout levels, stable dividends can serve as a mechanism to curb agency conflicts (Leary & Michaely, 2011; Suman & Singh, 2022). Regular and consistent dividend payments ensure that a firm is kept under continued scrutiny of capital market participants as it is forced to secure external financing frequently (Easterbrook, 1984). Consequently, the instances of expropriation of outside minority shareholders are minimized. Therefore, the payout policy should be rigid for dividends to be employed as an appropriate bonding mechanism.

In respect of the association between corporate governance mechanisms and dividend stability, it is again noted that they can either complement or substitute each other (La Porta et al., 2000; Leary & Michaely, 2011). Highly governed firms can enforce a stable payout policy to limit managerial expropriation (Allen et al., 2000). Thus, in this case, good governance practices will result in higher dividend smoothing.[4] Conversely, stable dividends and robust governance structures are alternate mechanisms for containing the problem of excess cash flow. Therefore, well-governed firms may exhibit lower dividend stability as smoothed dividends are required to a lesser extent for assuaging agency conflicts due to strengthened monitoring (Javakhadze et al., 2014; Koussis & Makrominas, 2019).

The empirical study is now extended to analyze the impact of corporate governance monitoring mechanisms on the extent of dividend smoothing. Correspondingly, the demeaned interaction term[5] between governance attributes and the lagged level of dividends is introduced in Eq. 6.1 to determine their effect on dividend stability. As the coefficient on the previous year's dividends alludes to the extent of smoothing, the interaction will capture the influence of corporate governance on their persistence or stability. The results from the empirical estimation of the augmented empirical model are presented in Table 6.11.

The existence of dividend smoothing is evinced as it is observed that current dividends (*DIVIDEND*) are positively affected by their previous year's values (*L.DIVIDEND*). Further, Column 1 reports that board independence weakens the positive association between the past dividend and contemporary dividend levels (*BIND x L.DIVIDEND*). Since independent directors are unaffiliated with the corporation and have reputational concerns, they tend to bring strict and objective scrutiny over managerial actions (Kanojia & Bhatia, 2022; Nazar, 2021). Hence, the enhanced state of governance with the inclusion of more independent directors on the board can reduce the need to pay out stable dividends to mitigate the misappropriation of cash. Contrastingly, it is noted that the extent of dividend smoothing increases with a higher level of board gender diversity (*BGD x L.DIVIDEND*). As expounded and noted in earlier sections, women directors exercise conservatism while formulating financial policies (García-Meca et al., 2022; Saeed & Sameer, 2017). Consequently, gender-diverse boards can pre-empt adverse market reactions to dividend cuts (Brav et al., 2005; Lintner, 1956) by disapproving of any drastic increases in payouts. Thus, female directors will adopt a cautious approach to dividend policy by recommending stable dividend payments.

[4] Dividend stability and smoothing are used alternatively.

[5] Mean-centering of the concerned variables are undertaken to address the problem of high correlation arising from their use for generating interaction terms.

Table 6.11 Corporate governance monitoring mechanisms and dividend stability

Dependent variable: *DIVIDEND*	Overall sample (2010–2019)	Pre-reform period (2010–2014)	Post-reform period (2015–2019)
Variables	(1)	(2)	(3)
L.DIVIDEND	0.491***	0.337***	0.436***
	(0.0502)	(0.0997)	(0.0634)
BSIZE x L.DIVIDEND	−0.00118	−0.00544	−0.00548
	(0.0213)	(0.0283)	(0.0266)
BIND X L.DIVIDEND	−0.00766**	−0.0152***	−0.00980**
	(0.00365)	(0.00436)	(0.00477)
CEODUAL x L.DIVIDEND	−0.112	−0.0799	−0.161
	(0.0839)	(0.150)	(0.118)
BGD x L.DIVIDEND	0.00772**	0.00844**	0.00283
	(0.00360)	(0.00428)	(0.00616)
PROMOTER x L.DIVIDEND	−0.00336	0.000659	−0.00764
	(0.00246)	(0.00508)	(0.00497)
NPD x L.DIVIDEND	0.0767	0.261	0.0473
	(0.119)	(0.236)	(0.115)
NAF x L.DIVIDEND	−0.124	−0.216	−0.104
	(0.0765)	(0.133)	(0.0969)
BSIZE	0.000892	0.000811	6.56e−05
	(0.000954)	(0.00115)	(0.000462)
BIND	−4.11e−05	−0.000125	−4.33e−05
	(5.30e−05)	(0.000109)	(9.55e−05)
CEODUAL	−0.00288	−0.00659	−0.00268
	(0.00354)	(0.00436)	(0.00326)
BGD	−0.000270**	−0.000309*	7.15e−06
	(0.000116)	(0.000175)	(0.000181)
PROMOTER	−5.16e−05	−8.09e−05	5.20e−06
	(4.33e−05)	(0.000190)	(6.62e−05)
NPD	−0.00349	−0.00448	0.00270
	(0.00249)	(0.00503)	(0.00529)
NAF	−0.00351	−0.00524	−0.00484**
	(0.00514)	(0.00849)	(0.00218)
FSIZE	0.00192*	0.000933	0.00390***
	(0.00110)	(0.00131)	(0.00106)
FAGE	6.98e−06	8.00e−05	1.98e−05
	(3.31e−05)	(7.15e−05)	(4.17e−05)

(continued)

Table 6.11 (continued)

Dependent variable: *DIVIDEND*	Overall sample (2010–2019)	Pre-reform period (2010–2014)	Post-reform period (2015–2019)
Variables	(1)	(2)	(3)
GROWTH	0.00322***	0.00470***	0.00285***
	(0.000862)	(0.00180)	(0.000833)
CASH	0.0344**	0.0109	0.0302
	(0.0160)	(0.0276)	(0.0218)
PROFIT	0.145***	0.123***	0.183***
	(0.0282)	(0.0312)	(0.0414)
BRISK	−0.00202	−0.00364	−0.0147
	(0.0288)	(0.0432)	(0.0413)
LEV	−0.00172	0.00443	−0.00260
	(0.0101)	(0.0131)	(0.0110)
SRTA	−0.0667**	−0.0827	−0.0370
	(0.0296)	(0.0754)	(0.0344)
AGENCYC	0.0176	0.0294	0.0201
	(0.0146)	(0.0251)	(0.0178)
Constant	−0.0510***	−0.0233	−0.0897***
	(0.0171)	(0.0271)	(0.0240)
Industry & Year FE	Yes	Yes	Yes
Wald F	66.61 (0.000)	29.65 (0.000)	39.66 (0.000)
AR2 (p-value)	0.921 (0.357)	0.127 (0.899)	0.654 (0.513)
Hansen J (p-value)	273.2 (0.112)	92.60 (0.463)	202.5 (0.110)

Notes This table summarizes the results from the two-step system GMM estimation of the augmented primary regression model obtained by including the interactions between corporate governance variables and lagged values of dividends in Eq. 6.1. Column 1 depicts the findings when the empirical analysis is carried out for the overall sample from FY 2010-FY 2019. Column 2 reports results for the period before the enactment of the Companies Act, 2013 (Pre-reform period). Column 3 indicates the findings for years when the Companies Act, 2013 is in effect (Post-reform period). Windmeijer's (2005) corrected-robust standard errors are shown in parentheses. ***, **, and * denote significance at 1, 5, and 10% levels, respectively

Columns 2 and 3 demonstrate the findings when the sample is divided into the pre-reform and post-reform periods based on the passage of the Companies Act, 2013. They indicate that the negative impact of board independence on the degree of dividend smoothing (*BIND x L.DIVIDEND*) is observed across both periods. In comparison, board gender diversity strengthens the positive relationship between the lagged and current value of dividends (*BGD x L.DIVIDEND*) in the pre-reform period. Its effect diminishes after the introduction of mandated board gender quotas.

6.5 Summary and Concluding Observations

This chapter evaluates the impact of corporate governance monitoring mechanisms on the amount and stability of dividend payouts. Dividends minimize the agency problem of free cash flow by reducing the surplus cash available at the discretion of corporate insiders (Jensen, 1986; Rozeff, 1982). In doing so, it also compels the management to acquire outside financing, which enhances the scrutiny of capital market participants on their actions (Easterbrook, 1984). Thus, dividends can serve as a bonding mechanism that can strengthen or substitute the role of corporate governance devices (Anwar et al., 2017; Kuo, 2017). In this relation, La Porta et al. (2000) propose two major hypotheses underlining the relationship between corporate governance and dividend payments. The outcome model predicts that higher and more stable dividend payouts are a result of robust corporate governance structures. On the other hand, the substitution hypothesis states that poorly governed firms make larger and rigid payouts to build a capital market reputation. Thus, the association between corporate governance attributes and dividends is ambiguous.

The present empirical examination attempts to clarify the nature of the linkage between corporate governance and dividend payments by employing the sample of non-financial companies listed on the NIFTY 500. The primary results obtained are presented in Table 6.12. Altogether, the findings pertaining to board gender diversity, board size, CEO duality, and additional large owners seem to be consistent with the presumptions of the outcome hypothesis. With respect to auditor independence, the empirical analysis highlights the beneficial role of taking non-audit services from the contracted auditor for younger entities. In relation to controlling owners, the results appear to be consistent with the substitution model.

The following chapter concludes the entire research study by summarizing all the findings from the empirical investigations undertaken in the preceding chapters. It also emphasizes its contributions and identifies important policy recommendations from the obtained results. Lastly, the study's limitations and future scope for research are also provided in the next chapter.

Table 6.12 Summary of results from empirical investigation of corporate governance monitoring mechanisms on dividends

Variables	Analyses	Results
Board size	Main effect	• No significant effect on dividend payout intensity • No significant effect on dividend stability
	Contingent effect	*CEO tenure* • Positive impact on dividend payout intensity in the late stages of a CEO's tenure *Firm growth opportunities* • Positive impact on dividend payout intensity in the case of low-growth firms *Other contingency factors* • No significant effect on dividend payout intensity
Board independence	Main effect	• No significant effect on dividend payout intensity • Negative impact on dividend stability, present across all the periods
	Contingent effect	• No significant contingent effect on dividend payout intensity
CEO duality	Main effect	• No significant effect on dividend payout intensity • No significant effect on dividend stability
	Contingent effect	*Firm growth opportunities* • Positive impact on dividend payout intensity in the case of low-growth firms • Negative impact on dividend payout intensity in the case of high-growth firms *Other contingency factors* • No significant effect on dividend payout intensity
Board gender diversity	Main effect	• Positive impact on dividend payout intensity, present in the pre-reform period • Positive impact on dividend stability, present in the pre-reform period
	Contingent effect	*CEO tenure* • Positive impact on dividend payout intensity in the late stages of a CEO's tenure *Firm size* • Negative impact on dividend payout intensity in the case of smaller firms *Firm growth opportunities* • Negative impact on dividend payout intensity in the case of high-growth firms *Other contingency factors* • No significant effect on dividend payout intensity
Controlling shareholder	Main effect	• No significant effect on dividend payout intensity • No significant effect on dividend stability

(continued)

Table 6.12 (continued)

Variables	Analyses	Results
	Contingent effect	*Industry concentration* • Positive impact on dividend payout intensity in the case of highly-concentrated industries *Other contingency factors* • No significant effect on dividend payout intensity
Non-controlling large shareholders	Main effect	• No significant effect on dividend payout intensity • No significant effect on dividend stability
	Contingent effect	*Firm financial condition* • Negative impact on dividend payout intensity in the case of financially distressed firms *Other contingency factors* • No significant effect on dividend payout intensity
Auditor independence	Main effect	• No significant effect on dividend payout intensity • No significant effect on dividend stability
	Contingent effect	*Firm age* • Negative impact on dividend payout intensity in the case of younger firms *Other contingency factors* • No significant effect on dividend payout intensity

Notes This table provides a brief overview of all the findings obtained from the present empirical examination

References

Abreu, J. F., & Gulamhussen, M. A. (2013). Dividend payouts: Evidence from US bank holding companies in the context of the financial crisis. *Journal of Corporate Finance, 22*, 54–65.

Abu Afifa, M., Saleh, I., Al-shoura, A., & Van Vo, H. (2024). Nexus among board characteristics, earnings management and dividend payout: Evidence from an emerging market. *International Journal of Emerging Markets, 19*(1), 106–133.

Allen, F., Bernardo, A. E., & Welch, I. (2000). A theory of dividends based on tax clienteles. *The Journal of Finance, 55*(6), 2499–2536.

Amidu, M., & Abor, J. (2006). Determinants of dividend payout ratios in Ghana. *The Journal of Risk Finance, 7*(2), 136–145.

Anderson, R. C., Mansi, S. A., & Reeb, D. M. (2004). Board characteristics, accounting report integrity, and the cost of debt. *Journal of Accounting and Economics, 37*(3), 315–342.

Anwar, S., Singh, S., & Jain, P. K. (2017). Impact of cash dividend announcements: Evidence from the Indian manufacturing companies. *Journal of Emerging Market Finance, 16*(1), 29–60.

Anwer, Z., Mohamad, S., Paltrinieri, A., & Hassan, M. K. (2020). Dividend payout policy of Shariah compliant firms: Evidence from United States. *Pacific-Basin Finance Journal, 69*, 101422.

Aoki, Y. (2014). How does the largest shareholder affect dividends? *International Review of Finance, 14*(4), 613–645.

Arora, R. K., & Srivastava, A. (2021). Ownership concentration and dividend payout in emerging markets: Evidence from India. *Global Business Review, 22*(5), 1276–1288.

Arslan-Ayaydin, Ö., Florackis, C., & Ozkan, A. (2014). Financial flexibility, corporate investment and performance: Evidence from financial crises. *Review of Quantitative Finance and Accounting, 42*(2), 211–250.

Baker, H. K., & Kilincarslan, E. (2019). Why companies do not pay cash dividends: The Turkish experience. *Global Finance Journal, 42*, Article 100419.
Balasubramanian, S. A., Radhakrishna, G. S., Sridevi, P., & Natarajan, T. (2019). Modeling corporate financial distress using financial and non-financial variables: The case of Indian listed companies. *International Journal of Law and Management, 61*(3/4), 457–484.
Ben-Nasr, H. (2015). Government ownership and dividend policy: Evidence from newly privatized firms. *Journal of Business Finance & Accounting, 42*(5–6), 665–704.
Bhatia, M., & Gulati, R. (2022). Are boards 'substitute' or 'complement' dividend payout? Econometric evidence for Indian banks. *Economic Notes, 51*(2), Article e12198.
Brav, A., Graham, J. R., Harvey, C. R., & Michaely, R. (2005). Payout policy in the 21st century. *Journal of Financial Economics, 77*(3), 483–527.
Brockman, P., & Unlu, E. (2011). Earned/contributed capital, dividend policy, and disclosure quality: An international study. *Journal of Banking & Finance, 35*(7), 1610–1625.
Brook, Y., Charlton, W. T., Jr., & Hendershott, R. J. (1998). Do firms use dividends to signal large future cash flow increases? *Financial Management, 27*(3), 46–57.
Cai, Y., Kim, Y., Park, J. C., & White, H. D. (2016). Common auditors in M&A transactions. *Journal of Accounting and Economics, 61*(1), 77–99.
Campbell, R. H. (1996). Letters to the Editor: CEO vs. Nun: It's a Draw, *Wall Street Journal*, August 12, Section A.
Carcello, J. V., Hermanson, D. R., Neal, T. L., & Riley, R. A., Jr. (2002). Board characteristics and audit fees. *Contemporary Accounting Research, 19*(3), 365–384.
Carter, D. A., D'Souza, F., Simkins, B. J., & Simpson, W. G. (2010). The gender and ethnic diversity of US boards and board committees and firm financial performance. *Corporate Governance: An International Review, 18*(5), 396–414.
Carter, D. A., Simkins, B. J., & Simpson, W. G. (2003). Corporate governance, board diversity, and firm value. *Financial Review, 38*(1), 33–53.
Chen, C. X., Lu, H., & Sougiannis, T. (2012). The agency problem, corporate governance, and the asymmetrical behavior of selling, general, and administrative costs. *Contemporary Accounting Research, 29*(1), 252–282.
Chen, Y. R. (2008). Corporate governance and cash holdings: Listed new economy versus old economy firms. *Corporate Governance: An International Review, 16*(5), 430–442.
Chen, Y. R., & Chuang, W. T. (2009). Alignment or entrenchment? Corporate governance and cash holdings in growing firms. *Journal of Business Research, 62*(11), 1200–1206.
Cheng, M., Dhaliwal, D., & Zhang, Y. (2013). Does investment efficiency improve after the disclosure of material weaknesses in internal control over financial reporting? *Journal of Accounting and Economics, 56*(1), 1–18.
Chintrakarn, P., Tong, S., Jiraporn, P., & Kim, Y. S. (2020). Using geographic density of firms to identify the effect of board size on firm value and corporate policies. *Asia-Pacific Journal of Financial Studies, 49*(1), 36–66.
D'Mello, R., Krishnaswami, S., & Larkin, P. J. (2008). Determinants of corporate cash holdings: Evidence from spin-offs. *Journal of Banking & Finance, 32*(7), 1209–1220.
Dahiya, M., Singh, S., & Chaudhry, N. (2023). Corporate social responsibility and dividend policy in India. *Management Decision, 61*(10), 3144–3168.
Davis, J. H., Schoorman, F. D., & Donaldson, L. (1997). Toward a stewardship theory of management. *Academy of Management Review, 22*(1), 20–47.
DeAngelo, H., DeAngelo, L., & Stulz, R. M. (2006). Dividend policy and the earned/contributed capital mix: A test of the life-cycle theory. *Journal of Financial Economics, 81*(2), 227–254.
Dhaliwal, D. S., Gleason, C. A., Heitzman, S., & Melendrez, K. D. (2008). Auditor fees and cost of debt. *Journal of Accounting, Auditing & Finance, 23*(1), 1–22.
Dhaliwal, D., Heitzman, S., & Zhen Li, O. (2006). Taxes, leverage, and the cost of equity capital. *Journal of Accounting Research, 44*(4), 691–723.
Donaldson, L., & Davis, J. H. (1991). Stewardship theory or agency theory: CEO governance and shareholder returns. *Australian Journal of Management, 16*(1), 49–64.
Duygun, M., Guney, Y., & Moin, A. (2018). Dividend policy of Indonesian listed firms: The role of families and the state. *Economic Modelling, 75*, 336–354.

Easterbrook, F. H. (1984). Two agency-cost explanations of dividends. *The American Economic Review, 74*(4), 650–659.
Elaoud, A., & Jarboui, A. (2017). Auditor specialization, accounting information quality and investment efficiency. *Research in International Business and Finance, 42*, 616–629.
Fama, E. F., & French, K. R. (2001). Disappearing dividends: Changing firm characteristics or lower propensity to pay? *Journal of Financial Economics, 60*, 3–43.
Finkelstein, S., & D'aveni, R. A. (1994). CEO duality as a double-edged sword: How boards of directors balance entrenchment avoidance and unity of command. *Academy of Management Journal, 37*(5), 1079–1108.
Flavin, T., Goyal, A., & O'Connor, T. (2021). Corporate governance, life cycle, and payout precommitment: An emerging market study. *Journal of Financial Research, 44*(1), 179–209.
García-Meca, E., López-Iturriaga, F. J., & Santana-Martín, D. J. (2022). Board gender diversity and dividend payout: The critical mass and the family ties effect. *International Review of Financial Analysis, 79*, Article 101973.
Gomes, A. (2000). Going public without governance: Managerial reputation effects. *The Journal of Finance, 55*(2), 615–646.
Gonzalez, M., Molina, C. A., Pablo, E., & Rosso, J. W. (2017). The effect of ownership concentration and composition on dividends: Evidence from Latin America. *Emerging Markets Review, 30*, 1–18.
Goyal, V. K., & Park, C. W. (2002). Board leadership structure and CEO turnover. *Journal of Corporate Finance, 8*(1), 49–66.
Grullon, G., & Michaely, R. (2002). Dividends, share repurchases, and the substitution hypothesis. *The Journal of Finance, 57*(4), 1649–1684.
Guay, W., & Harford, J. (2000). The cash-flow permanence and information content of dividend increases versus repurchases. *Journal of Financial Economics, 57*(3), 385–415.
Gupta, G., & Mahakud, J. (2022). Impact of financial distress on investment-cash flow sensitivity: Evidence from emerging economy. *International Journal of Managerial Finance, 19*(4), 713–743.
Gyapong, E., Ahmed, A., Ntim, C. G., & Nadeem, M. (2021). Board gender diversity and dividend policy in Australian listed firms: The effect of ownership concentration. *Asia Pacific Journal of Management, 38*, 603–643.
Gyimah, D., Siganos, A., & Veld, C. (2021). Effects of financial constraints and product market competition on share repurchases. *Journal of International Financial Markets, Institutions and Money, 74*, Article 101392.
Hair, J. F. J., Anderson, R. E., Tatham, R. L., & Black, W. C. (1998). *Multivariate data analysis*. Macmillan.
Haynes, K. T., Zattoni, A., Boyd, B. K., & Minichilli, A. (2019). Figureheads or potentates? CEO power and board oversight in the context of Sarbanes Oxley. *Corporate Governance: An International Review, 27*(6), 402–426.
Hendijani Zadeh, M. (2022). Auditee's payout policies: Does audit quality matter? *Managerial Auditing Journal, 37*(5), 542–564.
Hu, J., Jiang, H., & Holmes, M. (2019). Government subsidies and corporate investment efficiency: Evidence from China. *Emerging Markets Review, 41*, Article 100658.
Iatridis, G. E. (2012). Audit quality in common-law and code-law emerging markets: Evidence on earnings conservatism, agency costs and cost of equity. *Emerging Markets Review, 13*(2), 101–117.
Jagannathan, M., Stephens, C. P., & Weisbach, M. S. (2000). Financial flexibility and the choice between dividends and stock repurchases. *Journal of Financial Economics, 57*(3), 355–384.
Javakhadze, D., Ferris, S. P., & Sen, N. (2014). An international analysis of dividend smoothing. *Journal of Corporate Finance, 29*, 200–220.
Jiang, F., Cai, X., Jiang, Z., & Nofsinger, J. R. (2019). Multiple large shareholders and dividends: Evidence from China. *Pacific-Basin Finance Journal, 57*, Article 101201.
Jiang, Z., Kim, K. A., Lie, E., & Yang, S. (2013). Share repurchases, catering, and dividend substitution. *Journal of Corporate Finance, 21*, 36–50.

Jensen, M. C. (1986). Agency costs of free cash flow, corporate finance, and takeovers. *The American Economic Review, 76*(2), 323–329.
Jiraporn, P., & Lee, S. M. (2018). Do co-opted directors influence dividend policy? *Financial Management, 47*(2), 349–381.
Kanojia, S., & Bhatia, B. S. (2022). Corporate governance and dividend policy of the US and Indian companies. *Journal of Management and Governance, 26*(4), 1339–1373.
Klein, A. (2002). Economic determinants of audit committee independence. *The Accounting Review, 77*(2), 435–452.
Koussis, N., & Makrominas, M. (2019). What factors determine dividend smoothing by US and EU banks? *Journal of Business Finance & Accounting, 46*(7–8), 1030–1059.
Kuo, L. W. (2017). Reputation as a governance mechanism? Evidence from payout policy of insider-controlled firms in Taiwan. *Journal of Business Finance & Accounting, 44*(9–10), 1443–1476.
La Porta, R., Lopez-de-Silanes, F., Shleifer, A., & Vishny, R. W. (2000). Agency problems and dividend policies around the world. *The Journal of Finance, 55*(1), 1–33.
Lai, K. W., & Krishnan, G. V. (2009). Are non-audit services associated with firm value? Evidence from financial information system-related services. *Accounting & Finance, 49*(3), 599–617.
Leary, M. T., & Michaely, R. (2011). Determinants of dividend smoothing: Empirical evidence. *The Review of Financial Studies, 24*(10), 3197–3249.
Lee, B. S., & Suh, J. (2011). Cash holdings and share repurchases: International evidence. *Journal of Corporate Finance, 17*(5), 1306–1329.
Lintner, J. (1956). Distribution of incomes of corporations among dividends, retained earnings, and taxes. *The American Economic Review, 46*(2), 97–113.
Lorsch, J. W., & MacIver, E. (1989). *Pawns or potentates: The reality of America's corporate boards*. Harvard Business School Press.
Marchica, M. T., & Mura, R. (2010). Financial flexibility, investment ability, and firm value: Evidence from firms with spare debt capacity. *Financial Management, 39*(4), 1339–1365.
Mendiratta, A., Singh, S., Yadav, S. S., & Mahajan, A. (2023). When do ESG controversies reduce firm value in India? *Global Finance Journal, 55*, Article 100809.
Mittal, A., & Singh, S. (2025). Does CEO gender impact dividends in emerging economies? *International Journal of Disclosure and Governance, 25*, 165–176.
Monks, R. A., & Minow, N. (1995). *Corporate governance*. Blackwell.
Muth, M., & Donaldson, L. (1998). Stewardship theory and board structure: A contingency approach. *Corporate Governance: An International Review, 6*(1), 5–28.
Myers, S. C., & Majluf, N. S. (1984). Corporate financing and investment decisions when firms have information that investors do not have. *Journal of Financial Economics, 13*(2), 187–221.
Nadia, L. P., & Hanafi, M. M. (2023). Do women board members affect dividend policy and cash holdings? Evidence from ASEAN emerging economies. *Corporate Governance: The International Journal of Business in Society, 23*(4), 705–722.
Nazar, M. C. A. (2021). The influence of corporate governance on dividend decisions of listed Firms: Evidence from Sri Lanka. *The Journal of Asian Finance, Economics and Business, 8*(2), 289–295.
Ooi, J. (2001). Dividend payout characteristics of UK property companies. *Journal of Real Estate Portfolio Management, 7*(2), 133–142.
Pahi, D., & Yadav, I. S. (2022). Product market competition, agency cost and dividend payouts: New evidence from emerging market. *Journal of Management and Governance, 26*(3), 925–956.
Pathan, S., Faff, R., Méndez, C. F., & Masters, N. (2016). Financial constraints and dividend policy. *Australian Journal of Management, 41*(3), 484–507.
Pham, H. Y., Chung, R., Bao, B. H., & Min, B. S. (2021). Corporate payout policy: Does product market competition matter? Evidence from Australia. *International Journal of Managerial Finance, 17*(2), 342–357.
Pindado, J., Requejo, I., & De La Torre, C. (2012). Do family firms use dividend policy as a governance mechanism? Evidence from the Euro zone. *Corporate Governance: An International Review, 20*(5), 413–431.

Pinto, G., & Rastogi, S. (2022). Corporate governance impact on dividend policy of NIFTY-500 indexed Indian pharmaceutical companies (2014–2019). *Corporate Governance: The International Journal of Business in Society, 22*(7), 1547–1566.

Prakash, N., Singh, S., & Sharma, S. (2024). Technological diffusion, bank performance, and Solow's paradox: Insights from an emerging economy. *Journal of the Knowledge Economy, 16*(3). Advanced online publication. https://doi.org/10.1007/s13132-024-02347-4

Pucheta-Martínez, M. C., & Bel-Oms, I. (2016). The board of directors and dividend policy: The effect of gender diversity. *Industrial and Corporate Change, 25*(3), 523–547.

Renneboog, L., & Szilagyi, P. G. (2020). How relevant is dividend policy under low shareholder protection? *Journal of International Financial Markets, 64*, Article 100776.

Rozeff, M. S. (1982). Growth, beta and agency costs as determinants of dividend payout ratios. *Journal of Financial Research, 5*(3), 249–259.

Saeed, A., & Sameer, M. (2017). Impact of board gender diversity on dividend payments: Evidence from some emerging economies. *International Business Review, 26*(6), 1100–1113.

Sanan, N. K. (2019). Impact of board characteristics on firm dividends: Evidence from India. *Corporate Governance: The International Journal of Business in Society, 19*(6), 1204–1215.

Sarkar, J., & Selarka, E. (2021). Women on board and performance of family firms: Evidence from India. *Emerging Markets Review, 46*, Article 100770.

Sawicki, J. (2009). Corporate governance and dividend policy in Southeast Asia pre-and post-crisis. *The European Journal of Finance, 15*(2), 211–230.

Schmidt, K. M. (1997). Managerial incentives and product market competition. *The Review of Economic Studies, 64*(2), 191–213.

Shaheen, R., Luo, Q., & Bala, H. (2023). Untying the role of board gender diversity in dividend policy of politically embedded Chinese firms. *Journal of Applied Accounting Research, 24*(1), 170–198.

Shamsabadi, H. A., Min, B. S., & Chung, R. (2016). Corporate governance and dividend strategy: Lessons from Australia. *International Journal of Managerial Finance, 12*(5), 583–610.

Shen, W. (2003). The dynamics of the CEO-board relationship: An evolutionary perspective. *Academy of Management Review, 28*(3), 466–476.

Shen, W., & Cannella, A. A. (2002). Power dynamics within top management and their impacts on CEO dismissal followed by inside succession. *Academy of Management Journal, 45*(6), 1195–1206.

Smith, D. D., Pennathur, A. K., & Marciniak, M. R. (2017). Why do CEOs agree to the discipline of dividends? *International Review of Financial Analysis, 52*, 38–48.

Suman, S., & Singh, S. (2022). The role of multiple large shareholders in dividend payouts: Evidence from India. *American Business Review, 25*(1), 120–151.

Tian, J. J., & Lau, C. M. (2001). Board composition, leadership structure and performance in Chinese shareholding companies. *Asia Pacific Journal of Management, 18*, 245–263.

Upadhyay, A., & Sriram, R. (2011). Board size, corporate information environment and cost of capital. *Journal of Business Finance & Accounting, 38*(9–10), 1238–1261.

Walker, M. D., & Wu, Q. (2019). Equity issues when in distress. *European Financial Management, 25*(3), 489–519.

Windmeijer, F. (2005). A finite sample correction for the variance of linear efficient two-step GMM estimators. *Journal of Econometrics, 126*(1), 25–51.

Yang, X., Li, M., & Yang, Y. (2023). Signing auditors' experience and client investment efficiency. *Asia-Pacific Journal of Accounting & Economics, 30*(6), 1444–1476.

Ye, D., Deng, J., Liu, Y., Szewczyk, S. H., & Chen, X. (2019). Does board gender diversity increase dividend payouts? Analysis of global evidence. *Journal of Corporate Finance, 58*, 1–26.

Zhu, B., & Hou, R. (2022). Carbon risk and dividend policy: Evidence from China. *International Review of Financial Analysis, 84*, Article 102360.

Zona, F. (2016). Agency models in different stages of CEO tenure: The effects of stock options and board independence on R&D investment. *Research Policy, 45*(2), 560–575.

Chapter 7
Conclusions and Recommendations

This chapter concludes the book by providing an overview of the overall research work and enumerating recommendations based on the results obtained from the conducted studies. The book is conceptualized with the aim of examining the effectiveness of corporate governance monitoring mechanisms by focusing on their implications on major corporate financial decisions that have been shown to affect a firm's value. Accordingly, the research objectives have been defined to explore the impact of corporate governance on select investment, capital structure, and dividend decisions. Besides the universal linkages, the contingent effects of corporate governance devices are also probed to determine their boundary conditions.

The examination of research objectives is centered around non-financial corporations from India to identify the universal and contingent effects of corporate governance mechanisms. By utilizing system GMM estimation, the first objective looks into corporate governance's impact on the efficiency of long-term investment decisions. It also ascertains its influence on short-term investment decisions concerning cash holdings determination. Further, the second objective premised on a company's capital structure encompasses the evaluation of corporate governance's ramifications on the leverage ratio and cost of capital. Finally, the third objective deals with assessing the effects of corporate governance mechanisms on cash dividend policy.

In consideration of the analyses undertaken, this chapter is structured to recapitulate the key findings for each objective in Sect. 7.1. Section 7.2 delineates the corresponding recommendations for investors, the company's management, and policymakers. The contributions of the study are underscored in Sect. 7.3. Section 7.4 acknowledges the limitations of the work and highlights the future scope for research. Lastly, Sect. 7.5 concludes the chapter.

S. Singh and S. Suman, *Corporate Governance Monitoring Mechanisms and Corporate Performance and Valuation*, India Studies in Business and Economics,
https://doi.org/10.1007/978-981-96-9736-6_7

7.1 Key Findings from the Study

The main observations noted from the empirical investigation of the research objectives are summarized as follows:

7.1.1 *Corporate Governance and Investment Decisions*

The empirical results obtained from the examination of the impact of corporate governance monitoring mechanisms on investment decisions are described in Table 7.1.

7.1.2 *Corporate Governance and Capital Structure Decisions*

The significant findings obtained from the empirical investigation undertaken to uncover the ramifications of corporate governance on debt levels and weighted average cost of capital are presented in Table 7.2.

7.1.3 *Corporate Governance and Dividend Decisions*

The notable outcomes from the empirical investigation of the relationship between corporate governance monitoring mechanisms and dividend decisions are recounted in Table 7.3.

Collectively, the results across all the research objectives demonstrate that the effect of corporate governance monitoring mechanisms on corporate finance decisions is not universal and is contingent upon varied organizational circumstances.

7.2 Recommendations from the Study

The study proffers recommendations based on the obtained findings to the major stakeholders that affect a company's governance environment in the following manner:

Table 7.1 Summary of key findings from analysis of investment decisions

Investment decisions		
Analyses	Investment efficiency	Cash holdings
Main effect	Controlling owner discourages investment efficiency through over-investment and under-investment	Negative impact of board independence and non-controlling large shareholder on amassed cash
Role of the Companies Act of 2013	Negative effect of controlling owners is prominent in the pre-reform period Negative impact of CEO duality in the post-reform period	Negative influence of independent directors and non-controlling blockholders is stronger in the post-reform period
Role of CEO tenure	Negative influence of controlling ownership in the case of early-tenured CEOs Positive impact of board size in the case of long-term CEOs	Independent directors and non-controlling large owners reduce cash more when CEOs have completed considerable tenure in their office
Role of firm size	Negative effect of controlling owners and independent directors in smaller corporations	Negative effect of board independence and non-controlling large shareholders in small companies
Role of firm age	Positive influence of CEO duality in older companies	Large board and non-controlling blockholders decrease discretionary cash in younger businesses
Role of firm growth opportunities	Negative effect of CEO duality in high-growth entities	Negative influence of independent directors and non-controlling large owner in high-growth firms
Role of firm financial condition	Negative impact of controlling ownership in financially sound companies Positive influence of non-controlling large shareholders in financially sound corporations	Negative impact of board independence and non-controlling blockholders in corporations with financially sound conditions
Role of industry concentration	Controlling owners lower investment efficiency in medium-concentrated industries Negative effect of dual CEOs in highly concentrated markets Positive impact of non-controlling blockholders in highly concentrated industries	Non-controlling large owners decrease accumulated cash in highly concentrated industries

Table 7.2 Summary of key findings from the analysis of capital structure decisions

Capital structure decisions		
Analyses	Leverage ratio	Cost of capital
Main effect	Controlling owners negatively influence the leverage ratio	Controlling owners lower the cost of capital
Role of the Companies Act of 2013	Negative effect of controlling ownership stronger in the pre-reform period Positive influence of board independence in the post-reform period	Diminishing effect of controlling owners is more salient in the post-reform period Negative impact of independent directors in the post-reform period
Role of CEO tenure	A higher proportion of non-audit fees negatively affects the leverage ratio when long-term CEOs lead the corporation	Negative influence of controlling owners in the case of long-tenured CEOs
Role of firm size	Positive impact of independent directors in large-sized firms	Negative impact of controlling ownership in smaller corporations
Role of firm age	Positive effect of highly independent boards in older entities	Non-audit fees magnify the cost of capital in younger firms Dual CEOs bring down the cost of capital in older companies
Role of firm growth opportunities	Controlling shareholders decrease the leverage ratio more in low-growth companies	Negative influence of CEO duality in high-growth entities
Role of firm financial condition	Controlling owners and non-controlling blockholders keep the leverage ratio down in financially distressed companies	Negative effect of board independence and controlling owners in firms with financially distressed conditions
Role of industry concentration	A higher proportion of non-audit fees negatively influences the leverage ratio in medium-concentrated markets Negative effect of controlling ownership in highly concentrated industries	Non-controlling large shareholders affect the cost of capital negatively in the case of highly concentrated industries

7.2.1 Recommendations for the Investors

The primary observations and corresponding recommendations identified for investors are enumerated below:

Table 7.3 Summary of key findings from the analysis of dividend decisions

Dividend decisions	
Analyses	Dividend payouts
Main effect	Board gender diversity negatively influences dividend payout levels
Role of the Companies Act of 2013	Negative effect of gender-diverse boards is more salient in the pre-reform period
Role of CEO tenure	Larger and gender-diverse boards encourage dividends more in the case of long-term CEOs
Role of firm size	Negative influence of board gender diversity in smaller firms
Role of firm age	A higher proportion of non-audit fees is negatively associated with dividend payout intensity
Role of firm growth opportunities	Positive impact of board size and CEO duality in low-growth corporations Negative effect of CEO duality and board gender diversity in high-growth companies
Role of firm financial condition	Negative influence of non-controlling large owners in financially distressed corporations
Role of industry concentration	Larger boards and controlling shareholders distribute dividends in highly concentrated markets
Extent of dividend stability	Independent boards are associated with lower dividend stability Gender-diverse boards pay more stable dividends, the impact is prominent in the pre-reform period

i. As inferred from the reported findings, higher controlling ownership and the existence of CEO duality can lower the required rate of return demanded by investors in the case of small and high-growth firms, respectively. However, controlling owners and dual CEOs in these entities adversely affect the allocation of acquired funds as they are noted to invest inefficiently.

   In line with these observations, it is suggested that besides considering growth prospects and the current potential for earning higher returns, external capital providers should give due regard to the cash allocation procedures and proposed investment projects. They should focus on the planned and actual investment outlay and relative ex-post returns on projects to ensure that the private interests of corporate insiders do not drive a company's investment decisions.

ii. The study also evinces that as the degree of industry concentration increases, the severity of agency conflicts can also be magnified. For instance, the results indicate that promoters incur more inefficient investment expenditures and avoid the bonding mechanism of debt when the company competes in concentrated markets. Although these controlling owners are inferred to allay investors' concerns by paying more dividends when market concentration is high, the issue of unproductive capital allocation can hurt a corporation's future performance. Therefore, outside financing suppliers are strongly advised to pay heed to the industry structure in which businesses operate along with their governance arrangements to ensure the safety of their invested capital.

iii. The findings also demonstrate that independent directors waste away corporate cash on sub-optimal projects in smaller firms as they may lack true independence or the required expertise to make informed investment decisions. Hence, investors in small enterprises are recommended to be wary of perceiving independent directors as wholly objective. They should consider the effectiveness of independent directors in conjunction with a company's overall governance environment.

iv. Across the multiple empirical investigations, the study provides evidence in favor of the governance role of non-controlling large owners. Correspondingly, non-controlling large investors are exhorted to monitor corporate decisions actively to minimize rent extraction by the promoter owners.

7.2.2 Recommendations for the Company's Management

Based on the relevant inferences from the study, the main recommendations that can be of interest to a company's management are summarized as follows:

i. The findings highlight that higher promoter shareholding can reduce the expected rate of return demanded by external capital providers, particularly when the likelihood of agency conflicts and financial constraint issues is more salient. Accordingly, promoters or controlling owners are advised against a significant diminution in their equity ownership as their substantial stakeholding assures investors that they will not misappropriate corporate resources.

ii. The study also notes that highly independent boards can bring down the cost of financing as they are presumed to bring an impartial judgment on managerial actions. Resultantly, firms are guided to incorporate more independent directors on their boards to mitigate the expropriation concerns of minority shareholders and debtholders.

iii. The results also indicate that excessive non-audit fees can inflate the risk premiums charged by outside financing suppliers in younger corporations. Hence, these entities are cautioned to regulate their usage of non-audit services as the payment for these services can be perceived to impair auditor independence.

iv. The empirical analyses also suggest that women directors can bring fresh viewpoints, which can enhance the quality of board decisions. For instance, it was reported that gender-diverse boards accumulate precautionary cash reserves in middle-aged firms to capitalize quickly on any strategic opportunities to prevent organizational decline. They were also shown to limit dividend distribution when the company has attractive growth prospects.

In light of these observations, corporations are encouraged to enhance the gender diversity on the boards to take advantage of the distinctive human capital provided by female directors.

v. The study also deduces that CEO duality can be beneficial in older companies since a joint CEO-Chair is noted to lessen their under-investment tendencies and cost of capital. As an aged firm is prone to organizational inertia, a combined CEO-Chair position can provide it with the stronger leadership required to implement strategic changes swiftly. Therefore, older companies can consider having a consolidated CEO-Chair post, provided other checks and balances are in place.

7.2.3 *Recommendations for Policymakers*

The key recommendations that are tendered to policymakers based on the empirical evidence obtained from the study are summarized below:

i. The findings across several empirical investigations collectively underscore that the effectiveness of various corporate governance attributes is dependent upon different organizational circumstances. For example, dual CEOs are reported to invest inefficiently in high-growth entities. On the other hand, they are also noted to make large dividend payments in low-growth enterprises. Similarly, the research showcases that while employment of non-audit services makes external financing costly in younger firms, the valuable advisory rendered by auditors can aid in making better capital-gearing decisions in medium-concentrated industries. In essence, the study deduces that corporate governance mechanisms do not uniformly affect all corporate financial decisions.

   Consistent with the previous discussion, the study calls the attention of the policymakers to the observation that a one-size-fits-all approach may not be suitable for regulating agency problems. A more balanced regulatory framework that accommodates environmental contingencies can be helpful in addressing corporate governance challenges.

ii. The study demonstrates that independent directors in smaller corporations can be ineffective in executing their monitoring function as they are inferred to invest corporate cash inefficiently. These directors may be under the undue influence of promoters or have inadequate knowledge and skills, which prevent them from making sound investment decisions. Therefore, regulators are suggested to improve the functioning of independent directors in small-sized firms through increased accountability and enforcement of stringent qualification criteria for their appointment. Further, they are also advised to assist these companies in hiring experienced independent directors. The newly established independent directors database can be useful in this regard.[1]

iii. The results also indicate that the benefits of increased monitoring by larger boards are realizable when agency problems are severe. For instance, empirical

[1] Source: https://iica.nic.in/cid_databank.aspx.

analyses reveal that large boards curtail inefficient investment spending and stimulate higher payouts when long-term CEOs lead corporations. Hence, the study renders tacit support to the minimum board size requirements, which the regulators have recently prescribed.

iv. The observations from the research mostly allude to the more robust functioning of corporate governance mechanisms post the introduction of governance reforms by the Companies Act of 2013. Thus, policymakers are encouraged to continue improving and strengthening the corporate governance regulatory framework.

7.3 Contributions of the Study

The major contributions of the study are emphasized as follows:

i. The research focuses on the examination of Indian corporations that follow the Anglo-Saxon model[2] of corporate governance despite having a high level of insider ownership (Banerjee & Homroy, 2018; Reed, 2002). In this regard, the study's findings mostly allude to the observation that controlling owners of Indian companies dominate and primarily drive corporate finance decisions. Hence, the underscored results enhance one's understanding of the efficacy of borrowed corporate governance practices from the U.S. or U.K. in a developing economy context where principal-principal agency issues are more pronounced. They also serve as a cautionary direction to academics and policymakers alike to eschew a one-size-fits-all approach to corporate governance for all countries without taking into account their varied agency conflicts and institutional diversity.

ii. The study attempts to consider the effect of multiple corporate governance variables simultaneously in contrast to previous studies that are based on specific few corporate governance attributes or a composite corporate governance index. By avoiding the use of the corporate governance index and considering the influence of several monitoring mechanisms together, the findings bring to light the actual governance factors that are critical in shaping corporate financial policies.

iii. It also extends the literature on the non-controlling large owners or multiple large shareholders (MLS) by highlighting their governance role in an institutional context that has rarely been studied in this regard. Further, it augments the relevant literature by demonstrating the universal and conditional effects of the monitoring performed by the MLS.

[2] The origination of Anglo-Saxon model took place in the U.S. and U.K. to protect the interest of dispersed owners of widely-diffused firms against managerial entrenchment (Jeffers, 2005). In comparison, Indian corporations present the risk of expropriation of minority shareholders due to substantial stakeholding of controlling owners (Varottil, 2009).

iv. The results from the study add to the limited literature on the link between auditor independence and financial management decisions. They underline that the impact of the provision of non-audit services is contingent upon an organization's context and not universally detrimental. Correspondingly, the findings serve as a ground of thought for academics and regulators to deliberate on the blanket restriction of non-audit services.
v. It also contributes to an improved understanding of the practice of CEO duality by noting that the stewardship role of a joint CEO-Chair assumes prominence in environments that require swift implementation of strategic actions. Hence, the study evinces both the agency and stewardship theory by stressing that the cost–benefit tradeoff of the combined CEO-Chair position varies according to a company's circumstances. Accordingly, it guides academics to delve deeper into the boundary conditions of CEO duality to assist policymakers in approaching the regulatory stance on the combined CEO-Chair post from a thoroughly examined perspective.
vi. The research also considers the passage of the Companies Act of 2013 to illustrate how the effectiveness of various monitoring mechanisms differs after the institution of corporate governance reforms by this new legislation.
vii. The findings from the study extend the literature on the performance of corporate governance devices by bringing their contingent effects to the fore. They demonstrate that the impact of corporate governance attributes varies according to different organizational situations. Hence, the research conveys that the relationship between corporate governance and financial decisions may not always be universal. Consistently, the study exhorts academics to build a contingency theory of corporate governance, which can aid regulators in formulating better investment protection regulations.
viii. It also augments the disparate literature on dividend smoothing by observing that board independence and board gender diversity can affect the stability of cash dividend payouts.
ix. Lastly, this study enriches one's understanding of how corporate governance mechanisms may influence a firm's value by evaluating their implications on its important determinants, i.e., investment, capital structure, and dividend decisions. Consequently, the study broadens the bases for assessing the effectiveness of corporate governance devices.

7.4 Limitations and Future Scope of Research

The limits of the study and future direction for research are defined as follows:

7.4.1 Limitations of the Study

The identified limitations of the study are stated below:

i. The scope of the study is restricted to the Indian non-financial entities that are listed on NIFTY 500.
ii. Although the study sincerely attempts to incorporate the effect of various governance attributes, the empirical analyses are undertaken using only the dominant monitoring mechanisms of corporate governance.
iii. The issue of measurement error is dealt with by defining the variables in line with the extant literature and employing system GMM estimation. Despite following the established practices, the problem with variable measurement can persist.

7.4.2 Future Scope of Research

Based on the present work, the future scope of research is proposed as follows:

i. The study can be extended to financial companies to evaluate the implications of corporate governance devices on their investment, capital structure, and dividend decisions.
ii. As the governance systems vary across different countries, a similar study can be conducted in the context of other economies. Furthermore, a cross-country investigation can also be undertaken, which will help in addressing the contingency role of country-level factors, such as national governance quality and macroeconomic situation.
iii. Similarly, the role of other contextual factors, such as economic policy uncertainty, the extent of media coverage, industry type, and CEO age, can also be considered in future empirical investigations.
iv. Future research can also focus on other corporate governance attributes, including board committee composition, board interlocks, multiple directorships, and auditor tenure and reputation, that are noted to affect the monitoring of corporate insiders. In addition, governance aspects related to CEO remuneration can also be addressed.

7.5 Summary and Concluding Observations

Despite a growing emphasis on corporate governance by regulators and activist shareholders alike, the extant literature produces inconclusive evidence concerning its effects on a corporation's value (Aguilera et al., 2008; Pandey et al., 2022). The current research attempts to disentangle the underlined dichotomy by adopting a two-pronged approach to understand better the efficacy of various corporate governance monitoring mechanisms. First, the purview of the examination is shifted to focus on the implications of corporate governance on select financial management decisions, which have been reported to affect a company's value (Fama & French, 1998). By doing the same, one can comprehend how effective corporate governance devices drive the firm value. In addition, the role of different organizational contexts is also addressed to identify the boundary conditions of corporate governance attributes.

Employing a sample of non-financial entities from India, the initial analyses investigate the corporate governance's impact on investment decisions by concentrating on the efficiency of long-term investment projects and the level of cash holdings. The study is then augmented to discern how corporate governance mechanisms affect a company's capital structure composition and, subsequently, its cost of financing. Lastly, the linkages between corporate governance devices and dividend policy are also examined.

The findings from all the investigations collectively underscore that the effects of corporate governance monitoring mechanisms on corporate finance decisions are conditional rather than universal. Correspondingly, it is deduced that the effectiveness of corporate governance devices depends upon a company's environment. Based on the outcomes of the study, scholars and policymakers are called on to re-think the one-size-fits-all approach to corporate governance practices.

References

Aguilera, R. V., Filatotchev, I., Gospel, H., & Jackson, G. (2008). An organizational approach to comparative corporate governance: Costs, contingencies, and complementarities. *Organization Science, 19*(3), 475–492.

Banerjee, S., & Homroy, S. (2018). Managerial incentives and strategic choices of firms with different ownership structures. *Journal of Corporate Finance, 48*, 314–330.

Fama, E. F., & French, K. R. (1998). Taxes, financing decisions, and firm value. *The Journal of Finance, 53*(3), 819–843.

Jeffers, E. (2005). Corporate governance: Toward converging models? *Global Finance Journal, 16*(2), 221–232.

Pandey, N., Kumar, S., Post, C., Goodell, J. W., & García-Ramos, R. (2023). Board gender diversity and firm performance: A complexity theory perspective. *Asia Pacific Journal of Management, 40*(3), 1289–1320.

Reed, A. M. (2002). Corporate governance reforms in India. *Journal of Business Ethics, 37*(3), 249–268.

Varottil, U. (2009). A cautionary tale of the transplant effect on Indian corporate governance. *National Law School of India Review, 21*(1), 1–49.

MIX
Papier aus verantwortungsvollen Quellen
Paper from responsible sources
FSC® C105338
FSC
www.fsc.org

If you have any concerns about our products,
you can contact us on
ProductSafety@springernature.com

In case Publisher is established outside the EU,
the EU authorized representative is:
Springer Nature Customer Service Center GmbH
Europaplatz 3, 69115 Heidelberg, Germany

Printed by Libri Plureos GmbH
in Hamburg, Germany